FROMMER'S

COMPREHENSIVE TRAVEL GUIDE

MINNEAPOLIS & ST. PAUL
3RD EDITION

by Lucille Johnsen Stelling

PRENTICE HALL TRAVEL

NEW YORK • LONDON • TORONTO • SYDNEY • TOKYO • SINGAPORE

This book is dedicated to
Three Honorary Minnesotans,
Molly and Homer Johnsen
and
Bart Johnsen-Harris

FROMMER BOOKS

Published by Prentice Hall General Reference
A division of Simon & Schuster Inc.
15 Columbus Circle
New York, NY 10023

ISBN: 0-671-84677-9
ISSN: 1051-6980

Design by Robert Bull Design
Maps by Geografix Inc.

FROMMER'S MINNEAPOLIS & ST. PAUL

Editorial Director: Marilyn Wood
Senior Editors: Judith de Rubini, Alice Fellows, Lisa Renaud
Editors: Thomas F. Hirsch, Peter Katucki, Sara Hinsey Raveret, Theodore
    Stavrou
Assistant Editors: Margaret Bowen, Ian Wilker
Managing Editor: Leanne Coupe

Special Sales

Bulk purchases of Frommer's Travel Guides are available at special discounts. The publishers are happy to custom-make publications for corporate clients who wish to use them as premiums or sales promotions. We
can excerpt the contents, provide covers with corporate imprints, or create
books to meet specific needs. For more information write to Special Sales,
Prentice Hall Travel, Paramount Communications Building, 15 Columbus
Circle, New York, NY 10023

CONTENTS

ACKNOWLEDGMENTS

Many Minnesotans offered valuable suggestions and information for this book, and I thank them all, particularly Del Stelling, who remains my greatest resource in every sense.

LIST OF MAPS

INTRODUCING MINNEAPOLIS & ST. PAUL

Although they're known as the Twin Cities, Minneapolis and St. Paul are far from identical. Bound together by geography as well as history, they share a unique natural beauty thanks to an abundance of lakes and parks that greatly enhance the quality of life here. But through the years, Minneapolis and St. Paul have developed individual styles that complement rather than conflict with each other. More traditional than its younger sibling, St. Paul is often called "the last city of the East." And if St. Paul reminds you a bit of New England, then Minneapolis, "the first city of the West," may make you think of Los Angeles.

Which of the two will you prefer? That's a question that needn't be answered—or even asked. One of the best things about the Twin Cities is that you don't have to choose between them. With their downtown areas only ten minutes apart, they combine to offer a remarkable diversity of activities and attractions, and that's what makes them such an extraordinary vacation value. It's two great destinations for the price of one when you visit Minneapolis and St. Paul.

1. GEOGRAPHY, HISTORY & BACKGROUND

GEOGRAPHY

The 59 square miles that comprise Minneapolis are made up of relatively flat land, interspersed with a number of lakes. The Mississippi River divides parts of Minneapolis and St. Paul. St. Paul, with 55 square miles, also has several lakes within its city limits; much of the downtown area is surrounded by hills, with the Mississippi River on the south.

WHAT'S SPECIAL ABOUT THE TWIN CITIES

Museums
- ☐ The Minneapolis Institute of Art boasts a famous collection, as well as a 2,000-year-old mummy.
- ☐ The Walker Art Center, noted for contemporary art, year-round film screenings, and stage performances.

Parks
- ☐ Como Park, famous for its zoo and conservatory.
- ☐ Lake Harriet Park, with rose gardens and a music band shell, entertains Twin Citians and visitors alike.

For the Kids
- ☐ The Children's Museum combines education and entertainment with hands-on exhibits.
- ☐ Fort Snelling, where visitors experience 19th-century life.

Events/Festivals
- ☐ St. Paul Winter Carnival, an annual 12-day celebration of winter, features ice sculpture, activities, and competitions.
- ☐ Minneapolis Aquatennial, with sailboat races and lots of other summertime contests and activities.

Architecture
- ☐ The state capitol, inspired by St. Peter's Cathedral in Rome, overlooks St. Paul and the Mississippi.
- ☐ The IDS Building in downtown Minneapolis, considered one of the finest works of noted architect Philip Johnson.

After Dark
- ☐ Orchestra Hall, home of the Minnesota Orchestra, hosts distinguished international performers.
- ☐ Ordway Music Hall, a European-style building, is itself a work of art. Enjoy a concert, a play, or a touring musical here.
- ☐ The Tyrone Guthrie Theater offers plays, as do the Children's Theatre, the Old Log, and many others.

Zoos
- ☐ The Minnesota Zoo, home to koalas, sharks, and tropical birds.
- ☐ Como Zoo, where a multitude of animals await you, including the beloved trained seal, Sparky.

Shopping
- ☐ The Mall of America, in suburban Bloomington, the world's largest retail and entertainment complex.

Major League Sports
- ☐ Something for every enthusiast: baseball, the Twins; football, the Vikings; hockey, the Northstars; basketball, the Timberwolves.

Although every Minnesota license plate declares this the land of 10,000 lakes, there are really more than 12,000 in all—and that's only counting the ones that measure 10 acres or more. A total of 31 large lakes lie within the metropolitan area of Minneapolis and St. Paul, making outdoor recreation an important part of Twin Cities life throughout the year. Boating, fishing, and swimming in the summer and ice-skating, skiing, snowmobiling, and ice-sailing during the winter are all easily accessible.

The suburbs offer an interesting introduction to local geography: in Apple Valley, cross-country skiers can glide past elk, bison, and moose on authentically landscaped terrain at the Minnesota Zoo.

HISTORY

THE FIRST EXPLORERS

French explorers, traveling south from Canada, thought the Mississippi River might be a northwest route to the opulent East which Marco Polo had written so vividly about. During the 17th century at least one of these adventurous souls, the self-confident Jean Nicolet, brought along a change of clothes he thought appropriate for the exotic world of China. Imagine the astonishment of Dakota tribespeople when Nicolet stepped ashore in an intricately decorated robe "all strewn with flowers and birds of many colors."

Disappointed in their search for a new continent, these explorers found consolation in the region's abundance of furs—the Native Americans were more than willing to exchange their beaver and muskrat pelts for blankets, knives, tobacco, tools, and other unfamiliar and intriguing items.

In time the Ojibwa tribes from the East joined the Dakota, moving into this area in advance of the white men who had given them rifles, liquor, and other trappings of civilization. The name "Ojibwa" sounded like "Chippewa" to white men's ears, and that's the name by which the tribe is still known today. These advancing tribes disparaged the Dakota, calling them "Nadouessioux," or "little vipers," a name the white men shortened to "Sioux." Different from each other in language and cus-

DATELINE

- **1654** French traders Pierre Radisson and Sieur de Grosseilliers are the first Europeans to reach Minnesota.
- **1763** The Treaty of Paris ends the French and Indian War and cedes French territory east of the Mississippi River to England.
- **1803** Through the Louisiana Purchase, President Thomas Jefferson acquires a part of Minnesota from Napoleon Bonaparte.
- **1818** Following the Convention of 1818 with England, all of Minnesota is under the American flag.
- **1819** Fort St. Anthony (later renamed Fort Snelling) is established.
- **1837** Treaties are signed with the Ojibway and Dakota *(continues)*

DATELINE

tribes that allow white settlements within the Minnesota area.

● **1838** Pierre Parrant builds a shanty on the present site of St. Paul, calling it "Pig's Eye."

● **1841** Father Lucien Galtier builds the Chapel of St. Paul; the name endures today as the state capital of Minnesota.

● **1849** Minnesota becomes an official territory of the United States.

● **1853** The first state capitol is constructed.

● **1854** St. Paul is incorporated as a city.

● **1858** Minnesota becomes the 32nd state, third in size only to Texas and California.

● **1862** Minnesota's first railroad is built. An uprising occurs by members of the Dakota tribe frustrated with the government.

● **1867** Minneapolis is incorporated as a city.

● **1870–1880** Minneapolis becomes the flour mill
(continues)

toms, the Sioux and the Chippewa waged fierce and bloody warfare that threatened not only the white men's fur trade but also their own settlements.

French domination in the area ended in 1763, at the conclusion of the French and Indian War, when France surrendered to Great Britain all the land east of the Mississippi River. British rule was short-lived, however: Just 20 years later Britain relinquished the land to the newly formed United States of America, and in 1803, by terms of the Louisiana Purchase, Napoleon sold to the United States the territory that would one day include the state of Minnesota.

At this point President Thomas Jefferson sent army troops out to prepare for the construction of a "center of civilization" at the juncture of the Mississippi and Minnesota rivers. Fort Snelling became a refuge for traders, explorers, missionaries, and settlers, among them several Swiss families. Essentially squatters on land that had been ceded to the military by the Sioux, these families made their homes and livelihood in the protective shadow of the fort until a treaty with the tribes in 1837 officially opened new lands for settlement. The families then crossed the Mississippi to live and work on land that was to become St. Paul.

Awaiting the settlers when they arrived was an unsavory Canadian *voyageur,* Pierre "Pig's Eye" Parrant, who did a brisk business bootlegging rum to soldiers. The new settlement was known as "Pig's Eye" until 1841, when Father Lucien Galtier named his recently constructed log chapel in honor of St. Paul. The name stuck when townspeople made that the name of their community as well.

NEW SETTLERS POUR IN

Until as late as 1848, many of the inhabitants of this area spoke only French, but when Minnesota became an American territory in 1849 settlers from the eastern United States began to arrive in large numbers. And then came more immigrants from Europe. During the decades between 1860 and the turn of the century, thousands of newcomers arrived from northern European countries, including Sweden, Norway, Denmark, and Germany, along with some from the British Isles, particularly Ireland. Pamphlets printed in various languages and distributed abroad offered deals that were impossible to refuse—reduced ship and railway rates and inexpensive food, clothing, and shelter while the newcomers searched for land.

St. Paul, now the port of entry to the frontier beyond, was also the acknowledged center of business and culture in the new territory. Incorporated as a city in 1854, St. Paul became the state capital in 1858.

Minneapolis, off to a somewhat slower start, didn't become a city until 1867. But in 1872 it absorbed the village of St. Anthony, whose waterfall powered the sawmills and flour mills that would make the "Mill City" a prosperous industrial center. By the end of the decade, Minneapolis was declaring itself superior to St. Paul in numbers as well as importance. Competition grew more and more intense, and finally, in 1890, sibling rivalry erupted into internecine warfare when census results showed the population of Minneapolis to be greater than St. Paul. Amid cries of foul play, a recount showed that both cities had substantially inflated their numbers. Both embarrassed, the cities' free-swinging antagonism toward each other gradually faded away.

MODERN ACHIEVEMENTS

At present, the region proudly boasts about the numerous modern trends it initiated. American regional theater was born in Minneapolis when the Tyrone Guthrie Theater first raised its curtain back in 1963. And enclosed shopping malls and pedestrian skyways also debuted here, as did the popular sports of waterskiing and rollerblading.

DATELINE

ing capital of the world.

- **1883** The Northern Pacific Railroad connects Minnesota to the Pacific and the Atlantic.
- **1905** The present state capitol building is occupied.
- **1918** Minnesota congressman Andrew J. Volstead writes the legislation that enforces Prohibition.
- **1927** Minnesotan Charles A. Lindbergh makes the first solo transatlantic flight from New York to Paris.
- **1930** Minnesotan Frank B. Kellogg, U.S. secretary of state, wins Nobel Prize for his work on the 1928 Kellogg-Briand peace pact.
- **1931** Sinclair Lewis of Sauk Centre, Minnesota, wins the Nobel Prize in literature.
- **1987** The Minnesota Twins win the World Series.
- **1991** The Twin Cities host the 1991 International Special Olympics.
- **1991** The Minnesota Twins win the World Series for the second time.

2. FAMOUS PEOPLE

Harry A. Blackmun (1908–   ) This U.S. Supreme Court justice once taught at the St. Paul College of Law and at the University of Minnesota Law School.

Warren E. Burger (1907–   ) Former chief justice of the U.S. Supreme Court. Burger was a judge of the U.S. Court of Appeals from 1956 to 1969.

F. Scott Fitzgerald (1896–1940) Famous American author who wrote his first novel, *This Side of Paradise,* while living on Summit Avenue in St. Paul.

Judy Garland (1922–1969) The renowned singer and popular Hollywood star was born and raised in Grand Rapids, Minnesota.

Dr. Laurence Gould (1896–   ) Geologist, explorer, and author. Accompanied Admiral Byrd to Antarctica (1928–30) and further explored the South Pole region in 1957.

James J. Hill (1838–1916) U.S. railroad magnate, financier, and founder of the Great Northern Railroad.

Hubert H. Humphrey (1911–1978) Well-known U.S. statesman who began his political career as mayor of Minneapolis and later served as a U.S. senator and vice president of the United States.

Garrison Keillor (1942–   ) Author and radio personality. Born in Anoka, Minnesota, he graduated from the University of Minnesota in 1966. His radio show "A Prairie Home Companion" won a Peabody Award.

Frank B. Kellogg (1856–1937) Jurist and statesman. Elected U.S. senator from Minnesota, he later served as secretary of state under Calvin Coolidge. He was awarded the Nobel Prize in 1929 for drawing up the Kellogg-Briand peace pact.

Jessica Lange (1950–   ) This talented film actress was born in Cloquet, Minnesota, and studied at the University of Minnesota for two years. She starred in films such as *Frances, Sweet Dreams,* and *Cape Fear.* She won an Academy Award for her supporting role in *Tootsie.*

Sinclair Lewis (1885–1951) Born and raised in Sauk Centre, Minnesota, he achieved national fame in 1920 with the publication of his first novel, *Main Street.* Other famous novels include *Babbit* (1922), *Arrowsmith* (1925), *Elmer Gantry* (1927), and *Dodsworth* (1929). In 1927 he declined the Pulitzer Prize, but in 1930 he accepted the Nobel Prize in literature, becoming the first American ever to receive this prestigious award.

Charles A. Lindbergh, Jr. (1902–1974) Born in Detroit, Michigan, he was brought up on a farm near Little Falls, Minnesota.

IMPRESSIONS

When I was born, St. Paul had a population of three persons, Minneapolis had just a third as many. The then population of Minneapolis died two years ago; and when he died he had seen himself undergo an increase, in forty years, of fifty-nine thousand nine hundred and ninety-nine persons. He had a frog's fertility.
—MARK TWAIN, *LIFE ON THE MISSISSIPPI* (1883)

He gained fame in 1927 by making the first nonstop solo flight from New York to Paris.

Dr. William W. Mayo (1819–1911) and his two sons William and Charles founded the world-famous Mayo Clinic in Rochester, Minnesota, which remains one of the prominent medical centers of the world.

Walter [Fritz] Mondale (1928–   ) Born in southern Minnesota, he served as U.S. senator and later as vice president under President Jimmy Carter.

Gordon Parks (1912–   ) Probably best known as a photographer, he also excels as an artist, musician, author, and film editor. One of his most popular books is his autobiography, *A Choice of Weapons*. His film *The Learning Tree* was placed in the National Film Archives.

Prince (Prince Rogers Nelson) (1958–   ) Musician, actor, singer, and songwriter. Born in Minneapolis, he achieved international fame but returned home to establish a state-of-the art recording complex called Paisley Park.

3. ART, ARCHITECTURE & CULTURAL LIFE

ART

Art fanciers will find more than 130 galleries throughout Minneapolis and St. Paul and several major museums as well. The Minneapolis Institute of Art and the Walker Art Center are both widely known, not only for their local holdings, but for their successful touring exhibitions. More than a quarter of a million people visited the Walker in early 1980 to see 160 Picasso paintings, sculptures, collages, and drawings that the artist had kept for his own collection; later these works were sent to New York City for incorporation into the Picasso retrospective at the Museum of Modern Art.

ARCHITECTURE

Maybe the greatest strides of the Twin Cities during the past decade have been architectural. Prize-winning skyscrapers like the World Trade Center in St. Paul and the IDS Building in Minneapolis tower above older, more familiar structures. The Investors Diversified Services Tower, centrally located on Minneapolis's Nicollet pedestrian mall, was designed by famed architect Philip Johnson, who said of its glass expanses, "God changes my wallpaper four times each year." In fact, the outer appearance of this handsome reflective structure changes several times each day. Along with the creation of new Twin Cities landmarks, there's a healthy respect here for distinguished old buildings, many of which are listed on the National Register of Historic Places.

In Minneapolis, the shops, restaurants, and galleries of Riverplace reside in restored brick and limestone warehouses and mills on the banks of the Mississippi, not far from the waterfalls that powered Minneapolis's early industries.

In both cities, at any time of year, you can walk from one end of downtown to the other with no concern for rain or snow or anything else our weatherpersons may forecast; the extensive skyway systems are absolutely weatherproof. In Minneapolis, the network of glassed-in second-story thoroughfares is the world's longest privately owned skyway, while St. Paul's 4.7 mile skyway is the world's longest publicly owned system.

Besides mobility, the skyways can provide fascinating views. In Minneapolis you'll be able to look down on busy Nicollet Mall, surrounded by striking new structures like the Conservatory, the IDS Tower, and City Center. St. Paul has some impressive structures of its own for skyway viewing: the new World Trade Center and Town Square, among others. But nothing can beat the St. Paul Skyway view of the magnificent Minnesota State Capitol.

CULTURAL LIFE

Musical performances play a prominent role in Twin Cities cultural life, most notably at two world-class symphony halls: the elegant Ordway Music Theatre in St. Paul and the modern Orchestra Hall in Minneapolis. And there's music for the eye as well as the ear in downtown Minneapolis, where 32 windows of the Schmitt Music Center were bricked up on the parking-lot side of the building to accommodate a mammoth mural of a segment from the score of Maurice Ravel's *Gaspard de la Nuit*. Van Cliburn, in town for an appearance at Orchestra Hall, was so intrigued by the mural that he agreed to perform portions of the piece on a 9-foot Steinway that was pushed out into the parking lot for the occasion.

Perhaps, theater is the Twin Cities' most significant contribution to culture. *Time* evidently thought so when it highlighted the Tyrone Guthrie Theater in a cover story called "The Good Life in Minnesota," which described the fine art, music, and theater that is found here.

Since its opening performance in 1964, the Guthrie Theater has staged dozens of exciting productions, none more unique, though, than the history cycle which ushered in the 1990–91 season. In fact, by offering *Richard II, Henry IV,* parts 1 and 2, and *Henry V* in rotating repertory, the Guthrie made history of its own. This was the first time that a professional American theater company had ever performed these four great Shakespearean history plays in a single season. But the Guthrie is only one of dozens of playhouses in and around Minneapolis and St. Paul. No other city in the country besides New York has more theaters per capita, and no city except New York spends more on the performing arts than the Twin Cities do.

Theater in the Round, near the University of Minnesota's main campus, is one of the oldest continuously operating community theaters in the country; the Old Log, on the banks of Lake Minnetonka, houses the longest-lived theatrical stock company; and the Minneapolis Children's Theatre, adjoining the Institute of Art, is the largest of all American theaters for children; Great North American History Theater offers original historical plays based on Minnesota events and people. And Curt Wollan's Troupe America stages small-cast comedies and off-Broadway musicals at theaters throughout the country, including three in the Twin Cities.

4. RECOMMENDED BOOKS

GENERAL

The Story of Minnesota's Past by Rhoda R. Gilman (Minnesota Historical Society Press, 1992) covers the broad sweep of the state's history from prehistoric times to the present. Beautifully illustrated,

IMPRESSIONS

Minneapolis and St. Paul . . . are nicknamed the Twin Cities. They are divided by the Mississippi River, and united by the belief that the inhabitants of the other side of the river are inferior.
—TREVOR FISHLOCK, *AMERICANS AND NOTHING ELSE* (1980)

the book provides an accessible account for those interested in Minnesota's history.

James J. Hill and the Opening of the Northwest by Albro Martin (Minnesota Historical Society Press, 1992) is a fascinating account about the "empire builder" who created a gigantic railroad empire that extended from Chicago to the Pacific Coast.

Saint Paul: The First 150 Years by Virginia Brainard Kunz (The Saint Paul Foundation, 1991) is an interesting and handsomely illustrated book about St. Paul, covering the days of the early settlers to the present.

Everyone's Country Estate: A History of Minnesota's State Parks by Roy W. Meyer (Minnesota Historical Society Press, 1992) outlines the growth and development of more than 100 parks, monuments, waysides, and trails throughout Minnesota and reveals aspects of the state's history that have frequently been overlooked.

City of Lakes: An Illustrated History of Minneapolis by Joseph Stipanovich (Windsor Publications, Inc., 1982) is a lavishly illustrated book covering the history of Minneapolis from the days of the early explorers.

The WPA Guide to Minnesota (Reprinted by the Minnesota Historical Society Press, 1985) includes a vast amount of general information about the Twin Cities and Minnesota, as well as a number of recommended tours to areas throughout the state.

FICTION

Sinclair Lewis and F. Scott Fitzgerald have long been Minnesota's most acclaimed authors. Lewis etched an acid portrait of small-town America in *Main Street* and *Babbitt:* Needless to say, these novels did little to endear him to the townspeople of Sauk Centre when they were first published in the 1920's. By now, of course, the town is delighted to bask in his glory. Fitzgerald's first successful novel, *This Side of Paradise,* was written while he lived in St. Paul and was followed by a string of successful novels and short stories.

Among contemporary Minnesotans, Jon Hassler has provided the greatest number of fine novels, all of them set in this state. Any of them—*Staggerford, The Love Hunter, Grand Opening, A Green Journey,* or *North of Hope*—will help to familiarize visitors with Minnesota. Garrison Keillor is probably best known as the radio personality who recounted the hilarious goings-on in his mythical hometown, Lake Wobegon, Minnesota. Keillor's short writings have appeared frequently in the *New Yorker,* while his most recent novel is *A Radio Romance.*

Red Earth, White Earth by Will Weaver depicts the coming-of-age of a young Minnesotan during the 1950's, and the struggle of his friend, an American Indian trying to regain the land and self-respect of his people.

ART & ARCHITECTURE

Homecoming: The Art Collection of James J. Hill (Minnesota Historical Society Press, 1991) features rich color reproductions of the art pieces collected by the famous railroad magnate.

CHAPTER 2

PLANNING A TRIP TO MINNEAPOLIS & ST. PAUL

This chapter is devoted to the what, where, when, and how of your trip—the advance planning required to get it together and take it on the road. After deciding where to go, most people have lots of questions ranging from how to get there to when is the best time to go to what's the weather like. This chapter will answer all of these questions and more.

1. INFORMATION

SOURCES OF INFORMATION

The **Minnesota Office of Tourism** (tel. 612/296-5029, toll free 800/657-3700, or Canada toll free 800/766-8687) is staffed with travel counselors who can answer your general questions and also key into a data base listing the hotels, motels, and campgrounds that offer the specific amenities you desire.

Among the information you can get by phone or mail is listings of accommodations with no charge for children, weekend packages, senior citizen rates, pets permitted, babysitting and day care available, indoor pool, whirlpool, tennis, water beds, limousine and shuttle service, and scheduled entertainment. At your request the office will send you a travel newspaper, the *Minnesota Explorer,* and a variety of brochures.

For information on Minneapolis, contact the **Greater Minneapolis Convention and Visitors Association,** 1219 Marquette Ave., Minneapolis, MN 55403 (tel. 612/348-4313). For information concerning St. Paul, contact the **St. Paul Convention and Visitors Bureau,** 101 Norwest Center, 55 E. 5th St., St. Paul, MN 55101 (tel. 612/297-6985).

2. WHEN TO GO — CLIMATE & EVENTS

CLIMATE

In the Twin Cities there are four distinct seasons, with temperatures and precipitation that vary accordingly. The common perception of Twin Cities winters is that they're similar to those in outer Siberia or, closer to home, those in International Falls, the northernmost Minnesota town whose bone-chilling temperatures regularly make national news. Actually, weather in Minneapolis and St. Paul tends to be similar to that in other northern American cities, except that for most of the year there's relatively little humidity, so you probably won't feel as cold (or warm) as the thermometer might indicate.

The winter ushers in a dry cold unlike what you might have experienced in windy cities like Chicago or oceanside cities like New York. When the temperature really dips, the temptation is to stay indoors, but as often as not, proper clothing, including hats and gloves, will enable you to enjoy the clean, crisp, invigorating outdoors. In any event, you'll be comfortable downtown because of the extensive skyway system.

The Twin Cities' Average Monthly Temperatures and Rainfall

	Jan	Feb	Mar	Apr	May	Jun	Jul	Aug	Sep	Oct	Nov	Dec
Temp °F	11.2	17.5	29.2	46.0	58.5	68.1	73.1	70.6	60.6	49.6	33.2	19.2
Rainfall "	.82	.85	1.7	2.05	3.20	4.07	3.51	3.64	2.50	1.85	1.29	.87

MINNEAPOLIS & ST. PAUL CALENDAR OF EVENTS

JANUARY/FEBRUARY

✪ *ST. PAUL WINTER CARNIVAL* The largest winter celebration in the nation features ice sculptures, hot-air balloon races, ice-fishing contests, and other festivities. King Boreas, a mythical monarch, reigns over all of the merry proceedings.

Where: Events take place downtown and on various lakes. *When:* Usually the last Wednesday of January through the first Sunday of February. *How:* Call 297-6953 for specific dates and details.

MARCH

☐ **St. Patrick's Day Celebration.** Every March 17 finds downtown St. Paul and Minneapolis hosting what are reportedly the largest celebrations outside of New York City. The pubs and bars are full of revelers, and the festivities culminate in parades in both St. Paul and Minneapolis.

APRIL/MAY

☐ **Twin Cities Marathon.** A 26.2 mile course through one of the most picturesque marathon routes in the country takes runners from downtown Minneapolis to the state capitol area in St. Paul. First Sunday in April.

○ *FESTIVAL OF NATIONS* The St. Paul Civic Center plays host to a giant celebration of ethnic diversity that has been a local attraction for more than sixty years. Food, entertainment, and a wide variety of crafts for sale make this a particularly popular annual event.
   Where: St. Paul Civic Center, located downtown.
   When: Last weekend of April or first weekend of May.
   How: Tickets may be purchased at the door.

☐ **Syttende Mai.** Costumed participants celebrate Norwegian Constitution Day. A popular feature of this annual event is the parade on Nicollet Mall. Third week in May.

JUNE

☐ **Svenskarnes Dag.** This annual celebration of the Twin Cities' Swedish heritage takes place each year at Minnehaha Falls Park in Minneapolis. Fourth Sunday in June.
☐ **Grand Old Day.** Grand Avenue hosts an annual St. Paul celebration with festivities that include music, food, and a variety of events. For more details, call 224-3324. First Sunday in June.

JULY

☐ **Independence Day Celebration.** Costumed participants re-enact the 1827 Fourth of July celebration at Historic Fort Snelling. Call 726-1171 for details.
☐ **Taste of Minnesota.** An abundance of food and fun await

celebrants next to the state capitol, as some of the area's best known restaurants sell snack-size portions of their most popular dishes. Fireworks provide a fitting finale to the festivities. Usually held during the Fourth of July weekend.

☐ **Minneapolis Aquatennial.** A city-wide celebration of summer and the lake-related fun to be enjoyed in these parts. Call 377-4621 for further information. Usually the third week in July.

JULY/AUGUST

✪ *SOMMERFEST The great composers of Europe are saluted by the Minnesota Orchestra through a series of performances, and a wide variety of delectables are available, most of them European.*

Where: Peavey Plaza, on the Nicollet Mall, between 11th and 12th streets. How: Call 371-5656 for specific details and dates.

☐ **Concerts at the Minnesota Zoo.** Jazz is mostly what you'll hear on every Sunday during July and August at the picturesque Minnesota Zoo in the southern suburb of Apple Valley.

AUGUST/SEPTEMBER

✪ *THE RENAISSANCE FESTIVAL Re-creates the activities and atmosphere of 16th-century England with an assortment of events that involve visitors as well as costumed performers.*

When: Every weekend from the middle of August to the end of September (including Labor Day). How: Tickets are available at the Renaissance Festival Office, located 5 miles south of Shakopee on Highway 169.

✪ *MINNESOTA STATE FAIR One of the largest state fairs in the nation, this annual "get-together" features nationally known entertainers as well as a variety of homegrown exhibitions, demonstrations, and entertainments. Call 642-2200 for more information.*

Where: The Minnesota State Fairgrounds in St. Paul, near the intersection of Snelling Avenue and Midway Parkway. When: The 12-day event ends on Labor Day. How: Tickets are available at the front gate.

SEPTEMBER

☐ **Burnsville Fire Muster.** Held in the southern suburbs, this event includes a parade of fire trucks, a variety of outdoor musical entertainment, games, block parties, and fireworks. Altogether it's a very entertaining end-of-summer event. Second week in September.

☐ **Folkways of Christmas.** Forty-four historic homes comprise a 19th-century village called Murphy's Landing; Christmas is celebrated here in accordance with the various ethnic customs that prevailed in the village from the 1840s to 1890s. Costumed "interpreters" will lead you through kitchens in which you can watch the preparation of old-time Christmas goodies.

Where: On Highway 101, about halfway between Savage and Shakopee. *When:* Three weeks before Christmas.

3. HEALTH, INSURANCE & OTHER CONCERNS

Every traveler should have on hand whatever health-insurance identification cards or documents are necessary for treatment that might be required during an out-of-town trip. (Your local insurance agent can inform you about additional short-term coverage that might be appropriate.)

In addition to checking your health coverage, you may want to check your home and auto insurance as well to find out whether a short-term complementary policy may be advisable during your trip.

Diverse services are available to travelers through **United Way's Travelers Aid** (tel. 335-5000), where volunteers can meet children or elderly travelers at their destinations or help them make transportation connections. The organization can also provide interpreters for non-English speaking travelers as well as help for people with visual and hearing impairments.

4. WHAT TO PACK

You'll probably want to dress somewhat formally if you're going to a restaurant (some require that men wear a jacket and tie for dinner), but by and large, dress tends to be casual in the Twin Cities. Light clothing will see you through every warm-weather occasion, but remember that evenings tend to be cool, so bring along a light jacket or sweater.

During the winter you'll certainly want to bring boots to keep your feet dry in case of snow. In fact, here, as in metropolitan centers around the country, women's boots have become a fashionable wardrobe accessory. And don't forget your woolen hat and gloves. Then you'll be ready for anything that might transpire during our "theater of seasons."

5. GETTING THERE

Situated midway between the Atlantic and the Pacific, Minneapolis and St. Paul are readily accessible from anywhere in the world. All flights land in the Minneapolis/St. Paul International Airport.

BY PLANE

THE MAJOR AIRLINES

Northwest Airlines (toll free 800/225-2525) brings international visitors here daily from Europe, Asia, Mexico, and the Caribbean; its nonstop service includes flights from London, Amsterdam, and Tokyo. **Continental Airlines** (toll free 800/525-0280) flies in daily from Paris, Madrid, and Frankfurt.

United Airlines (toll free 800/241-6522) also serves the Twin Cities, with flights from Paris, London, Amsterdam, Brussels, Tokyo and Sydney, among other international cities.

 FROMMER'S SMART TRAVELER:
AIRFARES

1. Shop all the airlines that fly to Minneapolis–St. Paul.
2. Always ask for the lowest-priced fare, not just a discount fare.
3. Be aware that some inexpensive fares depend on advance booking; don't let a deadline go by without making your reservation.
4. At this writing, airline price wars are erupting. Newspaper ads and articles will keep you up-to-date on skirmishes that can save you lots of money.
5. Keep calling the airlines to check fares. Availability of inexpensive seats changes daily, and as your departure date draws nearer, more seats may be sold at lower prices.
6. Ask about senior citizen discounts (usually 10%) or about seniors' coupon books which will give you hefty discounts if you're willing to pay for four or eight one-way tickets at one time.

American Airlines (toll free 800/433-7300) and **KLM** (toll free 800/777-5553) are also among the nearly two dozen international, national, and regional airlines serving the Minneapolis–St. Paul airport.

BY TRAIN

Amtrak (toll free 800/872-7245) offers round-trip fares to Minneapolis and St. Paul from New York for $279; from Chicago it's $105; and from Los Angeles it's $279. Amtrak also offers a Monday-through-Thursday 15% discount to travelers over 62 and an everyday 25% discount for handicapped passengers and military personnel.

BY BUS

Although bus rates fluctuate, at this writing **Greyhound/Trailways** offers a round-trip fare from New York to Minneapolis–St. Paul for $251 with a 15% cancellation fee; if you purchase your ticket 14 days in advance, you'll pay a nonrefundable $125.50. From Chicago to the Twin Cities, the round-trip fares range from $108 with a 15% cancellation fee to a nonrefundable $54 with 14-day advance purchase. And from Los Angeles, round-trip prices range from $220.50 with a 15% cancellation fee to a nonrefundable $110.25 with 14-day advance purchase. Senior citizen discounts range from 5% to 10% for all but 14-day advance tickets. Military personnel pay $169 round-trip to anyplace Greyhound/Trailways goes.

The Greyhound/Trailways terminal in Minneapolis is located at 29 N. 9th St. (tel. 371-3320); in St. Paul it's situated at Ninth Street and St. Peter Street.

BY CAR

As for highway accessibility, Interstate 35, which extends from the Canadian border to Mexico, and Interstate 94, which extends from the Atlantic to the Pacific, intersect in downtown Minneapolis and downtown St. Paul. Within the Twin Cities, Interstate 35 divides, becoming Interstate 35E in St. Paul and Interstate 35W in Minneapolis. Interstate 35E goes all the way through St. Paul, while Interstate 35W goes north to south through Minneapolis. Interstate 94 goes through both cities in an east-west direction. A Belt Line freeway system encircles the Twin Cities area, with Interstate 494 extending through the southern and western suburbs and Interstate 694 traveling through the eastern and northern suburbs. The Belt Line has interchanges with all the major highway routes.

A new interstate, Interstate 394, now runs from the Lowry Hill tunnel off Interstate 94 in Minneapolis west to Interstate 494. Highway 169 extends through the western suburbs from U.S. 10 to Interstate 494 and continues on to the southwestern part of the state.

CHAPTER 3

FOR FOREIGN VISITORS

Although American fads and fashions have spread across Europe and other parts of the world so that America may seem like familiar territory before your arrival, there are still many peculiarities and uniquely American situations that any foreign visitor will encounter.

1. PREPARING FOR YOUR TRIP

ENTRY REQUIREMENTS

DOCUMENTS Canadian nationals need only proof of Canadian residence to visit the United States. Citizens of Great Britain and Japan need only a current passport. Citizens of other countries, including Australia and New Zealand, usually need two documents: a valid **passport** with an expiration date at least six months later than the scheduled end of their visit to the United States and a **tourist visa** available at no charge from a U.S. embassy or consulate.

To get a tourist or business visa to enter the United States, contact the nearest American embassy or consulate in your country; if there is none, you will have to apply in person in a country where there is a U.S. embassy or consulate. Present your passport, a passport-size photo of yourself, and a completed application, which is available through the embassy or consulate. You may be asked to provide information about how you plan to finance your trip or to show a letter of invitation from a friend with whom you plan to stay. Those applying for a business visa may be asked to show evidence that they will not receive a salary in the United States. Be sure to check the length of stay on your visa; usually it is six months. If you want to stay longer, you may file for an extension with the Immigration and Naturalization Service once you are in the country. If permission to stay is granted, a new visa is not required unless you leave the United States and want to reenter.

MEDICAL REQUIREMENTS No inoculations are needed to enter the United States unless you are coming from, or have stopped over in, areas known to be suffering from epidemics, particularly cholera or yellow fever.

If you have a disease requiring treatment with medications containing narcotics or drugs requiring a syringe, carry a valid signed prescription from your physician to allay any suspicions that you are smuggling drugs.

CUSTOMS REQUIREMENTS Every adult visitor may bring in, free of duty, one liter of wine or hard liquor; 200 cigarettes or 100 cigars (but no cigars from Cuba) or three pounds of smoking tobacco; and $100 worth of gifts. These exemptions are offered to travelers who spend at least 72 hours in the United States and who have not claimed them within the preceding six months. It is altogether forbidden to bring into the country foodstuffs (particularly cheese, fruit, cooked meats, and canned goods) and plants (vegetables, seeds, tropical plants, and so on). Foreign tourists may bring in or take out up to $10,000 in U.S. or foreign currency with no formalities; larger sums must be declared to Customs on entering or leaving.

INSURANCE

Unlike most other countries, there is no national health system in the United States. Because the cost of medical care is extremely high, we strongly advise every traveler to secure health coverage before setting out.

You may want to take out a comprehensive travel policy that covers (for a relatively low premium) sickness or injury costs (medical, surgical, and hospital); loss of, or theft of, your baggage; trip-cancellation costs; guarantee of bail in case you are arrested; and costs of accident, repatriation, or death. Such packages (for example, "Europe Assistance" in Europe) are sold by automobile clubs at attractive rates, as well as by insurance companies and travel agencies.

2. GETTING TO THE U.S.

Travelers from overseas can take advantage of the **APEX (Advance Purchase Excursion) fares** offered by all the major U.S. and European carriers. Aside from these, attractive values are offered by

Icelandair on flights from Luxembourg to New York and by **Virgin Atlantic** from London to New York/Newark.

Some large American airlines (for example, TWA, American Airlines, Northwest, United, and Delta) offer travelers—on their transatlantic or transpacific flights—special discount tickets under the name **Visit USA,** allowing travel between any U.S. destinations at minimum rates. They are not on sale in the United States, and must, therefore, be purchased before you leave your foreign point of departure. This system is the best, easiest, and fastest way to see the United States at low cost. You should obtain information well in advance from your travel agent or the office of the airline concerned, since the conditions attached to these discount tickets can be changed without advance notice.

The visitor arriving by air, no matter what the port of entry, should cultivate patience and resignation before setting foot on U.S. soil. Getting through immigration control may take as long as two hours on some days, especially summer weekends. Add the time it takes to clear Customs and you will see that you should make very generous allowance for delay in planning connections between international and domestic flights—an average of two to three hours at least.

In contrast, for the traveler arriving by car or by rail from Canada, the border-crossing formalities have been streamlined to the vanishing point. And for the traveler by air from Canada, Bermuda, and some places in the Caribbean, you can sometimes go through Customs and Immigration at the point of departure, which is much quicker and less painful.

FAST FACTS *FOR THE FOREIGN TRAVELER*

Business Hours   While most banks in the Twin Cities are open from 9am to 3pm Monday through Friday and from 9am to noon on Saturday, it's well to call the bank you plan to use to find out the particular hours it observes. Stores in the Twin Cities are usually open daily, with shorter hours on Saturday and Sunday.

Climate   See Chapter 2, "When to Go—Climate & Events."

Currency & Exchange   The U.S. monetary system has a decimal base: one American **dollar** ($1) = 100 **cents** (100¢).

Dollar **bills** commonly come in $1 ("a buck"), $5, $10, $20, $50, and $100 denominations (the last two are not welcome when paying for small purchases and are not accepted in taxis).

There are six **coin** denominations: 1¢ (one cent or "penny"); 5¢ (five cents or "nickel"); 10¢ (ten cents or "dime"); 25¢ (twenty-five cents or "quarter"); 50¢ (fifty cents or "half-dollar"); and the rare—and prized by collectors—$1 piece (both the older, large silver dollar and the newer, small Susan B. Anthony coin).

If you must exchange your foreign currency, the following banks will provide the service: **First Bank Minneapolis,** 120 S. 6th St., Minneapolis (tel. 612/370-4141); **First Bank St. Paul,** 332 Minnesota St., St. Paul (tel. 291-5000); **Norwest Bank Minnesota** in Minneapolis, 77 S. 7 St. (tel. 667-2793), and Norwest Bank Minnesota, 55 E. 5th St., St. Paul, (tel. 291-2211).

Travelers Checks are usually accepted as readily as cash. For foreign travelers in particular, they're a highly recommended safety measure. **Credit Cards** are invaluable not only as a method of payment but for establishing identification. Credit cards used in the Twin Cities are American Express, Discover, MasterCard, and Visa (the last two are the most commonly accepted). Others, including Carte Blanche and Diners Club, are widely accepted as well.

Customs See "Preparing for Your Trip" in this chapter.

Electric Current The United States uses 110 to 120 volts, 60 cycles, rather than 220 to 240 volts, 50 cycles, as in most of Europe. Besides a 100-volt converter, small appliances of non-American manufacture, such as hair dryers or shavers, will require a plug adapter with two flat parallel pins.

Embassies & Consulates All embassies are located in the capital of the United States. Embassies for English-speaking foreign visitors include:

Australian Embassy, 1601 Massachusetts Ave. NW, Washington, DC 20036 (tel. 202/797-3000).

Canadian Embassy, 1746 Massachusetts Ave. NW, Washington, DC 20036 (tel. 202/785-1400).

Irish Embassy, 2234 Massachusetts Ave. NW, Washington, DC 20008 (tel. 202/462-3939).

New Zealand Embassy, 37 Observatory Circle NW, Washington, DC 20008 (tel. 202/328-4800).

United Kingdom Embassy, 3100 Massachusetts Ave. NW, Washington, DC 20008 (tel. 202/462-1340).

The following foreign countries have consulates in the Twin Cities: **Consulate of Colombia,** 6800 Telemark Trail, Edina (tel. 933-2408); **Danish Consulate,** 7600 Parklawn Ave., Edina (tel. 893-1305); **Finnish Consulate,** 224 Franklin Ave. W. Minneapolis (tel. 872-0014); **German Consulate,** First Bank Place, Minneapolis (tel. 338-6559); **Norwegian Consulate General,** Foshay Tower, Minneapolis (tel. 332-3338); and **Swedish Consulate General,** 706 2nd Ave. S. Minneapolis (tel. 332-6897).

Emergencies By dialing **911,** you can reach police, an ambulance, or a fire department at any time of day or night. If you encounter problems such as sickness, accident, or lost or stolen baggage, call **Traveler's Aid,** an organization that helps travelers, foreign or American. Check the telephone directory for the nearest office.

Gasoline [Petrol]   Prices vary, but at this writing you'll pay $1.15 to $1.35 in the Twin Cities for each U.S. gallon (about 3.75 liters) of regular unleaded gasoline. Higher-octane fuels are also available at gas stations for a slightly higher price. Taxes are always included in the posted price.

Holidays   Banks, government offices, post offices, and many stores, restaurants, and museums are closed on the following national holidays: January 1 (New Year's Day); third Monday in January (Martin Luther King Day); third Monday in February (Presidents' Day); last Monday in May (Memorial Day); July 4 (Independence Day); first Monday in September (Labor Day); second Monday in October (Columbus Day); November 11 (Veterans' Day); last Thursday in November (Thanksgiving Day); and December 25 (Christmas Day). Every four years (1992 is the latest), the Tuesday following the first Monday in November is Presidential election day, a legal holiday.

Information   See "Information" in Chapter 2.

Mail   The main post office of Minneapolis is at 100 S. 1st St. (tel. 349-9100). St. Paul's main post office is at 180 E. Kellogg Blvd. (tel. 293-3099). **Postal rates** in the United States, at this writing, are 19¢ for postcards and 29¢ for letters up to 1 ounce. Rates to foreign countries vary; again at this writing, 40¢ for letters to Canada, 40¢ for postcards, and 50¢ per half-ounce for letters to most (but not all) other countries. Consult a post office for verification. Major city post offices are open Monday through Friday from 8am to 4pm, Saturday from 9am to noon; smaller communities often have more limited hours.

Generally to be found at intersections, **mailboxes** are blue with a red-and-white logo and carry the inscription "U.S. MAIL." If your mail is addressed to a U.S. destination, don't forget to add the five-figure ZIP Code after the two-letter abbreviation of the state to which the mail is addressed (MN for Minnesota).

Medical Emergencies   See "Emergencies," above.

Newspapers & Magazines   There are two daily newspapers in the Twin Cities, the *Star Tribune,* published in Minneapolis, and the *St. Paul Pioneer Press.* There are also free weekly and semiweekly local newspapers available at many supermarkets and banks. Newspapers published in New York, Chicago, Los Angeles, and other American cities are available at some bookstores (Barnes and Noble and B. Dalton among others) and at some supermarkets. *Minneapolis St. Paul Magazine* is a well-written monthly magazine which offers a wide variety of articles and events listings.

Post   See "Mail," above.

Radio & Television   There are many radio and television stations available in the Twin Cities. Radio stations include WCCO at 830 on the dial, KSTP at 1500 on the dial, and KSJN at 99.5 on the dial. Among the television stations here are: KSTP-TV, Channel 5; WCCO-TV, Channel 4; and PBS, Channel 2.

Safety Whenever you're traveling in an unfamiliar city or country, stay alert. Be aware of your immediate surroundings. Wear a money belt and don't flash expensive jewelry and cameras in public. This will minimize the possibility of your becoming a crime victim. Be alert even in heavily touristed areas.

Telephone, Telegraph & Fax Public telephone booths can be found in hotels, shopping malls, and most public buildings, stores, and service stations. **Local calls** cost 25 cents; most public telephones will accept nickels, dimes, and quarters. At the airport and in large hotels, you'll find phones that accept credit cards, particularly handy for international and long-distance calls. For long-distance or international calls, stock up with a supply of quarters; the pay phone will instruct you when you should put them into the slot. For **long-distance** calls in the United States, dial 1 followed by the area code and the number you want. For direct **overseas calls,** first dial 011, followed by the country code (Australia, 61; Republic of Ireland, 353; New Zealand, 64; United Kingdom, 44; and so on), then by the city code (for example 71 or 81 for London), and then the number of the person you wish to call. Before calling from a hotel room, always ask whether there will be a telephone surcharge. Sometimes the surcharge is very high; in this case you can save money by calling from a public telephone in the lobby.

For **reversed-charge,** or **collect calls,** and for **person-to-person calls,** dial 0 (zero), followed by the area code and number you want; an operator will then come on the line. If your operator-assisted call is international, ask for the overseas operator.

For local directory assistance, the number is 411; for long distance information, the numbers are 1, then the appropriate area code, and then 555-1212.

Like the telephone system, **telegraph** services are provided by private corporations like MCI, ITT, and Western Union. You can bring your telegraph to the nearest Western Union office or dictate it over the phone at a toll-free number (800/325-6000). You can also telegraph money or have it telegraphed to you very quickly over the Western Union system.

Most hotels have **fax** machines available to their guests; sometimes there is a charge to use it. You will also see signs for public faxes in the windows of some small shops.

Time The United States is divided into six time zones. From east to west, these are: eastern standard time (EST), central standard time (CST), mountain standard time (MST), Pacific standard time (PST), Alaska standard time (AST), and Hawaii standard time (HST). The Twin Cities are on central standard time. Noon in New York City (EST) is 11am in Minneapolis–St. Paul (CST), 10am in Denver (MST), 9am in Los Angeles (PST), 8am in Anchorage (AST), and 7am in Honolulu (HST).

Tipping This is a part of the American way of life, on the principle that you must expect to pay for any service you get. If you're staying longer than a night or two in a hotel or motel, tip the chambermaid about $1 a night. Restaurant servers should get 15% to 20% of your check. You should also tip bartenders (10% to 15%), cab drivers (15%), hairdressers (15% to 20%), and valet parking-lot attendants (50¢). Don't hesitate, though, to leave more or less, depending on the quality of service. People who do not receive tips are cafeteria and fast-food restaurant personnel, ushers in theaters or movie houses, and gas station attendants.

Toilets Don't look for free public toilets on American streets; you'll find them instead in hotels, restaurants, department stores, and shopping malls. Gas stations have them too, but to gain entrance you usually have to ask the attendant for the key.

Yellow Pages Unlike the white telephone directories, which list residential phone numbers, the Yellow Pages list local businesses and services by category.

THE AMERICAN SYSTEM OF MEASUREMENTS

LENGTH

1 inch (in.)	=	2.54cm				
1 foot (ft.)	=	12 in.	=	30.48cm	=	.305m
1 yard (yd.)	=	3 ft.	=	.915m		
1 mile	=	5,280 ft.	=	1.609km		

To convert miles to kilometers, multiply the number of miles by 1.61. Also use to convert speeds from miles per hour (m.p.h.) to kilometers per hour (kmph).

To convert kilometers to miles, multiply the number of kilometers by .62. Also use to convert kmph to m.p.h.

CAPACITY

1 fluid ounce (fl. oz).	=	.03 liters			
1 pint	=	16 fl. oz.	=	.47 liters	
1 quart	=	2 pints	=	.94 liters	
1 gallon (gal.)	=	4 quarts	=	3.79 liters	
	=	.83 Imperial gal.			

To convert U.S. gallons to liters, multiply the number of gallons by 3.79.

To convert liters to U.S. gallons, multiply the number of liters by .26.

To convert U.S. gallons to Imperial gallons, multiply the number of U.S. gallons by .83.

To convert Imperial gallons to U.S. gallons, multiply the number of Imperial gallons by 1.2.

WEIGHT

1 ounce (oz.)   =   28.35g
1 pound (lb.)   =   16 oz.   =   453.6g   =   .45kg
1 ton   =   2,000 lb.   =   907kg   =   .91 metric tons

To convert pounds to kilograms, multiply the number of pounds by .45.

To convert kilograms to pounds, multiply the number of kilograms by 2.2.

AREA

1 acre   =   .41ha
1 square mile   =   640 acres   =   259ha   =   2.6km^2

To convert acres to hectares, multiply the number of acres by .41.

To convert hectares to acres, multiply the number of hectares by 2.47.

To convert square miles to square kilometers, multiply the number of square miles by 2.6.

To convert square kilometers to square miles, multiply the number of square kilometers by .39.

TEMPERATURE

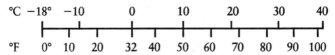

To convert degrees Fahrenheit to degrees Celsius, subtract 32 from °F, multiply by 5, then divide by 9 (example: 85°F − 32 × 5/9 = 29.4°C).

To convert degrees Celsius to degrees Fahrenheit, multiply °C by 9, divide by 5, and add 32 (example: 20°C × 9/5 + 32 = 68°F).

GETTING TO KNOW MINNEAPOLIS & ST. PAUL

The purpose of this chapter is to make you feel at home in the Twin Cities from the moment you arrive. Specific information about hotels, restaurants, special things to do and places to go will follow in succeeding chapters. For now, though, I'll tell you about the different neighborhoods in the Twin Cities and show you how to make your way around.

1. ORIENTATION

ARRIVING

BY PLANE

When your plane arrives in the Twin Cities, you'll be landing at the **Minneapolis–St. Paul International Airport,** just 10 miles from downtown Minneapolis and 8½ miles from downtown St. Paul. You'll exit your plane and walk into the upper level of the Charles Lindbergh Terminal Building; baggage-claim carousels and ground-transportation desks are on the lower level.

GETTING TO AND FROM THE AIRPORT As you leave the terminal you'll see a line of waiting cabs. **Taxi fares** average about $17 to downtown Minneapolis and $13 to downtown St. Paul. At press time, a 10% discount is available from Airport Taxi (tel. 721-6566) if you phone for an assigned cab number after picking up your luggage. You'll be picked up by your designated taxi on the ground level beyond the baggage carousels near Door #4.

If you'd like **limousine service** to Minneapolis, you can arrange for it across from baggage carousel #10 on the lower level of the terminal at the limousine service desk (tel. 827-7777). Service to downtown Minneapolis is $8 one way, $12.50 round-trip. For limousine service to St. Paul, go to the limousine service desk (tel. 726-5479) across from carousels #8 and #9. The fare to downtown St. Paul is $6 one way, $9.50 round-trip.

Cathedral of St. Paul	①
Greater Minneapolis Convention and Visitors Association	②
Minneapolis-St.Paul International Airport	③
St. Paul Convention and Visitors Bureau	④
St. Paul Downtown Airport	⑤
St. Paul/Minneapolis Minnesota Midway Station	⑥

The Metropolitan Transit Commission (tel. 827-7733) runs **buses** from the airport to Washington Avenue in downtown Minneapolis and to Robert Street in downtown St. Paul for $1.10 or $1.35, depending on whether you're traveling during rush hour. Bus #7 will take you to downtown Minneapolis at varying intervals throughout the day. Service to St. Paul is more limited. You may want

MINNEAPOLIS/ST. PAUL ORIENTATION

Falcon Heights

Como Park

Larpenteur Av.

Lake Phalen

Pierce

Butler Route

ST. PAUL

Minnehaha Av.

Dayton Av.

Summit Av.

St. Clair Av.

Mississippi River

George St.

St. Paul Downtown Airport

Randolph Av.

Highland Park

Annapolis St.

Pigs Eye Lake

Crosby Lake Park

Butler Av.

West St. Paul

Thompson Av.

Wentworth Av.

Mendota Rd.

Mendota Heights

South St. Paul

55th St.

Hudson Rd.

Indian Mounds Park

Church ✝

Information ⊙

to take the #7 bus for about two miles to the Mall of America, where you can transfer to a #4 bus that will take you to downtown St. Paul. (The #4 bus runs every 20 minutes throughout the day, less frequently at night.) You'll know the large MTC buses by their colors; the new fleet is white, the older, red. All are marked with a large "T" on the side.

During the morning or afternoon rush hour, an express bus will take you to either Minneapolis or St. Paul for $1.60.

BY TRAIN

Amtrak passengers to the Twin Cities pull in to St. Paul at the St. Paul/Minneapolis Minnesota Midway Station, 730 Transfer Rd., St. Paul (toll free 800/872-7245), located about 10 minutes from downtown St. Paul and 20 minutes from downtown Minneapolis. Cab service from the Amtrak terminal is $1.20 per mile.

BY BUS

Greyhound Bus Lines has terminals in both St. Paul and Minneapolis as part of its coast-to-coast service. In Minneapolis, the address is 29 N. 9th St. (tel. 371-3320); the St. Paul terminal is at Ninth Street and St. Peter Street (tel. 222-0509).

TOURIST INFORMATION

The **St. Paul Convention and Visitors Bureau** (tel. 612/297-6985) maintains a Visitor Information Booth on the street level of Town Square, at Seventh Street and Cedar Avenue, with plenty of brochures to help tourists get acquainted with the city. Hours are Monday through Friday from 8am to 5pm.

The **Greater Minneapolis Convention and Visitors Association** at 1219 Marquette Ave., Minneapolis, MN 55403 (tel. 348-4313), dispenses brochures and information Monday through Friday from 8am to 5pm. If requested, they will mail a tourist packet to you.

CITY LAYOUT

Although they share many miles of common border, Minneapolis and St. Paul are separated here and there by the Mississippi River.

In Minneapolis, avenues generally run north and south while streets run east and west. Main arteries are Hennepin Avenue, Nicollet Avenue, Lyndale Avenue, Park Avenue, Portland Avenue, and University Avenue.

In St. Paul, the main arteries are Summit Avenue, Grand Avenue, Selby Avenue, Marshall Avenue, University Avenue and West 7th Street (Fort Road).

NEIGHBORHOODS IN BRIEF

Downtown Minneapolis In recent years this section has become a somewhat prestigious address for young business and professional people as well as for retirees. High-rise condominiums and handsome townhouses stand amid cultural centers like Orchestra Hall and the Guthrie Theater. And just a short walk away,

Gavidae Common, the Conservatory, and City Center await with some of the finest shopping in this part of the country.

Uptown Minneapolis   Located some 3 miles to the south of downtown Minneapolis, this area has long been considered one of the trendiest parts of town. Home to a very diverse population—creative and commercial, artistic and academic, the neighborhood is great for people-watching. There are also lots of small specialty shops, foreign film theaters, and all kinds of ethnic restaurants.

Downtown St. Paul   Near the beautiful and majestic state capitol complex and the Cathedral of St. Paul, this area is home to many condominiums. Also in the neighborhood is the "Cultural Corridor" that connects some truly astonishing centers of music, art, and theater. On three sides of tiny Rice Park, you'll find the exquisite Ordway Music Theatre, the historic Landmark Center, and the distinguished St. Paul Public Library. Just two blocks away is the Minnesota Museum of Art and its popular tenant, the Park Square Theatre.

Grand Avenue   This section is St. Paul's answer to uptown Minneapolis. Filled with small shops selling distinctive wares and various ethnic restaurants, it's a stimulating and often trend setting part of town.

2. GETTING AROUND

BY BUS

Thanks to the Metropolitan Transit Commission's **"Dime Zone,"** a mere ten cents will take you to most offices, restaurants, and businesses in the downtown area.

For longer MTC expeditions, you can get maps, pocket schedules, and tokens in St. Paul at Town Square, Seventh Street and Cedar Avenue. In Minneapolis, you'll find them at the MTC Transit Store, 719 Marquette Ave.

Bus fares range from 60¢ to $1.25, depending on the time of day and distance traveled. You'll need the exact change when you board unless you've purchased a token or a commuter ticket (they won't reduce the cost of your ride, but will save you from scrounging for change).

For Metropolitan Transit Commission information, phone 827-7733.

BY TAXI

Cab fares are $1.10 per mile. Cab companies include **Airport Taxi** (tel. 721-6566), **Suburban Taxi** (tel. 884-8888), and **St. Paul**

Yellow Cab (tel. 222-4433). You may want to inquire about fares in advance, as they vary somewhat.

BY CAR

Unless you plan to spend all your time downtown, you'll want to rent a car for at least part of your visit to the Twin Cities. Otherwise you'll miss some of the many exciting attractions and activities in the environs.

Local car-rental companies include **Budget Rent-a-Car** (tel. 727-2000), **Hertz Rent-a-Car,** Minneapolis–St. Paul International Airport (tel. 726-1600); and **Avis Rent-a-Car,** Minneapolis–St. Paul International Airport (tel. 726-1526).

PARKING   Downtown parking is viewed by many Twin Citians as a good reason to shop in the suburbs. There's no lack of parking lots, but the rates can be high. In general, rates vary depending on location, time of day, and length of stay.

DRIVING RULES   State law permits a right-hand turn on red unless there's a sign indicating such a turn is not allowed.

SAFETY BELT LAW   State law requires that persons in the front seat of a car use a safety belt. Children must be securely fastened in protective children's seats.

BY BICYCLE

Bike and pedestrian paths run parallel in Twin Cities' parks so folks on foot and those on wheels don't compete for the same space. If you're interested in renting a bike call **Bennett's Cycle, Inc.** (tel. 922-0311) in the Minneapolis suburb of St. Louis Park or (tel. 633-3019) in St. Paul. In Excelsior, try **Area Wide Cycle** (tel. 474-3229), and in Minneapolis, **Downtown Bikes** (tel. 340-1812).

FAST FACTS MINNEAPOLIS & ST. PAUL

   Airport   See "Orientation" in this chapter.
   American Express   In St. Paul, the office (tel. 291-7081) is located in the St. Paul Center, 30 E 8th St. In Minneapolis, the office (tel. 343-5500) is located in the Pillsbury Center, 200 S. 6th St. To report a lost or stolen card, dial toll free 800/528-2121.
   Area Code   The telephone area code throughout the Twin Cities area is 612.

Babysitters   The concierge at your hotel or the desk clerk should be able to make arrangements for you.

Business Hours   Government offices usually open at 8am and close at 4:30 or 5pm. Stores tend to open at 9:30 or 10am; those downtown or in the suburbs usually stay open until 9pm. Banks usually open at 9am and remain open until 3 or 4pm, with extended hours on Friday afternoon and on Saturday morning.

Car Rentals   See "Getting Around" in this chapter.

Climate   See "When to Go" in Chapter 2.

Dentist   Call the **Dental Referral Service** at 222-3321.

Doctor   The **Physician's Referral Service** can be reached at 623-9555.

Driving Rules   See "Getting Around" in this chapter.

Drugstores   In Minneapolis, try **Dahl Pharmacy** (tel. 333-1593), 1200 Nicollet Mall, or **Loop Drug** (tel. 333-2481), 933 Marquette Ave. In St. Paul drugstores include **Carlson Pharmacy** (tel. 222-8594), 356 St. Peter St., and **Walgreen Drugstore** (tel. 222-0120), 425 Wabasha St.

Emergencies   Call 911 for fire, police, or ambulance.

Eyeglasses   Outfits in Minneapolis include **Moss Optical** (tel. 332-7907) at 10 S. 8th St., and **Vision World** (tel. 332-6656) at 733 Marquette Ave. In St. Paul, try **Benson Optical** (tel. 222-7625) at 62 E. 8th St., or **Christy Optical** (tel. 222-4970) at 355 Wabasha St.

Hairdressers/Barbers   In Minneapolis: **Crossings Skyway Barber** (tel. 341-2462), 250 2nd Ave. S.; and **Beauty Loft** (tel. 338-1763), 12 S. 6th St. In St. Paul: **Ken's Barber Shop** (tel. 224-4242), 275 E. 4th St.; and **Park Avenue Salon** (tel. 227-6677), 378 St. Peter St.

Hospitals   Abbott Northwestern Hospital (tel. 863-4095) offers 24-hour telephone consultations. Prescription medicine, emergency-room visits, or hospital care can be provided as needed, and specialist referrals can also be arranged at competitive fees. VISA, MasterCard, and personal checks are accepted.

Information   See "Information" in Chapter 2.

Laundry/Dry Cleaning   In Minneapolis, try **White Way Cleaners** (tel. 333-7995) at 800 Marquette Ave. In St. Paul, try **Lala and Keefe's** (tel. 227-3777) at 469 Wabasha St.

Libraries   The **Minneapolis Public Library** (tel. 372-6500) is located at 300 Nicollet Mall. The **St. Paul Public Library** (tel. 292-6311) is found at 90 West 4th St.

Liquor Laws   The legal drinking age in Minnesota is 21. Identification is required in nightclubs and bars.

Newspapers/Magazines   The Minneapolis newspaper is the *Star Tribune,* which is published daily. The *St. Paul Pioneer Press* also comes out every day.

Photographic Needs   There are now several 1-hour color-print developing and printing companies in the Twin Cities.

Many of them operate seven days a week in shopping centers. **Proex** (tel. 228-9608) one of the best, redevelops without charge any photos that customers find unsatisfactory.

Police   Call 911 to summon the police in an emergency.

Post Office   The main U.S. Post Office in Minneapolis is located at South 1st Street and Marquette (tel. 349-4970); in St. Paul it's at Kellogg Boulevard and Jackson Street (tel. 293-3011). There's 24-hour postal service available at the airport.

Radio   Program listings appear in the daily newspaper. WCCO, 830 on the AM dial, broadcasts news, sports, and popular music. On KSTP, 1500 on the AM dial, you'll hear talk shows, news, and popular music. For classical music and news, tune in to KSJN, 995 on your FM dial.

Religious Services   In Minneapolis, the **First Baptist Church** (tel. 332-3651) is located at 1021 Hennepin Avenue. The **St. Olaf Catholic Church** (tel. 332-7471) is at 215 S. 8th St. The **United Methodist Church** (tel. 871-5303) is found at 511 Groveland Avenue. **Temple Israel** (tel. 337-8680) is at 2324 Emerson Avenue.

St. Paul's houses of worship include the **Central Baptist Church** (tel. 646-2751), 420 N. Roy St.; **Cathedral of St. Paul** (tel. 228-1716), 239 Selby Ave.; **Central Presbyterian Church** (tel. 224-4726), 500 Cedar St., and **Mount Zion Temple** (tel. 698-3881), 1300 Summit Avenue.

Safety   You'll feel relatively safe in the Twin Cities, but remember that whenever you're traveling in an unfamiliar city or country you should stay alert. Be aware of your immediate surroundings. Wear a money belt and keep a close eye on your possessions. Be particularly careful with cameras, purses, and wallets, all favorite targets of thieves and pickpockets.

Shoe Repairs   In Minneapolis, try **Tony's Shoe Repair** (tel. 338-6957), 121 S. 8th St. or **Heels Plus** (tel. 338-1486), 625 Marquette Ave. In St. Paul, **Endicott Shoe Repair** (tel. 224-7173), 141 E 4th St. or **Heels Plus** (tel. 222-2758), Town Square, will get your shoes back in shape.

Taxes   The 6½% Minnesota state sales tax does not apply to clothing, prescription drugs, and food that is purchased in stores. At hotels, restaurants, and bars within the city limits of Minneapolis you'll pay an additional ½% tax on the same items that are subject to the state 6½% sales tax.

Taxis   See "Getting Around" in this chapter.

Television   There are six TV channels available here: Channels 2 (PBS), 4 (CBS), 5 (ABC), 9 (Independent), 11 (NBC), and 17 (PBS).

Time   Minnesota is in the central standard time zone, one hour behind the East Coast and two hours ahead of the West Coast (if it's 8pm in New York, it's 7pm in the Twin Cities, 6pm in Denver, and 5pm in San Francisco).

Transit Info For Metropolitan Transit Commission information, phone 827-7733.

Weather The weather bureau can be reached at 725-6090.

CHAPTER 5

TWIN CITIES ACCOMMODATIONS

1. MINNEAPOLIS
• FROMMER'S SMART
   TRAVELER: HOTELS
2. MINNEAPOLIS
   SOUTH SUBURBAN
3. ST. PAUL

Two types of accommodations have developed in the Twin Cities over the years: You can choose from the large, expensive, rather formal variety, or opt for lodgings that are smaller, more casual, and more moderately priced.

Recently, large and pricey hotels have sprouted beyond the city limits, but in general it's safe to say that you'll pay more for accommodations downtown than in the suburbs. Also, according to recent studies you'll pay more in Minneapolis than in St. Paul.

If you're going to be without a car for most of your stay, you may be better off in a downtown accommodation, where you can get around by foot or by bus to many of the most popular local attractions.

On the other hand, if you're going to have a car you might consider heading for the Interstate 494 "strip" where hotels and motels offer free parking and easy access to the airport as well as the freeways that connect the cities and suburbs. If you're here on business, you'll find that many of the Twin Cities' corporate offices are located in suburban rather than downtown areas.

I've selected hotels and motels in three price categories: expensive, moderate, and budget. Admittedly, one person's moderate is another person's expensive and a third person's budget, but use the following dollar amounts (which include tax) as guidelines: **expensive** hotels charge $85 or more per night double occupancy, **moderate** hotels range between $51 to $84, and **budget** lodgings run $50 and less.

By the way, don't hesitate to ask about discounts when you're making reservations, especially if you'll be here on vacation. Weekend rates, senior citizens' rates, and children's rates, among others, are widely available and can make a big difference in your total tab.

The **Minnesota Office of Tourism** (tel. 612/296-5029 or toll free 800/657-3700) will prepare you a customized printout of hotels and motels offering the kinds of amenities you need.

1. MINNEAPOLIS

EXPENSIVE

HOLIDAY INN METRODOME, 1500 Washington Ave. S., Minneapolis, MN 55454. Tel. 612/333-4646, or toll free 800/448-3663. Fax 612/333-7910. 265 rms. A/C TV TEL

$ Rates: $93 single; $103 double. Seniors receive 10% discount. AE, DC, DISC, MC, V. **Parking:** $6 for 24 hours.

One of the most central locations in the Twin Cities is offered by the Holiday Inn Metrodome. Situated on the eastern edge of downtown Minneapolis, with the University of Minnesota campus on one side and the Metrodome on the other, this hotel stands in the hub of the Seven Corners area, known for its top-notch ethnic restaurants and bars. Grandma's Restaurant is right next door, an exciting place famous for its eclectic decor and its varied American menu. You're also right in the heart of the West Bank theater district here, with the popular Hey City Theatre and Restaurant located just next door and Theater in the Round across the street. In the lobby, as well as in the guest rooms, you'll find decor that's been described as "subtle art deco."

Dining/Entertainment: In addition to a bar, there's the Restaurant Grill Room, which offers everything from sandwiches and burgers to seafood and steaks. Guests with children under 12 will be pleased to know that their kids can dine free of charge.

Services: Free shuttle service within a 3-mile limit, depending on availability.

Facilities: Indoor pool, whirlpool, sauna, exercise room.

HYATT REGENCY MINNEAPOLIS, 1300 Nicollet Mall, Minneapolis, MN 55403. Tel. 612/370-1234, or toll free 800/228-9000. Fax 612/370-1463. 533 rms, 21 suites. A/C MINIBAR TV TEL

$ Rates: $145–$165 weekday single or double; $89 weekend single or double; suites from $290. AE, DISC, ER, MC, V. **Parking:** $8 for 24 hours.

Luxury abounds at the downtown Hyatt Regency Minneapolis. A handsome fountain sculpture is the focal point of a large, decorative lobby where there's plenty of comfortable seating for prime people-watching. All rooms enjoy delightful views of the city and provide in-house pay movies, complimentary HBO and cable news, and AM/FM clock radios. Female travelers often ask for the rooms outfitted with hair dryers and lighted cosmetic mirrors.

Dining/Entertainment: Two of the most popular eating spots in town adjoin the main lobby of the Hyatt Regency: Taxxi, an American bistro, features casual dining with everything from hamburgers to prime ribs, halibut to walleye, and a choice of three pasta dishes daily. At Spike's Sports Bar and Grill, you'll find pool tables,

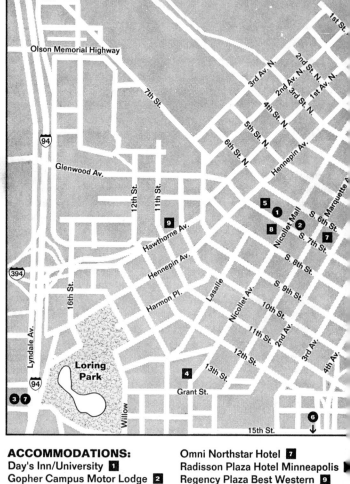

ACCOMMODATIONS:
Day's Inn/University **1**
Gopher Campus Motor Lodge **2**
Holiday Inn Metrodome **3**
Hyatt Regency Minneapolis **4**
Minneapolis Marriott **5**
Normandy Inn **6**

Omni Northstar Hotel **7**
Radisson Plaza Hotel Minneapolis ▶
Regency Plaza Best Western **9**

ATTRACTIONS:
City Center **1**
Gavidae Common **2**

dart boards, and minibasketball courts, along with a wide variety of appetizers, soups, salads, sandwiches, and main courses.

Services: Room service (from 6:30am to 2am), concierge.

Facilities: Large swimming pool; guest membership (for $8.50 per visit) in the sixth floor Greenway Athletic Club which offers weight lifting, racquetball, tennis, squash, a running track, sauna, and Jacuzzi; floors for nonsmokers.

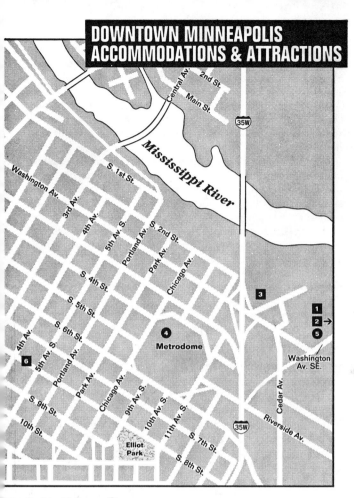

DOWNTOWN MINNEAPOLIS ACCOMMODATIONS & ATTRACTIONS

The Guthrie Theater **3**
Humphrey Metrodome **4**
James Ford Bell Museum of Natural History **5**
Minneapolis Institute of Art **6**
The Walker Art Center and the
   Minneapolis Sculpture Gardens **7**

MINNEAPOLIS MARRIOTT, 30 S. 7th St., Minneapolis, MN 55402. Tel. 612/349-4000, or toll free 800/228-9290. Fax 612/349-9223. 584 rms, 22 bi-level suites. A/C TV TEL
$ Rates: $159 weekday single, $179 weekday double; $74 weekend single or double. Seniors 10% discount. AE, DC, MC, V. **Parking:** $10 for 24-hour weekday parking; $3.50 weekend parking.

⭐ If you enjoy shopping, you'll be well situated at the Minneapolis Marriott. Rising above the three-level City Center downtown shopping mall, this luxury hotel is located barely a stone's throw away from Nieman Marcus, Saks Fifth Avenue, and Dayton's, one of the area's most distinguished department stores. There's a diversity of fine specialty shops accessible by skyway as well (see Chapter 9). But that's only part of the fun of staying at this sleek, modernistic 32-story triangular tower.

The decor in the Marriott's public places is stunning throughout and guest rooms are luxurious; many boast upholstered chairs and matching ottomans, built-in oak desks, and oversize beds. Also notable is the lighting provided by illuminated wall coves, which casts a soft glow over rooms that look out on beautiful cityscapes.

Dining/Entertainment: The hotel boasts two fine restaurants, Gustino's, featuring northern Italian cuisine, and Papaya's, a more casual family restaurant popular for its hamburgers and other standard American fare. The tunes of Gustino's singing servers add a musical touch from time to time, as do the piano melodies from the lobby lounge below.

Services: Room service (from 6:30am to 2am), concierge.

Facilities: Well-equipped health club with whirlpool and sauna; four floors for nonsmokers.

RADISSON PLAZA HOTEL MINNEAPOLIS, 35 S. 7th St., Minneapolis, MN 55402. Tel. 612/339-4900, or toll free 800/333-3333. Fax 612/337-9766. 357 rms, 30 suites. A/C TV TEL

$ Rates: $159 weekday single or double; $89 weekend single or double. Senior citizen discounts. AE, DC, DISC, MC, V. **Parking:** $10 per day weekdays; free on weekends.

⭐ A long-standing Twin Cities tradition was renewed in March 1987 with the opening of the Radisson Plaza Hotel Minneapolis. Since 1909 there's always been a Radisson Hotel on this site, but many qualms were expressed when the decision was made in 1981 to tear down the old familiar structure and replace it with a bigger and better one.

The Radisson Plaza Minneapolis is now the flagship of the Minneapolis based chain with over 200 hotels and affiliates worldwide. The hotel occupies one of the most centrally located sites in the Twin Cities: across the street from City Center, half a block from the Nicollet Mall, and attached by skyway to downtown shops, offices, and restaurants.

The first thing you'll notice is the elegant recessed entryway; the second is the main lobby's 1,200-pound marble pedestal, on which a huge 2,750-pound marble ball floats on half an inch of water. (It's 65 pounds of water pressure that keeps the ball suspended, in case you wondered—I did.)

The effort here has been to contrast the elegance of the public

**FROMMER'S SMART TRAVELER:
HOTELS**

1. Take advantage of the 30% to 50% discounts available during weekends.
2. If you're going to spend a week in Minneapolis or St. Paul, try to find a hotel offering weekly rates, which are cheaper.
3. Ask if parking or breakfast is included in the hotel rates.
4. Ask if there's a charge for local calls or a surcharge for long distance calls.
5. Does the hotel have a free airport shuttle service? This can save you the cost of a taxi.
6. Ask about summer discounts, corporate rates, and special packages. Many hotels don't tell you about promotional rates unless you inquire.

spaces with the residential feeling of the guest rooms. The colors throughout the hotel combine teal and mauve. The French provincial and Chippendale furnishings have an Old World look but offer modern convenience: The mahogany armoires have color TV sets hidden inside. Each bathroom has a TV speaker and telephone. Large desks are provided for business travelers.

Dining/Entertainment: The Festival Restaurant is popular for its Minnesota cuisine—walleye, steak, and wild rice. In the less formal Café, you'll find soups, sandwiches, and other hearty fare.

Services: Room service (from 6 to 1am), concierge.

Facilities: State-of-the-art fitness center with daily aerobics classes, computerized rowing and treadmill equipment, and a cross-country ski machine.

MODERATE

NORMANDY INN, 405 S. 8th St., Minneapolis, MN 55405. Tel. 612/370-1400. Fax 612/370-0351. 159 rms. A/C TV TEL

$ Rates: $69–$85 weekday single or double; $59–$85 weekend single or double. Seniors receive a 10% discount. AE, DC, DISC, MC, V. **Parking:** $5 per day Mon–Fri; free on weekends.

For decades, visitors to the Twin Cities have been welcomed at the Normandy Inn. The rustic, French-chalet-type exterior of this four-story building stands in sharp contrast to the high-rise structures that have grown up around it. The interior has a country look, with dark woodwork, marble tile floors, and a graceful central fountain. Guest rooms are done in earth tones of rust and beige.

The Normandy has a moderately priced coffee shop and restaurant with a full menu and a reputation for delicious high-rise popovers, beer-cheese soup, and pecan pie. There is a swimming pool.

OMNI NORTHSTAR HOTEL, 618 2nd Ave. S., Minneapolis, MN 55402. Tel. 612/338-2288, or toll free 800/THE-OMNI. Fax 612/338-2288. 24 rms, 3 suites. A/C TV TEL

$ Rates: Weekday $140 single, $160 double; weekend $59–$69 double. Suites from $250. AE, DC, DISC, MC, V. **Parking:** $9.45 per day Sun–Thurs; $7.95 per day Fri–Sat.

Twin Citians out for a special evening or event are apt to come to the Northstar Hotel. The reason for this handsome hotel's local popularity is its five-star restaurant, the Rosewood Room, and the intimate Rosewood Lounge where piano music is featured on Friday and Saturday evenings.

The handsome lobby is done in muted shades of beige and peach, and guest rooms feature muted brown and beige tones. A drive-up area makes for convenient arrivals and doormen are on duty 24 hours a day.

Facilities: The hotel is affiliated with the nearby YMCA, which issues guest memberships to its International Fitness Center at $5 per visit; the new Arena Health Club is available to guests at $10 per visit.

Services: Room service (from 6:30am to 11:30pm daily), laundry.

REGENCY PLAZA BEST WESTERN, 41 N. 10th St., Minneapolis, MN 55403. Tel. 612/339-9311, or toll free 800/423-4100. Fax 612/339-4765. 193 rms, 7 suites. A/C TV TEL

$ Rates: $66–$72 single or double; suites from $110. Seniors receive a 10% discount. AE, DC, DISC, MC, V. **Parking:** Free.

A winning combination of downtown location and suburban rates is available at this newly remodeled three-story hotel located at the end of Highway 12 on the edge of downtown Minneapolis.

Wood paneling and marble give the lobby a classical look, as does the library beyond. The rooms are large and pleasant, many of them enhanced by the beautiful prints of Les Kouba, a popular Minnesota nature painter. A raspberry and royal-blue color combination prevails in all the rooms, along with light-oak furnishings. Each room contains free in-house movies.

Dining/Entertainment: The Regency Café serves breakfast, lunch, and dinner from 6:30am to 7pm weekdays and from 7:30am to 5:30pm on weekends. Harrigan's Dining Room, offers burgers, steaks, seafood, and other American fare from 5 to 10pm. The Hub Cap Pub doles out soup, sandwiches, and dinner entrées; happy hour runs from 3 to 6pm.

Facilities: Large indoor swimming pool, children's wading pool, whirlpool.

Services: Free shuttle service to any downtown destination.

BUDGET

DAY'S INN/UNIVERSITY, 2407 University Ave. S.E., Minneapolis, MN 55414. Tel. 612/623-3999, or toll free 800/325-2525. Fax 612/331-2152. 130 rms. A/C TV TEL

$ Rates (including continental breakfast): $38–$50 single; $44–$60 double. Seniors receive a 10% discount. AE, CB, DC, DISC, MC, V. **Parking:** Free.

Located at University and Washington avenues, this hotel is six blocks east of the University of Minnesota's Minneapolis campus. Guest rooms, done in earth tones of rust, brown, and orange, offer two large chairs, a desk, and a credenza; most have a vanity area separate from the bath. There are no restaurants on the premises but there is a branch of the Embers chain right across the street. Free local phone calls, free shuttle service to local hospitals, and two nonsmoking floors are also offered here.

GOPHER CAMPUS MOTOR LODGE, 925 S.E. 4th St., Minneapolis, MN 55414. Tel. 612/331-3740. 44 rms. A/C TV TEL

$ Rates: $39 single; $49 double. Weekly rate $216 single; $282 double; $246 room with kitchenette. Seniors receive a 10% discount. AE, DC, DISC, MC, V. **Parking:** Free.

Low-cost weekly accommodations are available near the University of Minnesota at the Gopher Campus Motor Lodge. Thirty years after it first opened its doors, the Gopher Campus Motor Lodge remains a clean and comfortable place to stay. Brick walls in the guest rooms are a reminder of earlier times. Furnishings are simple and spare, as is the price structure.

2. MINNEAPOLIS SOUTH SUBURBAN

MODERATE

BEST WESTERN BRADBURY SUITES, 7770 Johnson Ave., Bloomington, MN 55437. Tel. 612/893-9999, or toll free 800/423-4100. Fax 612/893-1316. 126 rms. A/C TV TEL

$ Rates: $59.95 weekday double; $49.95 weekend double. AE, DC, MC. **Parking:** Free.

 Here, for the price of a single room, you'll be staying in a two-room suite with a small refrigerator and two TV sets. The suites, all done in shades of green and mauve, are comfortable

and spacious enough for an evening "at home," with dinner delivered by Lincoln Del, T.G.I. Friday, or some other local restaurant.

Services: Shuttle service within 1-mile radius to local restaurants and to airport.

Facilities: Free admission to nearby U.S. Swim and Fitness Club; whirlpool and exercise bike.

BEST WESTERN SEVILLE HOTEL, 8151 Bridge Rd., Bloomington, MN Tel. 612/830-1300. Fax 612/830-1535. 250 rms. A/C TV TEL
$ Rates: $55–$63 weekday single or double; $40–$45 weekend double. AE, DC, MC, V. **Parking:** Free.

You'll find the ambience of romantic Old Spain at the large and lovely Seville Hotel. Orange, brown, and yellow dominate the large lobby, while guest rooms are done in softer earth tones of beige and brown. Located right on Interstate 494, the Seville is about 20 minutes from the airport and 30 minutes from downtown Minneapolis and St. Paul. You're also close to fine suburban shopping at the nearby Southtown Center.

The dining facility here is Antonio's Steak and Pasta; there is also a bar. Facilities include a swimming pool, a sauna, and a whirlpool. There is also free shuttle service to and from the airport.

COMFORT INN, 1321 E. 78th St., Bloomington, MN 55420. Tel. 612/854-3400, or toll free 800/228-5150. Fax 612/854-2234. 276 rms, 4 suites. A/C TV TEL
$ Rates: Weekdays $53 single, $64 double; weekends $46 single or double. Suites from $75. Seniors 10% discount on weekdays only. AE, CB, DC, DISC, ER, MC, V. **Parking:** Free.

Located on the Bloomington "strip" just 5 miles from the airport, the Comfort Inn offers the convenience of a motel and the pleasing decor of a hotel. Rooms are attractively furnished in a variety of styles, and if you order king-size accommodations, you'll find a leisure recliner waiting along with the standard furnishings. Each of the rooms in this five-story complex offers free HBO.

Facilities: Exercise room, indoor heated pool.

Services: 24-hour shuttle service to and from airport.

EMBASSY SUITES HOTEL, 2800 W. 80th Street, Bloomington, MN. Tel. 612/884-4811, or toll free 800-EMBASSY. Fax 612/884-8137. 219 suites. A/C TV TEL
$ Rates: Weekdays, $104 for one person, $10 for each additional person. Weekends, $99 for up to four people in room with king-size and hide-a-bed; $109 for up to four people in room with two double beds and 1 hide-a-bed. AE, DC, DISC, MC, V. **Parking:** Free.

The Twin Cities Embassy Suites Hotel, located in suburban Bloomington, is as popular as ever. Morning in the handsome skylit indoor courtyard means a sumptuous cooked-to-order breakfast, while every afternoon brings a 2-hour cocktail party. New on the premises is a fine French bistro, Chez Daniel, where lunch and dinner are served.

HOLIDAY INN AIRPORT 2, 5401 Green Valley Dr., Bloomington, MN 55437. Tel. 612/831-8000, or toll free 800/ HOLIDAY. Fax 612/831-8000. 258 rms. A/C TV TEL

$ Rates: $65 single, $73 double; executive wing $77 single, $86 double. Seniors receive a 10% discount. AE, DC, DISC, MC, V. **Parking:** Free.

Just 7½ miles from the Minneapolis–St. Paul International Airport, this six-story Holiday Inn does a lot of fly-and-drive business: If guests stay for at least one night, they can leave their cars in the parking lot and take advantage of the free 24-hour airport shuttle service, thereby saving the cost of airport parking. Shuttle service is also available to nearby shopping malls and nearby restaurants. The two on-site restaurants to choose from here are Marti's and the Coffee Shop—both serve three meals daily from 7am to 10pm. The cocktail lounge is open from 8pm until 12:30am.

Facilities: Large swimming pool, whirlpool, sauna.

HOLIDAY INN EXPRESS, 814 E. 79th St., Bloomington, MN 55420. Tel. 612/854-5558, or toll free 800/HOLIDAY. Fax 854-4623. 142 rms. A/C TV TEL

$ Rates: Sun–Thurs $55 single, $61 double; Fri–Sat $49. Seniors receive a 10% discount. AE, DC, DISC, MC, V. **Parking:** Free.

You'll feel welcome at once in the attractive lobby here, with its sunken sitting room, brick-walled fireplace, and comfortable burgundy-and-beige seating. Like many other moderate and economy-priced motels, the Holiday Inn Express (formerly Dillion Airport Inn), has no restaurant of its own; but it's connected to Denny's and is only a few steps away from several informal and popular eating places. You can choose a room with a king-size bed, a water bed, or two double beds. All rooms contain a pair of upholstered chairs and a small desk; some have a balcony.

Services: Complimentary coffee around the clock; free shuttle service to and from airport from 5am to midnight.

HOLIDAY INN INTERNATIONAL, 3 Appletree Sq., Bloomington, MN 55420. Tel. 612/854-9000, or toll free 800/ HOLIDAY. Fax 612/854-9000. 432 rms, 132 suites. TV TEL

$ Rates: $83–$96 weekday double; $59 weekend double. Seniors receive 10% discount. AE, CB, DC, DISC, MC, V. **Parking:** Free.

This handsome 13-story building boasts a truly imposing lobby with a two-story atrium and furnishings done in peach and green. These same tones give an air of tranquility to the guest rooms as well.

Dining/Entertainment: Two appealing dining spots, the moderately priced Applebutter and the more elegant Pippins, are popular with local folks as well as with visitors. That's true of the Greenhouse Lounge as well.

Services: Free 24-hour airport shuttle service leaving every half hour; room service (from 6am to 11pm).

Facilities: Swimming pool, whirlpool, sauna, fitness center with Nautilus equipment and aerobics classes, suntan booth, hair salon.

SHERATON AIRPORT INN, 2525 E. 78th St., Bloomington, MN 55420. Tel. 612/854-1771, or toll free 800/325-3535. Fax 612/854-5898. 235 rms, 8 suites. A/C TV TEL

$ Rates: $75 weekday single or double; $59 weekend single or double; one-room suites from $80, two-room suites from $99. AE, DC, DISC, MC, V. **Parking:** Free.

For nearly 20 years visitors to the Twin Cities have enjoyed staying at the Sheraton Airport Inn. Now, a new beautifully landscaped four-story structure has been built adjacent to the original two-story building. The huge lobby contains cozy nooks and crannies that businesspeople find useful for private conferences, as well as an abundance of couches and coffee tables set amid plants and palm trees.

Dining/Entertainment: A full-service dining room, the Timbers, is popular. There's also a lounge with big-screen live TV coverage of major sporting events, as well as live music.

Services: Free 24 hour daily shuttle to and from the international airport (if you aren't picked up within 12 minutes of your initial call, your first night is free).

Facilities: Swimming pool, whirlpool, exercise room.

THUNDERBIRD MOTEL, 2201 E. 78th St., Bloomington, MN 55420. Tel. 612/854-3411, or toll free 800/328-1931. Fax 612/854-1183. 263 rms. A/C TV TEL

$ Rates: $65–$72 weekday single, $71–$78 weekday double; $57 weekend double for one to four guests. Seniors receive a 10% discount. AE, DC, MC. **Parking:** Free.

You'll find a lot more than a comfortable and convenient place to stay at the Thunderbird Motel. Located less than 5 miles from the Minneapolis–St. Paul airport, the Thunderbird is one of dozens of motels on the Bloomington strip, but it has certain notable features. A towering statue of a Native American chief dominates the front

---

IMPRESSIONS ·

I have lived in Minnesota . . . for thirteen years, a western Scandanavia where the birds sing in Swedish, the wind sighs its lullabyes in Norwegian, and the snow and rain beat against the windows to the tune of a Danish dirge.
—ANONYMOUS SAYING (1925)

lawn, and a graceful Apache rides his steed atop a granite pedestal near the main entrance.

The theme extends to the guest rooms as well, where paintings, draperies, and even the carpeting show a Native American motif. But there are 20th-century trappings at the Thunderbird too. This is the only motel on the strip with both an indoor and outdoor swimming pool. You'll have the use of a heat lamp, a whirlpool, a kiddie pool, and picnic tables in the vicinity of the spacious kidney-shaped indoor pool. And across the hall from these, a sauna and exercise room are available without extra charge to guests of the motel.

The Totem Pole dining room is open from 11am to 10pm Monday through Friday, with weekend dinners served from 5 to 10:30pm and all-you-can-eat brunches from 10:30am to 2:30pm. There is also free 24-hour shuttle service to and from the airport.

BUDGET

EXEL INN, 2701 E. 78th St., Bloomington, MN 55420. Tel. 612/854-7200, or toll free 800/356-8013. Fax 612/854-7200. 205 rms. A/C TV TEL
$ Rates: $34–$44 single or double. Seniors receive a 10% discount. AE, DC, DISC, MC. **Parking:** Free.

The Exel Inn is located just 4 miles from the Minneapolis–St. Paul International Airport. This brick complex of two two-story buildings offers attractive rooms at reasonable rates. The rooms, decorated in shades of brown and peach, are kept scrupulously clean. HBO is available in each room, at no additional cost.

FRIENDLY HOST INN, 1225 E. 78th St., Minneapolis, MN 55420. Tel. 612/854-3322, or toll free 800/453-4511. Fax 612/854-0245. 47 rms. A/C TV TEL
$ Rates: $38–$47 single or double. Seniors receive a $3 discount. AE, DC, DISC, MC, V. **Parking:** Free.

If you're interested in economical accommodations with cooking facilities, you'll be glad to learn about the Friendly Host Inn. They have single-bed rooms with a two-burner stove, a small sink, and a refrigerator. The much larger two-bed rooms contain a four-burner stove, a small refrigerator, and double cupboards.

Decor varies here, but the rooms are all attractive and comfortable. The motel is well located, just 5 miles from the airport. An indoor pool and whirlpool are available on the premises.

HOPKINS HOUSE HOTEL, 1501 Hwy. 7, Hopkins, MN 55343. Tel. 612/935-7711, or toll free 800/328-6024. Fax 612/933-3621. 164 rms. A/C TV TEL
$ Rates: $35 single; $40–$45 double; $65 room with hot tub. AE, DISC, MC, V. **Parking:** Free.

You'll find attractive, inexpensively priced accommodations at the suburban Hopkins Hotel. Located about 10 miles from Lake Minnetonka and 20 minutes from downtown Minneapolis, this seven-story complex offers an indoor pool, sauna, exercise room, and table tennis. The color scheme features shades of rose and blue, starting with the deep-rose cushioned couches and soft-blue table lamps in the lobby. Oak end tables and a brass ceiling punctuated with modern open globe lights complete the bright, cheery lobby decor. Your own room will doubtless be decorated in combinations of rose and blue as well, and if you like, it can also contain a heart-shaped water bed; just ask for a "happy-tub room." You'll find basic cable color TV here plus free HBO and ESPN sports.

3. ST. PAUL

EXPENSIVE

CROWN STERLING SUITES, 175 E. 10th St., St. Paul, MN 55101. Tel. 612/224-5400, or toll-free 800/433-4600. Fax 612/224-0957. 210 suites. A/C TV TEL

$ Rates: $102 single; $89 double. $99 weekend triple or quad. Seniors receive a 10% discount. AE, DC, DISC, MC, V. **Parking:** Free.

If you're familiar with Crown Sterling Suites hotels, you'll be glad to know that there are three of them here in the Twin Cities: one in downtown St. Paul as cited above; one in downtown Minneapolis at 425 S. 7th Street (tel. 612/333-7884, or toll free 800/433-4600; fax 612/333-7984); and one near the airport at 7901 34th Ave. S., Bloomington, MN 55420 (tel. 612/854-1000; fax 612/854-6557).

These value-packed hotels have effectively countered the old admonition: "If you want the comforts of home, stay home." Actually, the comforts awaiting you here may rival what you've left at home: not one but two handsomely furnished rooms with a TV and a phone in each, a kitchenette whose facilities include a microwave oven, and decor to suit your individual preference, with whole floors devoted to rooms decorated in tones of mauve, green, or blue. Just choose your floor and you choose your color.

A full cooked-to-order breakfast is yours each morning, and at the end of each day you can have your favorite drinks at the 2-hour cocktail party held in the attractive courtyard. Here, brick pillars, tile floors, fountains, and even a waterfall will remind you of your last visit to the Mediterranean, or of the visit you've yet to make. Facilities include a pool, a sauna, a whirlpool, and a steam room. There is also a free airport shuttle.

RADISSON HOTEL ST. PAUL, 11 East Kellogg Boulevard,

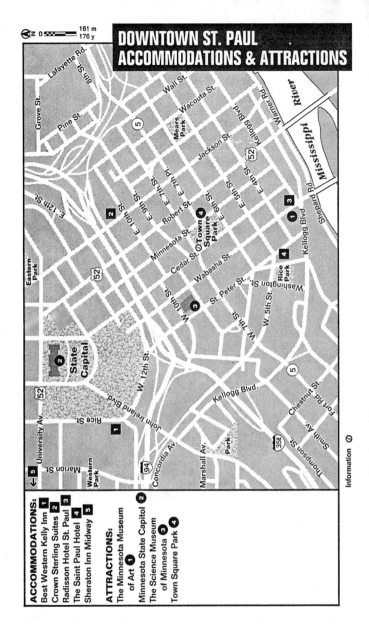

DOWNTOWN ST. PAUL
ACCOMMODATIONS & ATTRACTIONS

ACCOMMODATIONS:
Best Western Kelly Inn **1**
Crown Sterling Suites **2**
Radisson Hotel St. Paul **3**
The Saint Paul Hotel **4**
Sheraton Inn Midway **5**

ATTRACTIONS:
The Minnesota Museum of Art **1**
Minnesota State Capitol **2**
The Science Museum of Minnesota **3**
Town Square Park **4**

St. Paul, MN 55101. Tel. 612/292-1900, or toll-free 800-333-3333. Fax 612/224-8999. 465 rms, 10 suites. AC TV TEL
$ Rates: $95 weekday double, $110 weekday single; $65 weekend single or double. $125–$145 suite. Seniors $68, depending on availability.

Overlooking the Mississippi River and just 20 minutes from the Minneapolis/St. Paul International Airport, this hotel is connected by skyway to downtown businesses, shops and entertainment. Also close by is the Minnesota Museum of Art. Facilities here include an indoor garden court, a pool, and Le Carrousel, the Twin Cities' only revolving restaurant, which you'll find on the 22nd floor.

THE SAINT PAUL HOTEL, 350 Market St., St. Paul, MN 55102. Tel. 612/292-9292, or toll-free 800/292-9292. Fax 612-228-9506. 223 rms, 31 suites. AC TV TEL
$ Rates: Fri–Sat $79 single or double; Sun–Thurs $115 single, $130 double. $150–$625 suite. AE, DC, DISC, V.

You'll find a beautiful blend of the old and the new at the downtown St. Paul Hotel. In 1910 this was St. Paul's premier hotel, and now it has taken its place once more as a distinguished grand old hotel for those who expect and appreciate the best. Facing Rice Park and the Ordway Music Theatre, the St. Paul Hotel is situated between the beautiful St. Paul Public Library and the Landmark Center, the restored Old Federal Courts Building.

But if the St. Paul Hotel maintains close ties with the city's past, it's also an integral part of St. Paul's burgeoning present. Situated at one end of an extensive skyway system, it offers guests climate-controlled access to 38 downtown blocks of shops, banks, restaurants, and varied forms of entertainment.

Accommodations are appropriately elegant. Once past the lobby, with its antique crystal chandeliers, turn-of-the-century love seats and chairs, and large oriental screen, you'll be equally pleased with the guest rooms. Each is decorated uniquely, but all have either a king-size bed or two double beds, along with two comfortable chairs and an ample table. Deluxe rooms are outfitted with a love seat in place of the two chairs.

MODERATE

BEST WESTERN KELLY INN, 161 St. Anthony, St. Paul, MN 55103. Tel. 612/227-8711. 125 rms. TV TEL
$ Rates: $58 weekday single, $66 weekday double; $58 weekend single or double. AE, DISC, MC, V.

Located within easy walking distance of the State Capitol and the St. Paul Cathedral, this recently remodeled hotel overlooks downtown Saint Paul with its shops, museums and other popular tourist attractions and is only ten minutes away from the airport, the Metrodome and other downtown Minneapolis attractions. Amenities include an on-site restaurant, a lounge, an indoor pool, a whirlpool, a sauna, and a children's pool.

SHERATON INN MIDWAY, I-94 and Hamline Ave., St. Paul, MN 55104. Tel. 612/642-1234, or toll-free 800/535-2339. 200 rms. AC TV TEL

$ Rates: $82 weekday double, $72 weekday single; $60 weekend double, $50 weekend single. Senior weekday rates are $68. AE, DC, DISC, MC, V.

Conveniently located about ten minutes from downtown Minneapolis, and five minutes from downtown St. Paul, the Sheraton Inn Midway boasts Minnesota's largest sauna along with a popular swimming pool and whirlpool. The public space here is striking—a tasteful blend of natural plantings, polished brass and gleaming glass. You're sure to find the rooms clean and comfortable.

SUNWOOD INN, Bandana Square, 1010 Bandana Boulevard West, St. Paul MN 55108. Tel. 612/647-1637. 109 rms. AC TV TEL

$ Rates: $57–$62 single; $62–$67 double. Seniors, $52. AE, DC, DISC, MC, V.

Connected by skyway to the Bandana Square shopping and dining complex, Sunwood Inn offers an indoor pool, whirlpool, sauna and a wading pool. The two-story inn is a former railroad repair shop; the lobby retains a rustic quality with its wood-beamed ceiling and benches.

CHAPTER 6

TWIN CITIES DINING

The good news about dining out in the Twin Cities is that there's something here to suit every taste and every budget. Far from being the land of *lefse* and *lutefisk,* Minneapolis and St. Paul are remarkable for the variety, the quality, and the cosmopolitan nature of their restaurant cuisine. Actually, they're a little short on Scandinavian dining places, but there is plenty of good French, German, Greek, Italian, Chinese, Japanese, and Vietnamese fare to be found here. And there are fine eating spots that have a special way with basic American steaks, chops, and seafood.

A number of Twin Cities restaurants have won national and international awards, and they'll be called to your attention, along with those that have become favorites among knowledgeable local folks. Many of the places listed here, in fact, are the ones to which local hosts generally bring their own out-of-town guests.

I'll let you in on the not-to-be-missed restaurants in various parts of the cities and suburbs. They'll be listed in each area from the most expensive to the least expensive. Bear in mind that geographically some areas are relatively confined—the downtown Minneapolis, Warehouse, and Mill districts, for example. Others, like Minneapolis South Suburban, are rather spread out. Use the maps in this book to get oriented before you set out.

Two reminders about price: First, even the costliest eating spots tend to be moderately priced at lunchtime; thus, you can enjoy the finest in ambience, cuisine, and presentation for a nominal noonday cost. Second, prices in Twin Cities restaurants tend to be lower than in other metropolitan areas, so the "expensive" choice may seem quite reasonably priced to you. All the better. It's just one more benefit for visitors to these fair cities.

1. MINNEAPOLIS

VERY EXPENSIVE

DOWNTOWN

MORTON'S OF CHICAGO, 655 Nicollet Mall, Minneapolis. Tel. 673-9700.
Cuisine: STEAK HOUSE. **Reservations:** Required.
$ Prices: Appetizers $4.25–$8.95; main courses $15.95–$28.95. AE, DC, MC, V.
Open: Lunch Mon–Fri 11:30am–2:30pm; dinner Mon–Sat 5:30–11pm, Sun 5–10pm.

Like all Morton's of Chicago steak houses across the country, this one is situated one floor below street level. If you've left your car in the underground garage at the Nieman Marcus end of Gavidae Common, be sure to have your parking ticket validated at Morton's for complimentary parking. As you enter Gavidae Common from the garage, you'll see Morton's to your right. To gain access to the dining room, just open the large mahogany door and walk right in. You can also enter Morton's by descending a staircase just inside Nieman Marcus's Sixth Street entrance. A welcoming canopy with Morton's name on it will tell you you've come to the right place. Take time on your way down the stairs to look at the interesting black-and-white photographs on the wall. Collected from the Minnesota Historical Society, they depict the Twin Cities during bygone days.

Signature features at Morton's of Chicago steak houses are the open kitchens and the servers who provide you with a comprehensive show-and-tell presentation before taking your order. Tempting beef, lamb, chicken, veal, and fish, wrapped in plastic, will be displayed and discussed; a live lobster will be introduced as well. The portions, when they arrive, are easily large enough to share. (There's no charge for an extra plate.) The jumbo shrimp cocktail ($8.95) and broiled sea scallops wrapped in bacon with apricot chutney on the side ($7.50) are particularly popular appetizers. The Caesar salad ($4.95) and spinach salad ($4.75) are favorites as well. Among the entrées, shrimp Alexander ($17.50) and lemon oregano chicken ($15.95) rank high among the vegetarian dishes, but if you came for steak, you really can't go wrong with any of the choices, from the New York sirloin ($28.95) to the double filet mignon ($23.95) or the tenderloin brochette ($18.95). To accompany your entrée, consider sautéed fresh spinach and mushrooms ($3.95) or steamed fresh broccoli ($4.25) or asparagus ($6.50), both with hollandaise sauce. If you'd like a light

FROMMER'S SMART TRAVELER: RESTAURANTS

1. Eat your main meal at lunch, when prices are lower. You can eat at some of the Twin Cities' best restaurants for substantially less than what it would cost at dinner.
2. Choose set lunches and dinners when possible—many represent a 30% saving over à la carte menus.
3. Look for the daily specials on any à la carte menu; they're often cheaper than the regular listings.
4. Watch how much alcohol you drink; too much wine, beer, etc. can run up your tab.
5. Some expensive restaurants offer pasta dishes that are priced much lower than most entrées.
6. Ask if the entrée comes with a side dish like a vegetable or potato (this may be all you need to order).

and luscious soufflé for dessert, tell the waiter first off when you order; Mark Laurin, the gifted young chef, requires 30 minutes preparation time.

MANNY'S, in the Hyatt Regency Hotel, 1300 Nicollet Mall, Minneapolis. Tel. 339-9900.

Cuisine: STEAK HOUSE. **Reservations:** Required.

$ Prices: Appetizers $6.95–$7.95; main courses $17.95–$45.90. AE, DC, MC, V.

Open: Dinner Mon–Thurs 5:30–10pm, Fri–Sat 5:30–11pm, Sun 5:30–9pm.

One of the first things you'll notice at Manny's, along with the bright lighting and the hardwood floors, is the absence of centerpieces on the tables. Manny's makes no apologies for its lack of traditional ambience. What's important here, they explain, is what's on the plate; and what's on the plate has kept the phones ringing since Manny's first opened in June 1988.

When you do get a table at Manny's, you'll discover that everything is à la carte, and everything is large—your waiter will suggest you consider sharing a baked potato, an order of french fries, or a portion of creamed garlic spinach. And he won't be surprised if you ask to share your main course as well. Splitting portions is encouraged at Manny's, where there's no charge for an extra plate.

Although steak is what Manny's is mainly about, there are many other choices as well. Try lamb chops at $19.95, pork chops at $15.95, or lemon pepper chicken at $12.95. And if you're a shrimp fancier, be advised that the shrimp, lemon peppered and grilled, are king-size and utterly delicious. But steak, of course, is the most frequently ordered item, and you'll have a choice among memorable New York strip steak for $22.95, filet mignon at $18.95 or $21.95, or porterhouse at $22.95. If you want to go all the way, consider the 48-ounce double porterhouse steak that goes for $45.90. Maybe you can share the cost as well as the portion with a partner, but in any case keep in mind that the doggie bags, like everything else at Manny's, are super-size.

510, 510 Groveland Ave., Minneapolis. Tel. 874-6440.

Cuisine: FRENCH. **Reservations:** Required.

$ Prices: Appetizers $4.50–$8.50; main courses $15–$25; seven-course fixed-price meal $45. AE, DC, DISC, MC, V.

Open: Dinner Mon–Sat 5:30–10pm.

Where do celebrities head for lunch and dinner while they're in the Twin Cities? Likely as not, you'll find them at an elegant restaurant known simply as 510. Robert Redford has dined here, and so have Carol Channing, Charlton Heston, Pia Zadora, and Richard Dreyfuss. And while they were appearing in *Foxfire* at the nearby Guthrie Theater, Jessica Tandy and Hume Cronyn were here regularly.

This is probably the premier special-occasion restaurant in town, the place where lawyers, architects, and businesspeople confer with their peers. It's also a place where tourists come because they want to try 510's admirable cuisine for themselves.

Shimmering crystal chandeliers and sweeping blue-gray draperies provide a gracious and serene setting in which to enjoy the creativity and commitment to quality that have made Kathleen Craig's fine restaurant as popular as it is.

Unpredictability is one characteristic of 510, and your waiter will recite for you the specials of the day, including soups, appetizers, entrées, and desserts, as well as the fixed-price tasting menu, a seven- or eight-course dinner. Entrées include grilled marinated breast of chicken with radicchio and scallion ($18) and loin of beef with glazed garlic and bleu cheese ($24). The fish entrée changes daily.

A three-course theater menu is available from 5:30 to 6:30pm Monday through Saturday.

GOODFELLOW'S, 800 Nicollet Mall, Minneapolis. Tel. 332-4800.

Cuisine: AMERICAN. **Reservations:** Recommended.

$ Prices: Dinner appetizers $8–$10; main courses $18–$28; fixed-price four-course dinner $38; lunch main courses $9–$14. AE, DC, MC, V.

Open: Lunch Mon–Sat 11:30am–2:30pm; dinner Mon–Thurs 5:30–9pm, Fri–Sat 5:30–10pm.

For a special occasion, you can't do better than Goodfellow's.

Located on the top floor of the Conservatory, one of downtown Minneapolis's most unabashedly upscale shopping centers, Goodfellow's wide windows provide a dramatic view of the Nicollet Mall. The restaurant is accessible by skyway to major hotels and department stores, including Dayton's.

Goodfellow's has maintained its reputation for impeccable service, cuisine, and ambience. Prices here are relatively high, but the value is second to none. The menu changes seasonally with the availability of ingredients, but game, including venison, is available year round. Particularly popular are appetizers like grilled lamb tenderloin with spinach-and-warm-goat-cheese salad and fried eggplant, and fettuccine with grilled shrimp, oven-dried tomatoes, and basil sauce. Main-course favorites include braised pork tenderloin with wild rice cake and tomatillo-shallot sauce and grilled veal chop with herb cheese lasagne and roasted pepper sauce. Desserts are all tempting, but my personal favorite is the delectable lace cookie cup filled with raspberries, cream, and caramel.

The wine list here is widely and justifiably admired and includes over 400 selections, all of them American except for the champagne. (While most of the wines hail from California, a few are from the Finger Lakes of New York.) There's a wide variety of nonalcoholic wines and beers as well.

And then there's Goodfellow's vegetarian menu, devised with characteristic attention to detail. Vegetarians will be pleased with dinners featuring roast corn soup with cumin-seared tomatoes and cilantro, mixed green salad with red beet vinaigrette and parmesan cheese, fennel-and-pine-nut-stuffed phyllo leaves with white beans and grilled vegetables, and a choice of desserts or fresh fruit.

THE MILL DISTRICT

WHITNEY GRILLE, 150 Portland Ave., Minneapolis. Tel. 339-9300.
   Cuisine: AMERICAN. **Reservations:** Recommended.
$ Prices: Appetizers $4–$7.50; main courses $16.50–$24.95; Sun brunch buffet $17.95; lunch $4.25–$12.95. AE, DC, DISC, MC, V.
   Open: Breakfast Mon–Sun 7–10:30am; lunch Mon–Sat 11am–2pm; Sun brunch 9:30am–2pm; dinner Mon–Sun 5:30–10:30pm.

When this restaurant opened in March 1987, the Mill District (between the Metrodome and the Mississippi River) got its first upscale restaurant. There's an Old World atmosphere at the Whitney Grille, with its fabric-covered walls, African-mahogany woodwork, and marble appointments. The handsome traditional European chairs have been upholstered in tapestry and outfitted with gooseneck arms. An especially nice touch at dinnertime is the piano music offered from 6pm Monday through Friday and Sunday and from 6:30pm on Saturday.

The distinguished cuisine seems a natural extension of the setting. Executive chef Andy Nahler and executive sous-chef Richard Adams have won enthusiastic reviews for their regional American items, including West Coast halibut bisque, East Coast shellfish terrine, Colorado rack of lamb, and Wisconsin veal T-bone. Desserts are fabulous: A particularly popular summertime item is the exquisite raspberry roulade, a concoction of fresh raspberries and Chantilly crème wrapped in sponge cake soaked in Triple Sec. Cuisine and decor are special here, but so is the atmosphere of warmth and hospitality.

Breakfast prices range from $4.50 for pancakes with sliced fruit, maple syrup, and bacon, sausage, or ham to $8.50 for two eggs served with sirloin steak, scrapple, and toast. Sunday brunches are deservedly popular too. Luncheon entrées range from $8.50 for sautéed boneless breast of chicken to $13.50 for broiled prime sirloin. A selection of appetizers, soups, salads, sandwiches, and desserts is available. Dinner entrées include Minnesota walleye, veal T-bone, and chateaubriand for two, carved tableside.

NORTHEAST MINNEAPOLIS

JAX CAFÉ, 1928 University Ave. N.E., Minneapolis. Tel. 789-7297.
Cuisine: AMERICAN. **Reservations:** Recommended.
$ Prices: Appetizers $3.95–$10.95; main courses $10.95–$31.95; Sun brunch $12.95 adults, $5.95 children under 10. AE, DC, DISC, V.
Open: Lunch daily 11am–3pm; dinner Mon–Thurs 3:30–10:30pm, Fri–Sat 3:30–11pm, Sun 3:30–9pm; buffet brunch Sun 10am–3pm.

When lawyer/legislator Joseph Kozlak and his wife Gertrude decided to open a Minneapolis restaurant back in 1943, they were able to seat 56 diners. Today, the much-enlarged Jax, owned and operated by the founders' son Bill and his wife Kathy, can seat 300 people on each of its two floors, with room for 50 or so more on the beautifully landscaped patio. The handsome restaurant is known widely as a special-occasion place, where proms, weddings, anniversary celebrations, and other festive goings-on are enhanced by an ambience of dark woods, soft lighting, and impeccable service. You can enjoy piano music here on Thursday, Friday, and Saturday evenings from 6:30 to 10:30pm and at Sunday brunch.

The dessert temptations are many, but do consider the Bailey's Irish Cream banana torte, which recently won first prize in a cities-wide competition and a place on the menu of the annual gala Symphony Ball. Before dessert, though, there are other choices to be made: "classic cut" tenderloin, chicken marinara, broiled filet of walleye pike—the list is long and varied. Entrées are served with soup or salad and rice, pasta, potato, or vegetable. At lunch, entrées run from $6.50 to $10.50.

EXPENSIVE

DOWNTOWN

AZUR RESTAURANT, 651 Nicollet Mall, Minneapolis. Tel. 342-2500.

Cuisine: FRENCH MEDITERRANEAN. **Reservations:** Recommended.

$ Prices: Appetizers $6.50–$8.50; main courses $17.50–$24.50; fixed-price three-course dinner $21–$24; lunch $6–$13.50. AE, DC, MC, V.

Open: Lunch Mon–Sat 11:15am–2:30pm; dinner Mon–Thurs 5:30–9:45pm.

A few blocks away from D'Amico Cucina (see below), on the top level of Gavidae Common, this more recent enterprise of the D'Amico brothers has gained national recognition. Among its other laurels, the Azur Restaurant was named one of the best new restaurants of 1990 by *Esquire* magazine. The handsome decor was designed by Richard D'Amico in shades of black, purple, and green; the ambience is bustling and upbeat, thanks in part to the French rock-and-roll music that provides a spirited background. Service is correct but unpretentious. In fact, despite the fact that this is one of the most expensive restaurants in town, you'll eat dinner here without benefit of a tablecloth.

Featured here is chef Jay Sparks's version of the cooking you'd find in southern France's Côte d'Azur. Olive oil, roasted garlic, leeks, and fennel play an important part in Sparks's recipes. Popular dinnertime appetizers range from grilled tomato bread to yellowfin tuna with fried leeks and cucumber-melon sauce. Favorite entrées include gratin of prawns, field mushrooms, and fried artichokes and duck breast with caramelized balsamic vinegar, black olives, and pine nuts. There's an extensive wine list and a delightful variety of apéritifs and digestives. Complimentary valet parking is available in the Gavidae Common Parking Ramp.

GUSTINO'S, in the Minneapolis Marriott, 30 S. 7th St., Minneapolis. Tel. 349-4075.

Cuisine: NORTHERN ITALIAN. **Reservations:** Recommended.

$ Prices: Appetizers $5.25–$8.95; main courses $17–$24. AE, DC, MC, V.

Open: Dinner Sun–Thurs 6–10pm, Fri–Sat 6–11pm.

If you enjoy music in the foreground as well as the background when you dine, don't miss Gustino's. A talented group of singing servers are on hand here seven nights a week to bring you a beautiful blend of musical and culinary fare. Gustino's caters to the diverse performing schedules of these singers, who regularly appear in local operatic and musical-comedy productions.

There's a feast for the eye, as well, in this handsome art deco room with its panoramic view of downtown Minneapolis and, from March through October, spectacular Twin Cities sunsets. As you're led to your table through a glass alcove, you'll pass a white grand piano and a floor-to-ceiling triangular glass wine "cellar" displaying more than 200 bottles of Italian wine.

Veal is a specialty of the house and you can choose from veal scaloppine, veal in marsala sauce, breaded veal scallops with ham, mozzarella, and fresh tomatoes, or a delectable roast veal with the stuffing and sauce of the day. Gustino's offers fine Italian seafood and chicken too, with each entrée served with polenta or risotto and vegetables. You really can't go wrong with any of the soups, salads, pizzas, or pasta on the menu here, but do save room for a slice of pepperoni bread and one of the "painted desserts" concocted daily by the chef. The three-level *torre di pisa* is an extravaganza of assorted antipasti selections. Wine lovers will enjoy the "wines of the month," two selections that can be ordered by the glass that are ordinarily available only by the bottle.

KIKUGAWA, Riverplace, 45 Main St. S.E., Minneapolis. Tel. 378-3006.

Cuisine: JAPANESE. **Reservations:** Recommended.

$ Prices: Appetizers $3.25–$9.50; main courses $7.50–$16.75; fixed-price dinner $24.50; lunch $5–$10. AE, CB, DC, MC, V.

Open: Lunch Mon–Sat 11:30am–2pm; dinner Mon–Thurs 5pm–10pm, Fri–Sat 5pm–midnight, Sun 5–11:30pm.

Japanese cuisine, both traditional and contemporary, is featured at Kikugawa. Owner-operator John Omori recalls that since sushi first appeared on the menu during the early eighties, the raw-fish delicacy has gone from less than one-tenth of his food orders to about one-third. A full sushi bar is one of the features of his handsome restaurant with its pale-wood pillars and beams. *Nabemono* table cookery is available throughout the different dining rooms. Particularly popular are the tatami rooms, where diners leave their shoes at the door and experience traditional Japanese dining. There is also a main dining room and a room facing the river.

A favorite menu choice is beef shabu, paper-thin slices of filet mignon cooked for two or three seconds in hot shabu broth. Currently a favorite in Japan, the dish is particularly popular with the growing number of local residents who have visited the country. Omori has also introduced a yakitori bar, a broiling station for skewered chicken, beef, seafood, and vegetables. Other items you might try are sukiyaki and the nabemono table-prepared dishes, including shabu shabu (Japanese fondue). For haute cuisine Japanese style, try the combination tempura made of seafood, chicken, beef, and seasonal vegetables. There's a delicious selection of desserts here, including two inspired intercontinental inventions—tempura ice cream and green-tea ice cream.

MURRAY'S, 26 S. 6th St., Minneapolis. Tel. 339-0909.

Cuisine: AMERICAN. **Reservations:** Recommended.

$ Prices: Appetizers $5.25–$7.95; main courses $14.50–$24.95; steaks $18.50–$25.95; lunch $4.75–$9.50; afternoon tea $6.50. AE, MC, V.

Open: Lunch daily 11am–3pm; tea Mon–Fri 2–4pm; dinner Mon–Thurs 4–10:30pm, Fri–Sat 4–11pm.

For more than four decades Twin Citians have headed to Murray's. Butter-knife steak is the specialty of this handsome, family-managed restaurant, but you needn't live by beef alone at Murray's. The menu features broiled filet of walleye pike and T-bone veal steak, among other favorites. There are vegetarian selections as well.

Murray's has somehow managed to retain its intimacy after being enlarged a few years ago. Mirrored walls, dusty-rose draperies and valances, and wrought-iron chandeliers and balustrades provide the same warm and gracious setting that Art and Marie Murray cultivated back in the forties. Their grandson Tim, who now runs the restaurant, also kept the popular piano and violin accompaniment to the evening's dining experience.

Dinners here are in the expensive-but-worth-it category, but the ever popular downtowner menu, served from 4 to 6pm every day, features a full dinner including potato or vegetable and salad along with Murray's famous bread basket for $9.75 to $25.95.

NEW FRENCH CAFÉ, 128 N. 4th St., Minneapolis. Tel. 338-3790.

Cuisine: FRENCH. **Reservations:** Recommended.

$ Prices: Appetizers $4–$9; main courses $21–$26; lunch $8.95–$12.95; breakfast $5.75–$8.25; Sat–Sun brunch $8.85–$10.95. AE, DC, MC, V.

Open: Breakfast Mon–Fri 7–11am; lunch Mon–Fri 11:30–1:30pm; dinner Mon–Thurs 5:30–9:30pm, Sat–Sun 5:30–10pm; late-night supper Fri–Sat 10pm–midnight.

The New French Café, with its whitewashed brick walls and exposed wooden beams, is considered one of the smartest dining and drinking spots in the Twin Cities. This is the location of choice for that important breakfast meeting, the perfect spot for a casual lunch or a special dinner, and the place where many local artists get together late at night. It was the New French Café that began the transformation of Minneapolis's run-down warehouse district into a Soho on the Mississippi, where nearby art galleries attract crowds every week.

The cuisine features classic and contemporary French selections including ragoût of goose with red wine, crème fraîche, mushrooms, turnips, carrots, and leeks served with Savoyard potatoes. Desserts, baked on the premises, are a specialty here, including favorites like eclairs and fresh fruit tarts.

WAREHOUSE DISTRICT

D'AMICO CUCINA, 100 N. 6th St., Minneapolis. Tel. 338-2401.

Cuisine: ITALIAN. **Reservations:** Required.

$ Prices: Appetizers $6–$9; main courses $17–$25.

Open: Dinner Mon–Thurs 5:30–10pm, Fri–Sat 5:30–11pm, Sun 5–9pm.

No restaurant in the Twin Cities has proved more popular with the public and the press than D'Amico Cucina. Situated across the street from the Target Arena, D'Amico Cucina has been an unqualified winner since it was opened in September 1987 by the D'Amico brothers and their colleague, Steve Davidson. It is a handsome, casually sophisticated restaurant where the cuisine is imaginative, the service impeccable, and the atmosphere everything you could desire. The restaurant's brick wall and wood-beamed ceilings hearken back to the building's warehouse days, while the blend of peach and gray in the marble floor and the wall coverings is accented by steel and black leather chairs.

The menu choices here are varied and eminently tempting. The wine list, also, is extensive. Appetizers include the miniature thin-crusted pizza of the day, timbale of prosciutto, and charcoal grilled eggplant. Other notable items are the potato gnocchi with tomato, basil, thyme, and romano cheese and the savory quadrucci with chicken, walnuts, and sage.

Of the entrées, favorites include pork tenderloin with garlic, red beans, and smoked bacon; and grilled lamb with crispy lentils and black olives. The menu changes several times a year. Daily specials here are always worthy of careful consideration, and so are the pastries, custards, gelati, and sorbetti, all prepared on the premises.

On Sunday one of the best bargains in town is offered: a family-style dinner with soup, two pastas and one risotto, and lots of bread for $13.50 per person.

MODERATE

DOWNTOWN

BRIT'S PUB & EATING ESTABLISHMENT, 1110 Nicollet Mall, Minneapolis. Tel. 332-3908.

Cuisine: BRITISH. **Reservations:** Not accepted.

$ Prices: Appetizers $4–$6; main courses $6–$14. AE, DC, MC, V.

Open: Daily 7am–midnight.

 Situated directly across Nicollet Avenue from Orchestra Hall, Brit's is a relatively recent addition to downtown dining. It could hardly be more welcome. The proprietor, the cuisine, and the decor are all decidedly British, and the clientele is as eclectic as can be. Concertgoers in minks mingle affably with sports fans in jeans. Others come in not for a meal, but for a few pints and a game of darts or pool. Owner-manager Nigel Chilvers has imported an assortment of beers, as many if not more, he says, than are available in London. But, as in London, beer here is served at 54 degrees, which, he explains, enables a beer to best express its flavor.

The cuisine at Brit's is as delightful as the conviviality. Chilvers has shown that British food is not necessarily disappointing: the steak-and-kidney pie is a real treat, as are the tender and tasty tenderloin coins, served with Brit's own special sauce. For dessert, try the Thames River mud cake with crème à l'anglaise or the thoroughly British trifle.

PALOMINO, 825 Hennepin Ave., Minneapolis. Tel. 339-3800.

Cuisine: FRENCH/MEDITERRANEAN. **Reservations:** Required.

$ Prices: Appetizers $2.95–$7.95; main courses $6.95–$21.95. AE, MC, V.

Open: Lunch Mon–Sat 11:30am–2:30pm; dinner Mon–Thurs 5–10:30pm, Fri–Sat 5–11pm. Bar menu Mon–Sat 11am–1am, Sun 4pm–1am.

Located in LaSalle Plaza, an escalator ride above the historic State Theatre and a short distance from the Target Arena, Palomino opened in October 1991, intending to provide a special-occasion environment at moderate prices. They've accomplished that and a whole lot more. This is one restaurant in which the majority of diners tend to dress more formally in the daytime than at night. That's because the businesspeople who come for lunch tend to stop in during the evening as well, but much more casually clad.

Described as a "metropolitan bistro," Palomino features a south European cuisine that's predominately French, Italian, Greek, and Spanish. It also features one of the largest open kitchens you're likely to see anywhere. As you're led to your table in the beautiful two-level dining room, you'll pass an exhibition cooking area and see preparations of everything from spit-roast garlic chicken to oven-fired pizza, Roman style. Menus are printed daily or weekly here, depending on the availability of fresh items.

The dining rooms are at once elegant and comfortable. Marble dining tables, a large Matisse, and gleaming blown-glass fixtures combine with the mauve, purple, and black decor to make these rooms appropriate for all sorts of occasions. The handsome adjoining bar provides a pleasant alternative, including a menu of its own and a no-reservations policy. The bar, by the way, offers the largest grappa selection in the Midwest along with a large selection of ports and, among other favorites, the Pallini champagne and the peach schnapps that have become so popular here during spring and summer. Whether you come in for a meal or only for a pick-me-up, do consider one of the luscious desserts. The tiramisu is universally praised and for very good reason. Also be sure to try the house bread, baked by Baldinger's Bakery, with a mixture of seasonings devised by Palomino, with thoroughly delectable results. Many Twin Citians are thoroughly addicted to it.

PING'S, 1401 Nicollet Ave. S., Minneapolis. Tel. 874-9404.

Cuisine: CHINESE. **Reservations:** Recommended.

$ Prices: Appetizers $4–$6; main courses $7–$15; lunch buffet Mon–Fri $6.95; Sun buffet $8.95. AE, DC, DISC, MC, V.

Open: Mon–Thurs 11am–10pm, Fri 11am–midnight, Sat noon–midnight, Sun noon–9pm.

One of the best bargain buffets in the Twin Cities is found at Ping's, Monday through Friday from 11:30am to 2pm. Even more lavish buffets are available on Sunday. Pink Chinese kites contrast with gray walls and pillars in this attractive informal dining room, and a pink tile bar is the focal point of the lower of two dining levels. Chef Mingh Tran's selections attract downtown businesspeople, local residents, and others who savor the spicy Szechuan entrées that are featured here. One of the most renowned specialties is the crispy flavorful Peking duck. There is complimentary valet parking at Ping's nearby lot.

TEJAS, 800 Nicollet Mall, Minneapolis. Tel. 375-0800.

Cuisine: SOUTHWESTERN. **Reservations:** Recommended.

$ Prices: Appetizers $6–$9; entrées $10–$16. AE, DISC, MC, V.

Open: Mon–Sat 11am–10pm.

The cuisine at Tejas is not Tex-Mex; it's decidedly Southwestern. That means what you'll be tasting in this handsome dining room is a unique blend of Mexican and Southwestern-Native-American foods and flavors. The dining area is decorated in shades of peach, deep rose, and sea-foam green, and accented with Indian pottery. The meticulously arranged foods, many of them presented on plates "painted" with subtly seasoned sauces, are a treat for the eye. Visitors from as far away as California have been known to stop in the Twin Cities overnight in order to dine at Tejas. Reviews in *The New York Times, Esquire,* and *USA Today* have helped spread the word further yet.

The menu changes four times a year, but certain signature items are a permanent part of the offerings, such as tortilla soup with chicken, avocado, smoked tomato, and Jack cheese; Caesar salad with cayenne croutons and cumin-tamarind dressing; smoked shrimp enchilada with creamy barbecue sauce and jicama relish; smoked chicken nachos with Jack and Asiago cheeses and avocado and tomato salsas. For dessert, choices include flourless dark chocolate-ancho cake with Mexican vanilla sauce and warm upside-down pineapple skillet cake with rum-caramel sauce. Try any of these dishes and you'll understand what all the fuss is about.

If you're interested in take-out orders, Tejas will deliver anywhere in the downtown area. And one last bit of information—all the juices here are fresh squeezed, which accounts for the popularity of Tejas's lemonade and margaritas.

THE WAREHOUSE DISTRICT

MONTE CARLO BAR & GRILL, 219 3rd Ave. N., Minneapolis. Tel. 333-5900.

Cuisine: AMERICAN. **Reservations:** Recommended.

$ Prices: Appetizers $3.95–$7.95; main courses $6.95–$17.95; Sun breakfast $4.95. AE, DC, DISC, MC, V.

Open: Mon–Sat 11am–11:45pm, Sun 10am–10:45pm.

There's some question as to whether this popular art deco hangout is a restaurant with a bar or a bar with a restaurant. When the tin ceiling first went up some 70 years ago, the Monte Carlo was exclusively a drinking spot, and that's what it remained until the Warehouse District became chic back in the seventies. Now it has broadened its clientele, serving chicken soup, burgers, steaks, chops, and more at lunch and dinner to office workers, antique dealers, sales clerks, and shoppers. The best deal of all is the extended brunch, 10am to 4pm on Sunday: all the scrambled eggs, Canadian bacon, sausage, toast, and hash browns you can eat for $4.95.

The copper bar is still the focal point of Monte Carlo, with shelves of more than 500 bottles reaching up to the ceiling. Drinks are served club style—the mixer in a large tumbler, liquor in shot glasses, garnishes at the side. There's free parking in an adjoining lot. There's a relatively quiet front room off to the right as you enter Monte Carlo, preferred by those who find the rest of this lively restaurant a bit rambunctious.

UPTOWN

FIGLIO'S, 3001 Hennepin Ave., Minneapolis. Tel. 822-1688.

Cuisine: NORTHERN ITALIAN/AMERICAN. **Reservations:** Recommended.

$ Prices: Appetizers $4–$6; main courses $7–$15; lunch $5–$10. AE, MC, V.

Open: Daily 11:30am–1am; brunch Sun 11:30am–2pm.

Figlio's is a gem of an Italian restaurant, albeit one with a California accent. One of Figlio's dining rooms overlooks busy Lake Street, which has some of the best people-watching hereabouts. The other, larger room has a view of the busy kitchen with its built-in wood-burning oven flanked by brick walls.

The northern Italian cuisine is overseen by executive chef Rex Retneyer, who is famous locally for his version of carpaccio—paper-thin slices of raw beef tenderloin marinated in olive oil, shallots, capers, and herbs, topped with thinly sliced parmesan cheese, and placed on Italian bread, with three kinds of mustard at the ready.

Another specialty is something called *morto nel cioccolato,* "death by chocolate," of which happy locals contentedly declare, "What a way to go!" Do consider a portion of this extravagantly rich and utterly delicious concoction composed of alternating layers of chocolate cake and chocolate-amaretto gelato and served with a thick chocolate sauce.

The rest of the menu is a wide assortment of Italian and American favorites, from fettuccine Alfredo and stuffed tortellini to grilled swordfish and 10-ounce burgers.

There are a lot of nice touches to the service here, including the heated plates that keep your selection piping hot. Outdoor dining on Lake Street, take-out service, and Sunday brunch are some of the features that keep Figlio's popular.

LUCIA'S RESTAURANT, 1432 W. 31st St., Minneapolis. Tel. 825-1572.
Cuisine: CONTINENTAL/AMERICAN. **Reservations:** Recommended.
$ Prices: Appetizers $4.25–$4.95; main courses $7.95–$15.95. MC, V.
Open: Lunch Tues–Fri 11:30am–2:30pm; dinner Tues–Thurs 5:30–9:30pm, Fri–Sat 5:30–10:00pm, Sun 5:30–9pm; Sat–Sun brunch 10am–2pm.

Lucia Watson has been cooking since she was a small child growing up in Minneapolis, so her family and friends weren't surprised when she opened a small restaurant in 1985. What proved surprising about Lucia's new enterprise, though, was how fast it grew. A small room with a handwritten menu has now become a two-room restaurant with a bar. The handwritten menus have remained, though, adding a personal touch. And flexibility is something that Lucia considers important, especially for diners with dietary restrictions. "We're always open to special orders," she declares.

There are always two fresh soups on the menu, a choice of salads, a vegetarian entrée (usually pasta), as well as a fish dish, a poultry dish, and a meat dish. And among the tantalizing selection of desserts, there's always a variety of choice. The honey crushed-wheat bread is one of Lucia's own creations. Also popular are the moussaka with feta cheese for $6.25, the chicken, asparagus and lemon cream sauce on egg linguine for $7.95, the baked ratatouille under a phyllo crust for $7.95, and the Atlantic salmon with lemon, capers, and herbs for $15.95. The bar menu, popular for an afternoon snack or after attending a performance at night, features fresh pastries, cheese and fruit plates, pastas, salads, and soups.

NORTHEAST MINNEAPOLIS

YVETTE, in Riverplace, 1 Main St. S.E., Minneapolis. Tel. 379-1111.

   Cuisine: FRENCH/AMERICAN. **Reservations:** Recommended for indoor dining, not accepted for outdoor dining.

$ **Prices:** Appetizers $3.95–$6.95; main courses $9–$19; lunch $5–$11; Sun brunch $5–$11. AE, DC, MC, V.

   Open: Mon–Thurs 11am–11pm, Fri–Sat 11am–midnight, Sun 11am–10pm. Bar open until 1am Mon–Sat; Sun until 11pm.

A dimly lit dining room tastefully decorated in warm shades of mauve and gray. Sound romantic? It is, and it's part of what brings diners back again and again to Yvette. There's much to recommend this lovely restaurant that overlooks the Mississippi and historic St. Anthony Falls.

The dry-aged beefsteak here is among the best you'll find in the Twin Cities, and the daily seafood specials feature a mouth-watering selection flown in from Boston each day. Dinner entrées are served with potato and vegetable. Desserts are another specialty, with the top draw being the chocolate velvet cake, baked on the premises. The wine selection ranges in price from a Canteval house wine for $15 to Château Mouton Rothschild Pauillac 1897 for $3,000.

There's live jazz here every Tuesday through Saturday and a jam session each Monday night when Yvette's singer-pianist is joined by other musicians who are performing in other spots around town. When weather permits, there's outdoor dining on a flower-bordered terrace.

SOUTH MINNEAPOLIS

BLACK FOREST INN, 1 E. 26th St., Minneapolis. Tel. 872-0812.

   Cuisine: GERMAN. **Reservations:** Recommended.

$ **Prices:** Appetizers $1.50–$5; main courses $6–$16; lunch $3–$6. AE, DC, DISC, MC, V.

   Open: Lunch Mon–Sat 11am–5pm; dinner Mon–Sat 5–11pm, Sun noon–10pm; late menu Mon–Sat 11pm–midnight.

An extensive selection of domestic and imported beers and wines are served here amid the dark woods and stained glass of an authentic German "gasthaus." Luncheon entrées include Wiener Schnitzel and Sauerbraten, as well as chicken wings and corned beef on rye. The more comprehensive dinner menu includes German favorites like Schweinbraten (roast pork with apple dressing and red cabbage) and gefuellte krautrolle (stuffed cabbage with rice); entrées are served with a vegetable and often a potato pancake or spaetzel. The Black Forest features a long list of German, French, and California wines, as well as a variety of liqueurs, brandies, and cognac.

RUDOLPH'S BAR-B-QUE, Franklin and Lyndale aves., Minneapolis. Tel. 871-8969.

Cuisine: AMERICAN. **Reservations:** Recommended.

$ Prices: Appetizers $2.95–$4.95; main courses $7.95–$16.50; lunch $4.95–$5.50; Sun brunch $9.95. AE, MC, V.

Open: Mon–Thurs 11am–11pm, Fri–Sat 11am–1am, Sun 11am–10pm.

Wit, whimsy, and wonderful ribs are what you'll get at Rudolph's, which uses the steamy 1920s matinee idol as its theme. The barbecue sauce here has won innumerable national awards. If you're not a devotee of barbecued ribs, there are plenty of other entrées, ranging from Greek-style chicken to New York steak. Save room for the desserts; peach Melba is a real treat. On your way out, take a look at some of the wonderful vintage Hollywood photos that line the walls.

The other two Rudolph's are located at 815 E. Hennepin Ave., Minneapolis (tel. 623-3671), and 366 Jackson St., Galtier Plaza, St. Paul (tel. 222-2226). Hours vary by location, so call for specifics.

THE LORING AREA

LORING CAFÉ, 1624 Harmon Place, Minneapolis. Tel. 332-1617.

Cuisine: CONTINENTAL/AMERICAN. **Reservations:** Recommended.

$ Prices: Appetizers $5–$7; pasta $8–$11; main courses $11–$15; Sat–Sun brunch $5–$9; lunch $7–$11. MC, V.

Open: Lunch Mon–Thurs 11:30am–2:30pm; dinner Mon–Thurs 5:30–10pm, Fri–Sat 5:30–midnight, Sun 5–10pm.

You can have your choice of ambience at the Loring Café. Owner/manager Jason McLean has provided a variety of spaces, indoors and out, to suit a wide variety of tastes. This restaurant, bar, and arts center is located in a converted automobile showroom that dates back more than 50 years.

Dine on the main floor, in the loft, or, in the summertime, in the courtyard, one of the best outdoor settings in town (a saxophonist appears on a roof from time to time, playing some of the sweetest dinner music you'll ever hear). During less balmy times, other kinds of music are offered at the Loring Café—jazz, blues, folk, and classical music in the coffeehouse/bar.

During off-hours, the bar becomes a large studio available to painters, dancers, writers, and other artists. And in July 1991, the Loring Café launched the Loring Playhouse, which presents theater and dance performances. An example of the work here was the 1991 presentation of Sartre's *No Exit* with a dance interpretation by a company known as Ballet of the Dolls.

But it's the culinary achievements of the Loring Café that have made everything else possible. Appetizers like focacia served with roasted garlic bulb and French goat cheese are perennially popular. Entrées range from fresh vegetable sauté to veal loin chops with caramelized apples and calvados. And don't overlook the excellent pasta and pizza selections, the imaginative salads, and the long and excellent wine list.

BUDGET

DOWNTOWN

LOON CAFÉ, 500 1st Ave. N., Minneapolis. Tel. 332-8342.
   Cuisine: AMERICAN/MEXICAN. **Reservations:** Recommended.
 $ Prices: Appetizers $3–$7; main courses $4–$8. AE, DC, MC, V.
   Open: Mon–Sat 11am–1am, Sun 5pm–midnight.

Downtown office workers and shoppers find this a good place for a quick lunch. The oblong burger served on a sourdough bun is popular, and so are the "championship chilis." There's also a selection of soups, salads, and sandwiches.

Primarily, though, this is a bar that sells food, not a restaurant that sells drinks, and the Loon really comes into its own in the evening, when it's one of the busiest, noisiest spots in this chic neighborhood. Taped music, overpowering when you walk in, soon subsides into the general din and somehow doesn't inhibit conversation. Celebrities, local and national, wander in from time to time: Bob Dylan, Morgan Fairchild, and others have been sighted at the Loon.

UPTOWN

LOTUS, 3037 Hennepin Ave., Minneapolis. Tel. 825-2263.
   Cuisine: VIETNAMESE. **Reservations:** Recommended.
 $ Prices: Appetizers $2.15–$3.85; main courses $5–$6. No credit cards.
   Open: Sun–Thurs 11:00am–10pm, Fri–Sat 11am–11pm.

Budget dining doesn't get any better than at Lotus. Don't be put off by the minimal decor at this casual, congenial spot. The white Oriental lamp shades are about as far as Le and Hieu Tran went in 1983 when they decorated the first of what would become four busy neighborhood eating places.

Because sharing is encouraged, you can try a number of savory, nutritious entrées; everything from beginners' fare like chicken or beef with vegetables to less familiar selections such as curried mock duck sautéed with onion, garlic, and lemongrass and served in a spicy coconut gravy. The chow mein here is delectable—a hearty mixture of chicken, beef, and shrimp with crunchy slabs of cabbage, carrots, celery, onion, and broccoli that in no way resembles the gelatinous mound you find in many Chinese restaurants. The menu indicates which items are hotter than others, but the dishes can be adjusted to taste. You may have to wait for a table at the Lotus restaurants, but you'll be rewarded by the food.

You'll find other locations at 313 Oak St., Minneapolis (tel. 331-1781); 3907 W. 50th St., Edina (tel. 922-4254); Burnsville (tel. 890-5573); and 867 Grand Ave. in St. Paul (tel. 228-9156). Hours vary with each restaurant.

SOUTH MINNEAPOLIS

MALT SHOP, 809 W. 50th St. at Bryant, Minneapolis. Tel. 824-1352.
   Cuisine: AMERICAN/INTERNATIONAL. **Reservations:** Not accepted.
$ Prices: Appetizers $2.50; main courses $3.95–$6.25. MC, V.
   Open: Mon–Thurs 11am–10:30pm, Fri 11am–11pm, Sat 8:30am–11pm, Sun 8:30am–10:30pm.

Famous for its hamburgers and ice-cream desserts, the Malt Shop also offers an array of international specialties—everything from bird's-nest salad to feta salad. All soups, dressings, and sauces are made by the Malt Shop. Salads come in two sizes and so do the "gourmet hamburgers," which also come in many variations. Daily specials, served with soup or salad and a grilled onion roll, vary from Monday's lasagne to Sunday's chicken Monterey. Popular box lunches include a sandwich, potato chips, fruit or feta salad, a chocolate-pecan cookie, and condiments and utensils for $4.75. Breakfast is served daily at the other Malt Shop, 1554 Concordia, St. Paul (tel. 645-4643).

NORA'S, 2107 E. Lake St., Minneapolis. Tel. 729-9353.
   Cuisine: AMERICAN. **Reservations:** Recommended.
$ Prices: Appetizers $1.50–$2; main courses $5–$9. MC, V.
   Open: Daily 11am–10pm.
The decor, the prices, and the service at this economy restaurant have pleased patrons for the past 30 years. Among the perennial favorites here are fried chicken, shrimp with garlic butter baked in wine sauce, and tenderloin filets.

The breads, soups, and sauces are made on the premises. Popular items include broiled-to-order steak with onion rings and "Uncle Nels" broiled sandwich, a combination of turkey breast, mushrooms, cheddar cheese, and a light wine sauce on toast. Another, newer Nora's is located at 3118 W. Lake St. (tel. 927-5781), just a block from Lake Calhoun.

2. MINNEAPOLIS SOUTH SUBURBAN

EXPENSIVE

GREGORY'S, 7956 Lyndale Ave. S., Bloomington. Tel. 881-8611.
 Cuisine: AMERICAN. **Reservations:** Recommended.
 $ Prices: Appetizers $3.95–$4.95; main courses $13.95–$18.95; lunch $5.95–$8.95. AE, DC, DISC, MC.
 Open: Lunch Mon–Fri 11am–3pm; dinner Mon–Thurs 4–10pm; Fri–Sat 4–10:30pm. Bar open until 1am.

You'll think you've come to a small rustic restaurant as you approach Gregory's, but wait till you get inside! There are three floors of dining rooms and bars here, making Gregory's one of the largest and most popular restaurants in the burgeoning suburb of Bloomington.

The Old West prevails in the main dining room, with its split-log walls and wagon-wheel chandeliers. The other rooms offer a diverse ambience: the elegance of the Ritz, with its mahogany furnishings; the turn-of-the-century Parlor, warm and inviting with frosted gaslight globes and a hand-carved fireplace; the trendy black leather upholstery and stained glass windows of the Rafters.

You'll find a touch of Cajun here and a bit of nouvelle cuisine there, but primarily this is the place for prime rib, walleye pike, chicken, shrimp, and duck. There are soups made from scratch and three luncheon specials every day. The next day's specials are noted in each luncheon menu, so regulars can plan accordingly.

Lunch ranges from burgers and fries to broiled walleye. Dinnertime entrées are served with salad and potato or rice and range from baby beef liver to Cajun shrimp.

KINKAID'S, 8400 Normandale Lake Blvd., Bloomington. Tel. 921-2255.
 Cuisine: STEAK/SEAFOOD. **Reservations:** Recommended.
 $ Prices: Appetizers $5.50–$6.95; main courses $13.95–$26.95; Sun brunch $7.95–$13.95. AE, MC, V.
 Open: Lunch Mon–Sat 11am–2pm; dinner Mon–Thurs 5–10pm, Fri 5–11pm, Sat 4:30–11pm, Sun 5–9pm; Sun brunch 10am–2pm.

This beautifully appointed steak-and-seafood house is an elegant assemblage of marble, brass chandeliers, and cherry-wood furnishings. Kinkaid's offers a choice of top-notch steaks, chops, and mesquite-grilled fish, along with pasta, soups, and desserts.

Luncheon entrées, served with vegetable and herb bread, range from $7.50 for fish-and-chips to $12 for boneless New York steak. The dinner menu, which includes a lengthy wine list, carries a money-back guarantee that your steaks, chops, and roasts will be moist, flavorful, and tender. An elegant back bar has a dining area of its own, and a separate bar features fresh oysters flown in daily from the East Coast, West Coast, Canada, and New Zealand. Desserts are delicious too.

MODERATE

COCOLEZZONE, 5410 Wayzata Blvd., Golden Valley. Tel. 544-4014.
   Cuisine: NORTHERN ITALIAN. **Reservations:** Recommended.
$ **Prices:** Appetizers $4–$8; main courses $7–$27; pizza $7–$8. AE, MC, V.
   Open: Lunch Mon–Fri 11am–5pm, Sat 11am–1pm, Sun 11am–2:30pm; dinner Sun–Thurs 5–9:30pm, Fri 5pm–midnight, Sat 4:30pm–midnight.

The next best thing to a trip to Italy is a meal at CocoLezzone. Named for a popular trattoria in Florence, this large, lively, and very beautiful spot was an instant success when it opened in June 1985. With marble floors and a plenitude of imported artifacts, CocoLezzone is an altogether delightful place.

Because northern Italian fare is featured here, be prepared to see, along with the usual tomato-laden toppings, such relatively unfamiliar sights as seafood pizza and pizza with spinach, cheese, and a cooked egg in the center. Tomatoes make many appearances here, most notably in tortellini rosa, a delectable meat-filled pasta in a tomato and cream sauce.

Dining here can be very expensive or inexpensive, depending on how you approach the lengthy à la carte menu. Sharing is encouraged by the helpful waiters, who will explain the traditional succession of the Italian courses. The lunchtime menu lists a variety of antipasti, or you may prefer to select your own assortment from the tempting display case. Next comes the pizza, followed by soups, primi (a selection of pastas), meat, fish, and, finally, salad—for reasons of digestion, you'll be told.

DA AFGHAN, 929 W. 80 St., Bloomington. Tel. 888-5824.
   Cuisine: AFGHANI. **Reservations:** Recommended.
$ **Prices:** Appetizers $3.75–$6.25; main courses $6.95–$13.25; lunch $5.95–$10.95. MC, V.
   Open: Lunch Mon–Fri 11am–3pm; dinner Mon–Thurs 5–10pm, Fri–Sat 5–11pm.

You're in for a wide diversity of tastes at Da Afghan. Although many of the dishes feature shrimp, beef, lamb, and chicken, vegetarians will find a lot to enjoy as well. An appetizer listed as *pakawra*—potatoes, eggplant, and zucchini fried in a specially seasoned batter—is particularly delicious. Among the entrées, served with or without meat, try bahnjean bouranee, eggplant cooked with tomatoes and spices, served in korma sauce, topped with homemade garlic, yogurt sour-cream sauce, and dry mint. In addition to entrées, you'll have a wide choice here among sandwiches and kebobs, along with Afghani-style pizza and a large tossed salad featuring homemade Afghani cheese. The ambience here is noteworthy too—colorful rugs, serving trays, and costumes hang on the wall; soft Middle Eastern music provides a pleasant background. Da Afghan can be difficult to find, so call ahead for directions.

T.G.I. FRIDAY'S, 7730 Normandale Blvd., Bloomington. Tel. 831-6553.

Cuisine: AMERICAN. **Reservations:** Recommended.

$ Prices: Appetizers $3.95–$6.25; main courses $8.35–$12.95. AE, CB, DC, MC, V.

Open: Mon–Sat 11am–1am, Sun 10am–1am.

There's something for everybody at T.G.I. Friday's. As the name implies, this is a place for unwinding after work is done. It's also a place for lunch or dinner, weekdays and weekends alike. There is a large, square bar and several elegantly cluttered dining rooms, which abound with Tiffany-style lamps, stained-glass windows, and assorted antiques. The red and white striped tablecloths are a signature item at T.G.I. Friday's throughout the country.

Best described as an American bistro, this congenial gathering place is remarkable for its selection of nonalcoholic drinks. Prices are easy to take here too. Burgers with all sorts of extras are the most inexpensive option, although the beef, chicken, and seafood entrées are reasonably priced as well. The children's menu features everything kids love best, from hot dogs to grilled cheese to pigs-in-a-blanket.

There are two other locations, at 5875 Wayzata Blvd., St. Louis Park (tel. 544-0675); and 2480 Fairview Ave. N., Roseville (tel. 631-1101).

BUDGET

OLD COUNTRY BUFFET, 9 E. 66th St., Richfield. Tel. 869-1911.

Cuisine: AMERICAN. **Reservations:** Accepted only for large groups.

$ Prices: Breakfast $5.30; lunch $5; dinner $6.50. No credit cards.

Open: Mon–Thurs 11am–8:30pm, Fri 11am–9pm, Sat 8am–9pm, Sun 3am–8:30pm.

⑤ You'll understand the overwhelming success of the popular Old Country Buffet restaurants as soon as you step into one. With an abundance of booths and tables, the attractive country-style decor is done in shades of navy, rust, and white.

Certain items regularly appear, afternoon or evening, on the succession of buffet tables. You'll always find fluffy mashed potatoes and golden fried chicken, along with gravy, vegetables, salads, breads, beverages, desserts, make-your-own sundaes, and hot cinnamon rolls. But that's far from all. There's a long list of daily specials and, for dinner seven nights a week, you can have roast beef or ham carved to order as well. If you try Old Country Buffet once during your visit to the Twin Cities, you'll probably come back. It couldn't be more pleasant or more budget pleasing. Other locations are in Roseville at Roseville Commons, 2480 Fairview Ave. (tel. 639-1812); in Fridley at Holly Shopping Center, 6540 University Avenue (tel. 572-8627); and in Minnetonka at 7-Hi Shopping Center, 4801 Hwy. 101, Minnetonka (tel. 474-3210).

PANNEKOEKEN HUIS RESTAURANT, 3020 W. 66th St., Richfield. Tel. 866-7731.

Cuisine: DUTCH. **Reservations:** Not accepted.
$ Prices: Appetizers $2–$4.50; main courses $3–$8. AE, DC, DISC, MC, V.
Open: Mon–Sun 6am–11pm.

The most popular item on the menu in these attractive family restaurants is, of course, the pannekoeken, a soufflé-style pancake that is baked in the oven, flipped, and then rushed to the table before its puffiness disappears. The average deflation time is 20 seconds, and that's why you'll sometimes see a waitress dashing from the kitchen with a plate aloft as others clear out of her way. You can choose from 11 different toppings for your pancake or eat it with powdered sugar and lemon wedges. You'll love it either way.

There are other delights here as well—hearty Dutch stews and soups and omelets, for example. But much of the menu is Dutch-American: metworst sausage and eggs, pannekoeken burgers, Netherlander sandwiches. And, finally, there are wholly domestic items, like grilled Reuben sandwiches, barbecued ribs, and batter-fried chicken strips. Save room for some of the imported candies and fresh pastries you'll be invited to take with you on your way out. You'll be glad you did! Altogether there are 13 Pannekoeken Huis restaurants in the Minneapolis–St. Paul metropolitan area.

PEARSON'S FAMILY RESTAURANT, 3803 W. 50th St., Edina. Tel. 927-4464.

Cuisine: AMERICAN. **Reservations:** Not required.
$ Prices: Appetizers $3–$4; sandwiches $4–$7; main courses $6–$12. AE, DISC, MC, V.

Open: Mon–Sat 7am–9:30pm, Sun 9am–7pm.

Pearson's features the kind of down-home cooking that many Minnesotans grew up with. Brothers Paul and Marston Pearson, the second generation owners, share responsibility for the restaurant which their parents opened in 1973 as a coffee shop. That small diner has since been joined by the Oak Room and the Oak Room West, two elegant, handsomely paneled dining rooms with large stone fireplaces and brass chandeliers.

Local families enjoy Pearson's because the menu is varied enough so that everyone can find something to his or her liking, including the basic hamburger, omelets, or salads. Breakfasts are well under $5, most lunches and dinners under $10. Swedish meatballs, baked chicken, and roast prime rib rank high among the favorites here; and the pastries, soups, salad dressings, and dinner rolls all deserve high marks.

3. ST. PAUL & ENVIRONS

EXPENSIVE

DOWNTOWN

LE CARROUSEL, in the Radisson Hotel, 11 E. Kellogg Blvd., St. Paul. Tel. 292-1900.
   Cuisine: AMERICAN. **Reservations:** Recommended.
$ **Prices:** Appetizers $5.50–$6.50; entrées $17.95–$39. AE, CB, DC, DISC, MC, V.
   Open: Lunch Mon–Fri 11:30am–2:30pm; dinner Mon–Thurs 5:30–10:30pm, Fri–Sat 5:30–11:30pm; Sun jazz brunch 11:30am–2:30pm.

There's a lot to enjoy at Le Carrousel. Located on the 22nd floor of the Radisson Hotel St. Paul, this is the restaurant with the most spectacular view of downtown and the Mississippi River. Moreover, the central portion of this handsome dining room revolves almost imperceptibly so that from your table you'll be able to view the complete circle within a 45-minute period. But restaurants must be judged primarily on their cuisine, and the important news here is that executive chef Ronald Bohnert has created a remarkably eclectic menu, featuring a wide diversity of selections—everything from foccacia and escargot to beef prime rib and buffalo rib eye to Thai chicken stir-fry and Mediterranean swordfish.

Housed in a hotel that accommodates guests from all over the world, Le Carrousel routinely serves foreign visitors, however, a large proportion of its guests first came here on prom night and have been returning for wedding anniversaries and other important milestones ever since. There's enough in the way of tradition to provide a sense of continuity—favorites like onion soup gratinée, corn fed premium choice beef, pecan crusted walleye pike, and Bailey's Irish Cream torte. There are also innovative methods of preparing and presenting foods such as dinners for two served tableside—roasted rack of lamb in an herb mustard crust ($49 for two) and hardwood grilled tenderloin of beef ($45 for two). Also well received have been "Combinations" including samplers of chicken Oscar and veal marsala ($22) and grilled shrimp brochette with seared sea scallops served with ginger masno sauce and saffron rice ($21). All entrées are accompanied by the tasty house salad and loaves of freshly baked bread.

THE ST. PAUL GRILL, 350 Market St. Tel. 292-9292.

Cuisine: AMERICAN. **Reservations:** Recommended.

$ Prices: Appetizers $4.75–$8.50; main courses $8.95–$19.95; lunch $3.50–$6.95; Sun brunch $7.50–$11.50. AE, DC, DISC, MC, V.

Open: Lunch Mon–Sat 11:30am–2pm; dinner Tues–Sat 5:30–11pm, Sun–Mon 5:30–10pm; Sun brunch 11am–2pm.

This recently enlarged dining room can boast one of the loveliest views in the Twin Cities. Located on the ground floor of the distinguished St. Paul Hotel, the Grill overlooks tiny picturesque Rice Park, which is flanked by three other famous buildings as well—the St. Paul Main Library, the Ordway Music Theatre, and the Landmark Center. Popular with business, professional, and political figures at lunchtime, the Grill is the natural choice for dinner at any time, but particularly when something exciting is happening across the park at the Ordway Theatre. In those instances, manager Patrick Wandzel advises reservations as early as two weeks in advance. Celebrities who've dined here are numerous; they include Bernadette Peters, Tommy Tune, and Pavarotti. The decor is similar to what you might have found in Chicago and New York grills during the 1920s and 1930s when certain patrons appreciated the opportunity to dine—and especially to drink—in privacy. Here, opaque ribbed glass set upon mahogony panels separate the booths, giving diners a nice amount of privacy.

Whether at a booth or a table, though, what matters most is that you can be assured the highest quality of fare and service. Under the management of Patrick Wandzel, attention to individual requests is of great importance. Because this is an American grill, you'll find steaks, chops, and seafood among the offerings, but you'll find them served with a bit of a difference. For example, the lamb chops (widely regarded as the best in town) are served with jalapeño mint jelly. You'll wonder why this hasn't been done all along!

Signature items include the sourdough bread and the red flannel roast beef hash, made with prime rib, beets, potato, and topped with an egg. Three specials are offered each week, with a daily change of potato and soup, a different vegetable each day, and a different fresh grill item. The superlative desserts change too, thanks to pastry chef Lisa Steinhauer.

MODERATE

DOWNTOWN

FOREPAUGH'S, 276 S. Exchange St., St. Paul. Tel. 224-5606.
   Cuisine: FRENCH. **Reservations:** Recommended.
$ **Prices:** Appetizers $3.50–$8.75; main courses $11.95–$17.50; lunch $4–$8; brunch $11.75. AE, MC, V.
   Open: Lunch Mon–Fri 11:30am–2pm; dinner Mon–Sat 5:30–9:30pm, Sun 5–8:30pm; Sun brunch 10:30am–1:30pm.

One of the loveliest Victorian houses in the Twin Cities, Forepaugh's is also one of its finest French restaurants. Built in 1870 by businessman Joseph Lybrandt Forepaugh, this three-story mansion faces the home of Alexander Ramsey, first territorial governor of Minnesota. Now listed on the National Register of Historic Places, both houses are popular with visitors seeking fine examples of Victorian architecture and decor.

At Forepaugh's there are nine lovely dining rooms, each named for a past governor of Minnesota. From the Pillsbury Room you can enjoy a panoramic view of downtown St. Paul; in the Olson Room you can admire the richness of fine mahogany paneling; and in the Sibley Room you'll see historic photos of Victorian tea parties. The state fish takes on a delectably French aspect here in a dish called walleye à la meunière; New York sirloin, prepared to taste with a tangy green peppercorn sauce, is a favorite too. Entrées are served with salad, potato, and vegetable.

GALLIVAN'S, 354 Wabasha St., St. Paul. Tel. 227-6688.
   Cuisine: AMERICAN. **Reservations:** Recommended.
$ **Prices:** Appetizers $4.50–$7.95; main courses $6.45–$18.95; lunch $4.95–$8.45. AE, DISC, MC, V.
   Open: Mon–Sat 11am–1am.

This St. Paul landmark is comprised of three separate dining rooms with an adjoining bar and lounge. The spacious main dining room features dark woods and subdued lighting; the intimate library boasts a functioning fireplace along with bookshelves stocked with biographies, law books, and encyclopedias.

The loyal clientele here is composed largely of folks who work in the neighborhood—lawyers, judges, and civil servants from the nearby courthouse and city hall. The prices may prove a pleasant surprise to first-timers. Entrées, which include a choice of soup or salad and a choice of pasta, french fries, or baked potato, range from a crisp half-chicken to a T-bone steak. If you're a liver lover like me, you'll adore the broiled baby beef liver with bacon and onions; the broiled walleye pike is a favorite too. There's a long wine and liquor list.

THE DECO, 305 St. Peter St., St. Paul. Tel. 228-0520.
   Cuisine: SCANDINAVIAN/CONTINENTAL. **Reservations:** Recommended.
$ **Prices:** Lunch $5.95–$11.95; Sun brunch $13.95. AE, DC, DISC, MC, V.
   Open: Tues–Fri 11:30am–2pm, Sun 11am–1:30pm.

It's altogether fitting that Soile Anderson's restaurant is located on the top floor of the Minnesota Museum of Art, since the items that comprise her legendary Sunday brunches are themselves works of art. The same can be said for the items she offers Tuesdays through Fridays, along with a Scandinavian buffet. Everything that's served by Soile Anderson has been prepared on-site, and her emphasis is always on healthy foods seasoned with fresh spices. Along with the complimentary glass of champagne or sparkling cider that comes with Sunday brunch, there's a choice of soups, salads, entrées, breads, and desserts that's nearly dazzling. But Scandinavian fare is only part of what's offered at the Deco. Along with the salmon soup you may find borscht, Romanian tuna salad, Finnish chicken salad, lamb steak au poivre, and shrimp scampi. And the international diversity of the menu also extends to the desserts. Vienna Sachertorte is a frequent favorite, as is Scandinavian strawberry cake.

THE MIDWAY AREA

DAKOTA BAR AND GRILL, 1021 E. Bandana Blvd., St. Paul. Tel. 642-1442.
   Cuisine: AMERICAN. **Reservations:** Recommended.
$ **Prices:** Appetizers $4–$9; main courses $7–$18. AE, DC, DISC, V.
   Open: Dinner Mon–Thurs 5:30–10:30pm, Fri–Sat 5:30–11:30pm, Sun 5:30–9:30pm; Sun brunch 10:30am–2:30pm.

The accent is all-American at the Dakota Bar and Grill, a gathering place that's won many local awards. The daily menu features a full complement of seafood, beef, chicken, lamb, and pork, along with tasty vegetarian dishes that have converted many a carnivore. Most dishes are made with ingredients from Minnesota and Wisconsin.

Executive chef Ken Goff's imaginative use of spices and garnishes excels in popular items like brie-and-apple soup. Another popular creation is fresh walleye in a toasted wild rice crust with cucumber-tarragon tartar sauce.

The fabulous desserts include a tart cherry rice pudding with almond crust and caramel and—if calories are no object—chocolate mousse with strawberry cream. For lunch, consider fresh salmon hash with wild rice, sweet peppers, and mint or grilled smoked ham with raspberry-rhubarb sauce. The Sunday brunch buffet features muffins, granola, coffee cakes, yogurt, and several hot entrées. Outdoor dining is popular here during spring, summer, and early fall, when flowering shrubs enhance the setting.

GRAND AVENUE

LEXINGTON, 1096 Grand Ave., St. Paul. Tel. 222-5878.
   Cuisine: AMERICAN. **Reservations:** Recommended.
$ Prices: Appetizers: $3.95–$7.95; main courses $8.95–$25.95; lunch $6.95–$8.95. AE, CB, DC, MC, V.
   Open: Mon–Thurs 11am–10pm, Fri–Sat 11am–midnight; Sun brunch 10am–3pm; Sun dinner 4–9pm.

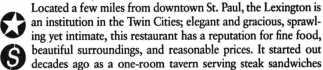

Located a few miles from downtown St. Paul, the Lexington is an institution in the Twin Cities; elegant and gracious, sprawling yet intimate, this restaurant has a reputation for fine food, beautiful surroundings, and reasonable prices. It started out decades ago as a one-room tavern serving steak sandwiches and hamburgers and has since evolved into a 360-seat restaurant with an extensive menu. You'll find traditional American fare like New York sirloin, spring lamb chops, Dover sole, lobster tails, and barbecued ribs. And then there are the specialties of the house—medallions of beef bourguignon glazed with a sauce of red wine, veal scaloppine sautéed in butter and simmered with sherry and mushrooms, and Minnesota ringneck pheasant braised in a sauce of cream and brandy and served over wild rice. Entrées are served with a choice of potato and salad. There are five different desserts served each night, ranging from bread pudding with homemade caramel sauce to cheesecake.

The setting is as carefully designed as the menu: dark polished woods, crystal chandeliers, fine oil paintings, and a variety of rare artifacts. You won't find a lovelier setting, friendlier service, or finer food than that of the Lexington.

ACROPOL INN, 748 Grand Ave., St. Paul. Tel. 298-0151.
   Cuisine: GREEK/AMERICAN. **Reservations:** Recommended.
$ Prices: Appetizers $4.95–$5.95; main courses $8.95–$12.95; lunch $5–$9. MC, V.
   Open: Mon–Thurs 11am–9pm, Fri–Sat 11am–10pm, Sun 11am–9pm.

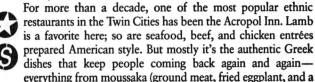

For more than a decade, one of the most popular ethnic restaurants in the Twin Cities has been the Acropol Inn. Lamb is a favorite here; so are seafood, beef, and chicken entrées prepared American style. But mostly it's the authentic Greek dishes that keep people coming back again and again—everything from moussaka (ground meat, fried eggplant, and a special topping) to dolmas (ground meat and rice wrapped in grape leaves and topped with lemon sauce) to stefado (beef in wine sauce with potatoes and onions). The Greek salads are delectable too, enhanced with imported feta cheese and olive oil. Dinner entrées include soup, salad, and homemade bread.

THE CATHEDRAL AREA

TULIPS, 452 Selby Ave., St. Paul. Tel. 221-1061.
   Cuisine: FRENCH. **Reservations:** Recommended.
$ Prices: Appetizers $3.95–$4.95; main courses $7.95–$17.95; lunch $3.95–$8.95. DC, DISC, MC, V.
   Open: Lunch Mon–Fri 11:30am–3pm; dinner Mon–Sun 5–10pm.

⭐ In a small restaurant that's been voted "most romantic" by a local newspaper, Angela and Bob Piper offer a French cuisine that's hearty, nourishing, and tasty. Background music features the likes of Ella Fitzgerald at lunchtime and classical music in the evening. Tablecloths and the paintings of local artists brighten the three small dining rooms. Menu items include "heart healthy" entrées like chicken Minceur (chicken dusted with three peppers, garlic and lemon wedges) for $8.95 and traditional French dishes like medallions of tenderloin with beurre café de Paris (garlic, parsley, and pepper) for $14.95. Vegetarian entrées appear on every menu as well, like the cheese ravioli with artichokes, olive oil, and butter for $9.95. All entrées are served with fresh vegetables. Desserts change regularly, though some, like flan with caramel sauce, make frequent appearances.

W. A. FROST AND COMPANY, 374 Selby Ave., St. Paul. Tel. 224-5715.
   Cuisine: AMERICAN. **Reservations:** Recommended.
$ Prices: Appetizers: $4.25–$8.95; main courses $9.95–$17.95. AE, DC, DISC, MC, V.
   Open: Lunch Mon–Sat 11am–2pm; dinner daily 5:30–10:30pm.

⭐ The ambience of bygone days dominates here, with tin Victorian ceilings, marble tables, Oriental rugs, and illuminated oil landscapes that date back to the turn of the century. There are two functioning fireplaces as well, a popular feature during the winter months. As the seasons change, though, diners look forward to some of the Twin Cities' most picturesque outdoor dining, amid flowering bushes and trailing vines and under a living canopy of trees.

Favorite appetizers include the savory smoked salmon and cream-cheese torte and crispy Chinese chicken wings. A wide range of seafood is served here, everything from walleye to monkfish. And there's a variety of beef, chicken, and pasta entrées, all of which include potato and fresh vegetable. You'll also find one of the largest selections of imported beers and fine liquors in the area. At this fine restaurant people customarily come just as they are; don't be surprised to see casually clad diners.

MACALESTER/GROVELAND

KHYBER PASS CAFÉ, 1399 St. Clair Ave., St. Paul. Tel. 698-5403.

Cuisine: AFGHANI. **Reservations:** Not required.

$ Prices: Appetizers $1.95–$2.95; main courses $5.25–$11.25; lunch $4.50–$6.25. No credit cards.

Open: Lunch Tues–Sat 11am–2pm; dinner Tues–Sat 5–9pm.

⑤ Faculty members and students from nearby Macalester College and the University of St. Thomas make up more than half the regular diners here. Afghani articles decorate the white walls and Afghani music provides an exotic background in the comfortable dining room. Owner Habib Amini, who does all the cooking, explains that unlike other Middle Eastern cuisines, Afghani cooking uses relatively few spices and aims to enhance rather than overpower the food's natural perfume. Chicken, lamb, and vegetarian dishes are among the favorites here. One popular selection is the *kebob-e murgh,* chunks of boneless chicken cooked on a skewer and served with tomatoes, onions, and chutney; *korma-e sabzee* is a delicious spinach dish served with chunks of lamb; *korma-e dahl,* another popular entrée, features chunks of lamb with yellow lentils cooked in onions and garlic.

A full dinner, served with basmati rice, salad, chutney, and flat bread, runs from $7.25 to $8.95. Desserts are delicious. If you like puddings, you're bound to enjoy the firni, rich and creamy and flavored with a blend of cardamom, rosewater, and pistachios. If you're a yogurt lover, try a glass of Doh, plain yogurt diluted with water, mixed with cucumber, and garnished with mint. It's delightfully refreshing!

RISTORANTE LUCI, 470 S. Cleveland Ave., St. Paul. Tel. 699-8258.

Cuisine: ITALIAN. **Reservations:** Recommended.

$ Prices: Appetizers: $4.50–$5.95; pasta $5.25–$9; main courses $8.95–$11.95. No credit cards.

Open: Dinner Tues–Thurs 5–9:30pm, Fri–Sat 5–10:30pm.

★ The decor of this very popular restaurant is simple—white walls, black wrought-iron light fixtures, and white tablecloths. The menu, which changes four times a year, is divided into sections for antipasti, soup, salad, pasta, and meat or fish. There's also a four-course "taster's dinner," which includes the day's antipasti, pasta, and fish special with a choice of soup or salad, all in reduced portions. All flat pasta as well as desserts and bread are made on the premises; and all the mozzarella cheese is made in house from fresh curd. Featured on the menu are antipasti like bruschetta con pecorino fresco (grilled home-baked bread with fresh goat cheese and dill), gazpacho Neapolitan style, rigatoni alla bolognese (with ground veal, lamb, and beef simmered with tomatoes, red wine, and fresh herbs), and linguine alla puttanesca (fresh tomatoes, olive oil, garlic, Calamata olives, and capers). Secondi (meat and fish courses) include pollo piacere (sautéed chicken breast) prepared several ways. And then there are the sweets—Luci cheesecake, flourless chocolate torte (made daily with Belgian chocolate), and a variety of fruit tarts. There is an extensive wine list.

BEYOND ST. PAUL

KOZLAK'S ROYAL OAK RESTAURANT, 4785 Hodgson Rd., Shoreview. Tel. 484-8484.
Cuisine: AMERICAN. **Reservations:** Recommended.
$ Prices: Appetizers $4.50–$8.95; main courses $13.95–$25.95; lunch $6–$9. AE, CB, DC, DISC, V.
Open: Lunch Mon–Sat 11am–2pm; dinner Mon–Thurs 4–9:30pm, Fri–Sat 4–10:30pm; Sun brunch 10:30am–2pm.

Whether you're seated indoors in one of the handsome dining rooms overlooking the outdoor gardens or outside on the veranda, you'll be pleased by the attentive service and reliable cuisine that has distinguished this restaurant for decades.

Four-course jazz brunches are particularly popular here, where your tab will depend on the entrée you select. The entrées range from eggs Benedict to veal and fettuccine to "brunch steak." The meal is modeled on the jazz brunches offered at Brennan's in New Orleans. Entrées are complemented by a trip to the salad bar or, if you choose, a house salad or a cup of the Boston clam chowder.

LAKE ELMO INN, 3442 Lake Elmo Ave., Lake Elmo. Tel. 777-8495.
Cuisine: AMERICAN. **Reservations:** Recommended.
$ Prices: Appetizers $3.75–$6.50; main courses $10.50–$19.95; Sun brunch $12.95 for adults, $6.95 for children. AE, DC, DISC, MC, V.
Open: Lunch Mon–Sat 11am–2pm; dinner Mon–Thurs 5–10pm, Fri–Sat 5–11pm, Sun 4:30–8:30pm; Sun brunch 10am–2pm.

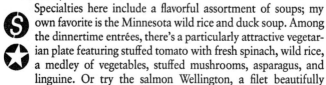

Specialties here include a flavorful assortment of soups; my own favorite is the Minnesota wild rice and duck soup. Among the dinnertime entrées, there's a particularly attractive vegetarian plate featuring stuffed tomato with fresh spinach, wild rice, a medley of vegetables, stuffed mushrooms, asparagus, and linguine. Or try the salmon Wellington, a filet beautifully prepared with spinach and wrapped in puff pastry. The chicken Alfredo is a winning combination of mostaccioli, chicken, and parmesan cream sauce. Desserts here are spectacular, particularly during the Sunday "champagne brunch," when 20 or so are presented for your selection.

VENETIAN INN, 2814 Rice St., Little Canada. Tel. 484-7215.

Cuisine: ITALIAN/AMERICAN. **Reservations:** Recommended.

$ Prices: Appetizers $3.50–$8.25; main courses $8.95–$19.50. AE, CB, DC, DISC, MC, V.

Open: Lunch daily 11am–3pm; dinner Mon–Thurs 3–9pm, Fri–Sat 3–10pm.

About 5 miles north of downtown St. Paul, this restaurant is readily accessible to both Twin Cities. The location was largely rural when Congie and Joe Vitale first opened a vegetable stand on this site years ago. Today, after a succession of remodelings, the dining room seats 300 people, with room for 600 in the banquet halls. And nearly 200 more attend performances in the Venetian Playhouse.

You'll be offered a bib with your order of ribs or pasta, both of which rank high with the regulars. Seafood is a specialty, along with Italian dinners including veal scaloppine, eggplant parmigiana, and chicken cacciatore. Dinner includes an antipasto tray, tossed salad, and Italian bread; some dishes also include a side of spaghetti or baked potato. Entrées range from rigatoni with meatballs to a seafood platter that includes haddock, stuffed shrimp, whitefish, scallops, and lobster tail.

THE OLIVE GARDEN, 1451 W. County Rd. 42, Burnsville. Tel. 898-4200.

Cuisine: ITALIAN. **Reservations:** Recommended.

$ Prices: Appetizers $3.45–$5.50; main courses $7.25–$11.95; pasta $6.50–$9.95; lunch $3.95–$6.25. AE, DC, DISC, MC, V.

Open: Lunch daily 11am–4pm; dinner Sun–Thurs 4–10pm, Fri–Sat 4–11pm.

If you liked the Olive Garden restaurants you've encountered before, chances are good that you'll be pleased with the ones you visit in the Twin Cities. The one in Burnsville is a particular favorite with folks living south of the Minnesota River and with shoppers at the nearby Burnsville Shopping Center. The manager of this branch, Tim Hall, reports that veal piccata, chicken marsala, and chicken Florentine are particular favorites, along with cannelloni and lasagne. At lunchtime, one of the best buys here would have to be the specialties that include an entrée—everything from spaghetti with tomato sauce to pasta and seafood—and a choice of soup or salad and garlic breadsticks for $3.95 to $5.85. Desserts are worth mentioning too: Try the scrumptious cannoli, a pastry shell filled with cream and topped with powdered sugar.

BUDGET

DOWNTOWN

WABASHA DELI & CAFÉ, 32 Filmore Ave. E., St. Paul. Tel. 291-8868.
  Cuisine: DELI.
$ Prices: Breakfast $1.20–$2.70; lunch $1–$3.40. No credit cards.
  Open: Mon–Thurs 6am–5:30pm, Fri 6am–2pm.

Whether you're interested in a ham and cheese omelet at breakfast time or a roast beef and Swiss croissant for lunch, the neat and friendly Wabasha Deli & Café is a very good bet. You'll be dining among state workers from nearby offices as well as neighborhood folks.

This is the only restaurant in town where you can find the full line of breads made by the nearby Baldinger Bakery, which supplies some of the finest restaurants in town. A rack in the dining room displays the loaves on hand; others—multigrain, caraway, you name it—are available in short order. You can also order take-out box lunches for less than $5 each, fruit and muffin trays for $4, and fruit baskets for $10 to $30 depending on the size.

GRAND AVENUE

CAFÉ LATTE, 850 Grand Ave., St. Paul. Tel. 224-5687.
  Cuisine: SANDWICHES/SALADS. **Reservations:** Not accepted.
$ Prices: Salads $3.50–$4.75; sandwiches $3.75–$4.75; soups $2–$3.75. AE.
  Open: Mon–Thurs 10am–11pm, Fri 10am–midnight, Sat 9am–midnight, Sun 9am–10pm.

You'll probably find a line at Café Latte, but don't hesitate to join the crowd. For the past eight years, this small restaurant has been providing the best in delicious and nutritious soups, sandwiches, and salads, along with some of the richest, most irresistible desserts in the entire Twin Cities area. Selections change each day, with the listing posted on a board near the doorway. Of the 100 varieties of bread baked on the premises here, four or five are offered everyday. You'll have your choice as well among four different kinds of soup along with a stew and the ever-present turkey chili, which may be a bit hot for some palates. Make sure you leave room for dessert. In fact, after-theater crowds testify to the lure of Café Latte's cakes, tortes, fruit tarts, and espresso. You can buy a whole cake for $17 to $22 or settle for an individual serving for $2.25 to $2.95.

SAVAGE

THE EVERGREEN, 4749 W. Hwy. 13, Savage. Tel. 890-3372.

Cuisine: AMERICAN/MEDITERRANEAN.

$ Prices: Appetizers $1.95–$4.55; main courses $5.65–$9.95; lunch $3.45–$8.25; noon buffet $6.25. MC, V.

Open: Mon–Fri 11am–10pm, Sat–Sun 11am–8pm.

One of the best dining values south of the Minnesota River can be found at the Evergreen Restaurant, where Greg and Tula Kalomas run a family restaurant with wholesome food at reasonable prices. Along with steaks, chops, seafood, and pastas, you'll find a delightful diversity of Greek specialties, including my own special favorite, a spectacular appetizer called saganaki that's made of Kasseri cheese, breaded, fried in olive oil, flambéed at the table, and then served with pita bread. Soups have always been a specialty here, and they're part of the daily all-you-can-eat buffet, which includes a soft drink, coffee, or tea. If you're in the mood for a beverage of a different kind, be advised that the Evergreen features a good selection of domestic and imported beers and wines.

CHAPTER 7

WHAT TO SEE & DO IN THE TWIN CITIES

- **DID YOU KNOW...?**
1. **THE TOP ATTRACTIONS**
2. **MORE ATTRACTIONS**
3. **COOL FOR KIDS**
4. **ORGANIZED TOURS**
5. **SPORTS & RECREATION**

A beautiful blend of the old and the new is what you'll find here in the Twin Cities. Many of the cities' buildings, like the splendid mansions on St. Paul's Summit Avenue, have been listed on the National Register of Historic Places; other spanking-new structures will dazzle you with their soaring expanses of reflective glass. Don't miss Gavidae Common, City Center, and Philip Johnson's award-winning IDS Tower in downtown Minneapolis. Be sure to visit Town Court, part of the handsome Town Square Center not far from the state capitol in downtown St. Paul. Note, too, that the internationally famed arts of the Twin Cities are often housed in buildings that are themselves works of art.

The lakes of Minneapolis and St. Paul are legendary, not only for their beauty but for the many popular activities that take place there throughout the year.

SUGGESTED ITINERARIES

IF YOU HAVE ONE DAY From downtown Minneapolis, drive through South Minneapolis via Portland Avenue to Minnehaha Parkway, then drive east to Minnehaha Park for a view of the beautiful Minnehaha Falls and the statue of the young couple immortalized by Longfellow's famous poem. Visit the nearby historic Stevens House, then continue by going south on Hiawatha Avenue which will lead you to Highway 62. Look for signs for Fort Snelling. (En route you'll pass the huge U.S. Veterans Hospital.) Tour the restored Fort Snelling, at the confluence of the Minnesota and Mississippi rivers, taking time if possible to visit the museum on the site and to view the historical film.

After the Fort Snelling visit, take Highway 55, crossing the Mendota Bridge. Turn left on the Sibley Memorial Highway (Minnesota Highway 13) for a visit to old Mendota, site of one of the earliest fur trading posts. Tour the preserved Sibley House and Faribault House.

At this point, you may wish to return to the Mendota Bridge via Highway 13. Take Highway 55 across the bridge to Highway 5. Turn south on 5, proceed past the Minneapolis–St. Paul International Airport to Interstate 494, then west to the recently completed Megamall, the largest retail and entertainment complex in the United States.

You can finish the day's adventures here, taking time out for the kind of refueling you most enjoy.

IF YOU HAVE TWO DAYS   A visit to the Twin Cities wouldn't be complete without at least a day dedicated to St. Paul. An excellent place to start is the recently completed new home of the Minnesota Historical Society located near the intersection of Kellogg Boulevard and John Ireland Boulevard. You'll find a wide variety of fascinating exhibits here describing the history of this "Land of 10,000 Lakes." Next door to the Historical Society is the impressive St. Paul's Cathedral, arguably the most magnificent structure overlooking the St. Paul skyline. Visit the nearby capitol, then drive downtown to a convenient parking spot near the World Trade Center and its adjacent shopping complex. Consider a stop for a bite here or across the street at Town Square, a major shopping complex that includes on its top level the world's largest indoor park. The carousel at Town Square Park will be of particular interest to the young members of your party. Before leaving St. Paul, take Fourth Street one way to Market Street for at least a look at Rice Park, which is bordered by four notable buildings: the Ordway Music Theatre, the St. Paul Central Library, the St. Paul Hotel, and the Landmark Center.

IF YOU HAVE THREE DAYS   If you're staying in Minneapolis, you may want to drive over the Third Avenue Bridge, where you can get a wonderful view of St. Anthony Falls and the Milling District that once distinguished Minneapolis as the Flour Capital of the World. After crossing the Mississippi River, turn right on University Avenue and proceed to and through the campus of the University of Minnesota. Continue on University Avenue into St. Paul, through the Midway District, then turn left on Lexington Avenue which will lead you to Como Park, the Como Zoo, and the newly renovated Japanese garden. When you've completed your Como Park visit, return to University Avenue and proceed east toward downtown St. Paul to Rice Street, adjacent to the state capitol.

After you turn onto Rice Street, proceed to John Ireland Boulevard, where you'll turn right again to the St. Paul Cathedral. At this juncture, you'll come to Summit Avenue, perhaps the most impressive avenue of homes anywhere. Traveling west on Summit, you'll pass the governor's mansion, William Mitchell College of Law, Macalester College, and the University of St. Thomas. At the end of Summit, you'll come to the East Mississippi River Boulevard, upon which you can return to Minneapolis, taking time, if you like, for a relaxed meal at the Lexington Café on the corner of Lexington Avenue and Grand Avenue. Incidentally, Grand Avenue is a marvelous place to browse, since it is filled with quaint shops and popular restaurants.

IF YOU HAVE FIVE DAYS OR MORE   If time permits, include an overnight stay in Rochester, Minnesota, less than a 2-hour drive from the Twin Cities. This is, of course, the home of the famous Mayo Clinic. Free tours of the clinic are available to the public on weekdays, as are tours of Mayowood, the lovely home and grounds that were originally the home of the late Dr. Charles Mayo. The Mayo Medical Museum, also open to the public, offers a variety of interesting and informative films, videotapes, and exhibits.

1. THE TOP ATTRACTIONS

FORT SNELLING, Hwy. 5 at Hwy. 55, 1 mile east of the Minneapolis–St. Paul International Airport. Tel. 726-9430 or 726-1171 for specifics on tours and special events.
   One of the most popular sight-seeing attractions in the Twin Cities

isn't in either Minneapolis or St. Paul, but in between them at the confluence of the Mississippi and Minnesota rivers. This is the place where in 1819 Col. Josiah Snelling and his troops began construction of a fort to establish an official presence in the wilderness that had recently been won from Great Britain. President Thomas Jefferson had hoped this outpost would become a "center of civilization," and that's what occurred, as families arrived and built homes on the perimeter of land that had been ceded to the army by the Sioux. In 1837, after a treaty opened additional land for settlement, these families moved across the river to establish a community of their own, one that would later be known as St. Paul.

Fort Snelling played another important role in U.S. history. In 1837 Dred Scott, the slave of an army surgeon, sued for his freedom on the basis of having lived for a time in the free state of Minnesota. He lost the case, but the now-famous Dred Scott decision is often cited as a contributing factor in the American Civil War. And in 1864 a young German military attaché named Count Zeppelin ascended 300 feet above the Old Round Tower in a large gas-filled canvas bag. Later, such vehicles, bearing the count's name, served as a common means of aerial transportation.

Since 1937 the Minnesota State Historical Society has maintained a living museum at Fort Snelling, where costumed guides re-create the activities and ceremonies of everyday army life during the 1820s. While you're here, don't overlook the interesting gift shop with its selection of authentic Native American handcrafted jewelry.

Admission: $3 adults, $1 children ages 6–15; children under 5, free.

Open: Mon–Sat 10am–5pm, Sun noon–5pm. **Directions:** From downtown Minneapolis, take 35W to Hwy. 62 which leads into Hwy. 55. Follow signs about 1 mile to Fort Snelling. From St. Paul, take 35E to 494N; then proceed west to Hwy. 55, which will take you to Fort Snelling.

THE MINNESOTA ZOO, 12101 Johnny Cake Ridge Rd., Apple Valley. Tel. 432-9000.

The terrain at the Minnesota Zoo has been carefully created to resemble the authentic grasslands and woodlands of the wild animals that now make their home here. What may be the world's most remarkable cross-country skiing takes place in the Minnesota Zoo, where, for the price of admission, you glide within full view of camels, Siberian tigers, Asiatic wild horses, moose, snow monkeys, musk oxen, red pandas, and more.

Six separate "trails" offer education so entertainingly that you won't even realize how much you've learned until you've left the 480-acre site, approximately half an hour from downtown Minneapolis and St. Paul.

The **Tropics Trail** is one of the most exotic areas of the zoo, an indoor oasis of plants and animals from far-away tropical areas.

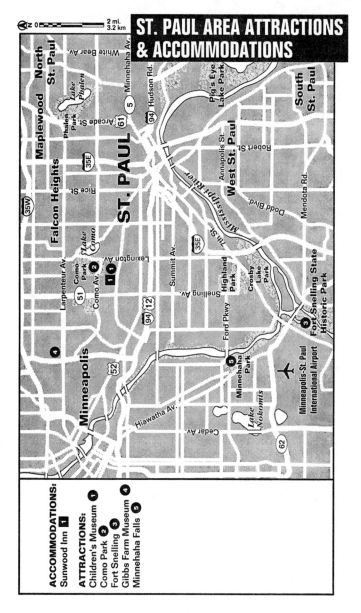

ST. PAUL AREA ATTRACTIONS & ACCOMMODATIONS

ACCOMMODATIONS:
Sunwood Inn **1**

ATTRACTIONS:
Children's Museum **2**
Como Park **2**
Fort Snelling **3**
Gibbs Farm Museum **4**
Minnehaha Falls **5**

(Don't miss the recently opened Coral Reef exhibit with its lovely formations which provide the habitat for colorful tropical fish.) This massive exhibit is housed in the largest structure in the zoo, with more than 650 animals and 500 different varieties of plants.

The **Minnesota Trail** features animals indigenous to these parts; a beaver pond provides amazing evidence of the inborn engineering know-how of these industrious creatures. Other native Minnesotan animals in daytime and nocturnal settings include otters, lynx, weasels, and an assortment of creatures hailing from Minnesota's lakes, prairies, and forests.

The **Discovery Trail** will introduce you to some unlikely new friends. Visited with a tarantula lately? Or a sea star? You'll have the opportunity for close encounters with these and other unusual beings in the **Zoo Lab.** And you'll be able to watch an intriguing bird show, ride a camel or an elephant, pet a goat, and enjoy other hands-on experiences here.

On the **Northern Trail,** you'll be surrounded by tigers, Asian lions, coyotes, musk oxen, camels, wild horses, and moose. And you'll get to meet what may be your first-ever pronghorn, a graceful antelope look-alike.

The **Sky Trail** is an option you can enjoy for an additional $3 per person. This monorail weaves in and out of hills and lakelands as you view wild terrain and listen to "nature narratives" provided by knowledgeable guides.

Admission: $6 ages 13–64, $4 ages 65 and up, $2.50 children ages 3–12; children under 3, free. Parking is free.

Open: Mon–Sat 10am–6pm, Sun 10am–8pm. **Directions:** From downtown Minneapolis, take 35W south to 62 east to Cedar Ave. So. (Hwy. 44). Zoo exit is marked on Hwy. 77 in Apple Valley.

THE MINNESOTA STATE CAPITOL, 700 Wabasha St., St. Paul. Tel. 296-2881.

The grandest of all Twin Cities sights is the Minnesota State Capitol, built in 1905 on a hill overlooking downtown St. Paul. Crowned by the world's largest unsupported marble dome, this magnificent structure was the design of Cass Gilbert, a young St. Paul architect whose later work included the Woolworth Building in New York City. At the base of the dome, modeled after the one Michelangelo created for St. Peter's in Rome, is a dramatic grouping of gilded figures titled *The Progress of the State.* Four prancing horses, symbolizing the power of Nature, are held in check by two women, representing Civilization. A charioteer, Prosperity, holds aloft a horn of plenty in one hand, while in the other he grasps a banner bearing the inscription "Minnesota."

The interior of the capitol building is equally impressive, with its marble stairways, chambers, and halls, and its fine oil paintings depicting important events in Minnesota history.

Tours: Free guided tours through the senate, house of representatives, and supreme court chambers offered Mon–Fri 9am–4pm, Sat 10am–3pm, Sun 1–3pm. **Directions:** From Minneapolis take I-94E; exit on Marion St.; turn left on John Ireland Blvd. From St. Paul, take 94 or 35E; exit at the capitol.

MINNEAPOLIS INSTITUTE OF ART, 3rd Ave. S. and E. 24th St., Minneapolis. Tel. 870-3046.

More than 70,000 objects of art representing more than 25,000 years of history await you here. Since the institute eliminated its general admission charge in September 1989 except for special exhibitions, there's been a remarkable increase in the number of visitors. Besides the institute's famous 2,000-year-old mummy, other favorites here are a fascinating assortment of African masks, a rare collection of Chinese jades, and Pre-Columbian gold objects from the Incas.

Faithfully re-created period rooms have long been popular, and so are more recent additions—everything from ethnic galleries to the meticulously restored Purcell-Cutts house, an example of the early 20th-century design movement known as the Prairie school. Other holdings here include work by Rembrandt and a number of French impressionists as well as superb examples of contemporary art. A photography collection adds to the diversity.

Even the exterior of the institute represents an intriguing blend of periods. On the 24th Street side is the original majestic classic revival structure, which faces Fair Oaks Park, while around the corner, extending past the main entrance, is the contemporary facade, a mixture of steel and brick whose color and texture blends gracefully with the original.

If you're here in June, check out the annual Father's Day Rose Fete, an extravaganza of fun, food, crafts, and entertainment. Throughout the year, you'll find an interesting schedule of lectures, gallery concerts, and films.

Open: Tues, Wed, Fri, Sat 10am–5pm; Thurs 10am–9pm, Sun noon–5pm. **Directions:** From downtown Minneapolis, take 3rd Ave. south. From downtown St. Paul, take I-94 to 11th St. exit. At second stoplight, turn left onto 3rd Ave. and proceed to 2400 Third Ave. South.

THE WALKER ART CENTER AND THE MINNEAPOLIS SCULPTURE GARDENS, 725 Vineland Place, Minneapolis. Tel. 375-7577 or 375-7622.

To reach this attraction from downtown St. Paul, take 94W to the Hennepin-Lyndale exit. From the left lane, turn right. Just before the second set of lights, turn left. The Walker will be at your left. From downtown Minneapolis, follow 1st Avenue North to 11th Street. Turn left on 11th and go one block to Hennepin Avenue. Turn right, pass St. Mary's Cathedral; go under the bridge, then turn left and, after one block, turn right. The Walker will be at your left.

The Walker Art Center, adjoining the Tyrone Guthrie Theater and facing the Sculpture Garden, is famous for its permanent collection of contemporary art. In addition, some of the most prestigious exhibitions that tour the country make stops at the Walker. In February 1980, "Picasso: From the Musée Picasso, Paris" brought Picasso's work to the United States for the first time; these works were later incorporated into the Picasso retrospective at the

New York Museum of Modern Art. The Walker is also known for the popular presentations it offers through its Department of Film and Video, its Department of Performing Arts, and its Department of Education.

Across Vineland Place, the Minneapolis Sculpture Garden, whose display of artworks and educational activities are managed by the Walker Art Center, has been attracting wide attention since it was dedicated in September 1988. The most extensive garden of its kind in the United States, it's been called the country's finest new outdoor space for displaying sculpture.

Probably the most readily recognizable work here is *Spoonbridge and Cherry* by Claes Oldenburg and Coosje van Bruggen—a 52-foot-long spoon bearing a cherry that measures 9½ feet in diameter, with a 12-foot stem. This sculptural fountain and reflecting pool stand in honor of William and Mary Weisman, parents of Minneapolis-born philanthropist and art collector Frederick R. Weisman.

The wide variety of 20th-century sculpture on display here includes work by artists Henry Moore, Isamu Noguchi, George Segal, and Jackie Ferrara. California architect Frank Gehry is represented by the dramatic *Standing Glass Fish* in the conservatory, which features horticultural displays throughout the year. To the surprise of many observers, the Sculpture Garden has become a year-round attraction, so come and see it for yourself, whatever the weather.

Admission: Art Center $3 adults, $2 students. Free on Thurs.
Open: Tues–Sat 10am–8pm, Sun 11am–5pm.

2. MORE ATTRACTIONS

ARCHITECTURAL HIGHLIGHTS

At the corner of Summit and Selby avenues, near the state capitol, stands one of St. Paul's proud architectural achievements, the 3,000-seat Renaissance-style **Cathedral of St. Paul,** constructed of Minnesota granite. John Ireland Boulevard, the street that extends just half a mile from the capitol to the cathedral, is named for the dynamic archbishop of St. Paul who served as a chaplain during the Civil War and later lent his energies toward raising the funds for this magnificent structure, which he dedicated to the people of St. Paul.

Beyond the cathedral, Summit Avenue, long the most prestigious of St. Paul's addresses, extends 4½ miles to the Mississippi River. On this distinguished street stands the country's longest span of intact **Victorian mansions,** and here, at 240 Summit Ave., you'll find one of the city's perennially popular tourist attractions, the mansion of "empire builder" James J. Hill, founder of the Great Northern

Railroad. (For information about tours, phone 297-2555.) Among the more modest homes on this avenue is the one at 599 Summit, where F. Scott Fitzgerald lived in 1918 while finishing his first literary success, *This Side of Paradise*. And farther down toward the Mississippi, at 1006 Summit, you'll find the governor's stately residence.

Perhaps the most dramatic of St. Paul's restored structures is the **Landmark Center,** facing Rice Park at 106 W. 6th St. This massive early French Renaissance building with Gothic towers and pillars, turrets and gables, 20-foot ceilings and hand-carved mahogany and marble decoration, served for decades as the Federal Courts Building and Post Office. Eventually it fell into disrepair and was slated for demolition until a determined coalition of private citizens and public officials intervened. Returned to its former grandeur, today it houses all sorts of offices and is open to the public for free guided tours.

GALLERIES

Most galleries are open from 11am to 4pm Tuesday through Saturday, by appointment. Some are open Thursday evening until 8pm. Phone ahead to confirm hours.

THOMAS BARRY FINE ARTS, 400 1st Ave. N., Suite 304, the Wyman Building, Minneapolis. Tel. 338-3656.

This gallery offers contemporary American work, including photography, prints, drawings, paintings, and sculpture. Artists include Don Gahr, Lynn Geesaman, Bruce Charlesworth, and Ken Moylan, as well as David Madzo, Scott Stack, and Steven Woodward.

FLANDERS CONTEMPORARY ART, 400 1st Ave. N., the Wyman Building, Minneapolis. Tel. 344-1700.

Flanders features museum-quality contemporary painting, drawing, and sculpture by nationally and internationally known American and European artists, among them Georgia O'Keefe, Albert Giacometti, Eric Fischl, Nancy Graves, and Tom Holland.

MCGALLERY, 400 1st Ave. N., Suite 332, the Wyman Building, Minneapolis. Tel. 339-1480.

McGallery is an avant-garde fine-art gallery offering works in a variety of forms—painting, sculpture, glass, ceramics, and others. Paul Benson, Sheldon Hage, Jean Murakami, Barbra Nei, and Chris Hawthorne are among the artists represented here.

THOMSON GALLERY, 321 2nd Ave. N., Minneapolis. Tel. 338-7734.

The Thomson Gallery offers contemporary drawings, paintings, prints, photography, and sculpture by such artists as Philip Larson,

Lance Kiland, Steven Sorman, and Tom Rose. Much of the work shown here is of museum quality.

SUZANNE KOHN GALLERY, 1690 Grand Ave., St. Paul. Tel. 699-0477.

Regional painters are featured here, and if you don't see what you want on the walls of this small gallery, you're welcome to go downstairs for a look through the works stored there. Among the artists represented are the established Midwestern artist Jerry Rudquist and regional artists like Tom Maakestad and Steven Carpenter. Suzanne Kohn also has a satellite gallery in Minneapolis at the International Design Center, 100 2nd Ave. N. (tel. 341-3441). Exhibits change here monthly.

ART RESOURCES, 494 Jackson St., St. Paul. Tel. 222-4431.

Art Resources features the work of Midwestern artists, with over 6,000 pieces of original art, ranging from abstract expressionism to classical realism.

KRAMER GALLERY, 229 E. 6th St., St. Paul. Tel. 228-1301.

The work of late 19th-century and early 20th-century regional artists is featured here, though other American and European painters of that period are exhibited also, along with turn-of-the-century Native American art and artifacts. Among the famous painters represented here are Alexis Fournier, who left St. Paul to study with Barbizon masters in France, and Nichola Brewer, another notable turn-of-the-century painter of the Barbizon school.

RAYMOND AVENUE GALLERY, 761 Raymond Ave., St. Paul. Tel. 644-9200.

If you're interested in bringing top-quality crafts back from your visit to Minnesota, try this gallery, where you'll find baskets, jewelry, and pottery.

LAKES

For information about Minneapolis's lakes, phone 348-2243. Three of the most popular lakes in Minneapolis form a chain that's believed to be part of the course followed by the Mississippi River some 25,000 years ago. Although the property close to **Lake of the Isles** is very expensive these days, you couldn't have given it away 100 years ago when it was a mess of swamps and marshes. The land was dredged in the late 1880s and by the turn of the century had become valuable real estate. Now a man-made lake, it's popular with fishermen because it's stocked with tasty sunfish and crappies. Lake of the Isles is popular with canoeists too for its irregular shoreline and varied landscape. During the winter a regulation hockey rink is set up, along with areas for general skating and a warming house. If you decide to walk around Lake of the Isles, remember that the path closest to the shore is for you; the other path is for bicyclists.

A channel connects Lake of the Isles to **Lake Calhoun,** so boaters can paddle from one to the other. No powerboats are permitted on city lakes, partly because of the noise and partly because the rapid churning of the water erodes the shoreline. Lake Calhoun is the largest of the chain of lakes, and at 90 to 100 feet, it's the deepest as well. Whatever the season, you're likely to see boats here, lots of one-man skimmers and sailboats in the summertime, iceboats (sailboats on blades) in the winter. This is perhaps the lake most popular with young adults.

The third link in the chain of lakes, **Lake Harriet,** may have the greatest appeal to families because of its delightful gardens and bird sanctuary. Lake Harriet Rose Gardens provides an annual display of glorious colors and scents for visitors. The Lake Harriet Rock Garden has been popular since 1929; it was refurbished in 1984. And the adjacent bird sanctuary features a wood-chip path for visitors who enjoy the solitude and serenity of an unspoiled woodland setting. If you're visiting the Twin Cities from late May until early September, join the crowds who arrive by boat, bike, or automobile to enjoy the nightly bandstand concerts at Lake Harriet. Along with Lake Calhoun and **Lake Nokomis,** Lake Harriet also features weekend sailboat races that draw throngs of participants and observers throughout the summer months.

MUSEUMS

THE AMERICAN SWEDISH INSTITUTE, 2600 Park Ave., Minneapolis. Tel. 871-4907.

The American Swedish Institute is a fairy-tale-like castle of pale limestone, with arches, turrets, a small balcony, and a tower. It's equally grand within, with decorative ceilings, intricately designed rugs of Swedish wool, and a glorious stained-glass window copied from a famous and historic Swedish painting.

This magnificent 33-room mansion was donated to the American Swedish Institute by Swan J. Turnblad, who came to this country in 1887 at the age of eight. By the time he was 27 Turnblad had become manager of the *Svenska Amerikanska Posten,* a Swedish-language weekly, and as its owner 10 years later he made it the largest Swedish-language newspaper in America. His general purpose for the institute, to "foster and preserve Swedish culture in America," has been admirably fulfilled. Artifacts in the mansion demonstrate over 150 years of the Swedish experience in the United States. On display are items Swedish immigrants brought with them from the old country and works of art by Swedish and Swedish-American artists. A film program is presented every Sunday at 2pm and musical programs are offered at 3pm on Sunday afternoons during the winter months.

Admission: $3 adults, $2 seniors and students under 19.

Open: Tues, Thurs–Sat noon–4pm; Wed noon–8pm and Sun 1–5pm.

JAMES FORD BELL MUSEUM OF NATURAL HISTORY, University Ave. and 17th Ave. S.E., Minneapolis. Tel. 624-1852 or 624-7083.

The oldest museum in the state of Minnesota is still one of the most popular. Located on the Minneapolis campus of the University of Minnesota, it's famous for its three-dimensional scenes of Minnesota wildlife, which have proved fascinating to generations of visitors. Animals and birds in their natural habitats are painstakingly reproduced and displayed here; accompanying legends provide information in a concise and interesting way.

In the popular "Touch and See" room, children can examine for themselves the skins, bones, and skulls of a wide variety of animals, including mammoths and dinosaurs. Among the creatures on hand are stuffed wildlife specimens such as moose, elk, and caribou, as well as Lenny, a live Gila monster, which is sometimes kept company by visiting animals from the Como Park Zoo.

Admission: $2 ages 17–61; $1 ages 62 and older and children ages 3–16; children under 3, free. On Thurs all are free.

Open: Tues–Sat 9am–5pm, Sun 1–5pm.

GIBBS FARM MUSEUM, Cleveland and Larpenteur Aves., Falcon Heights, St. Paul. Tel. 646-8629.

This popular museum re-creates life on a 7-acre farm at the turn of the century. Costumed guides are on hand to answer questions about the artifacts and activities on this homestead. You'll see how the Gibbs family's home grew from a one-room cabin to a large, comfortable farmhouse complete with parlor, sitting room, kitchen, bedrooms, and more. In a red barn you'll find farming, woodworking, and veterinary exhibits. Friendly animals await you behind the barn, and there's a one-room schoolhouse with wooden double desks, a pump organ, slate boards, and a school bell. A slide presentation explains what farming on the fringe of St. Paul was like in those days.

Information about individual programs, which vary from month to month, can be obtained from the Ramsey County Historical Society, 323 Landmark Center, 75 W. 5th St., St. Paul (tel. 222-0701).

Admission: $2.50 adults, $2 seniors, $1 children ages 2–18.

Open: May–Oct, Tues–Fri 10am–4pm, Sun noon–4pm; June–Aug, Tues–Fri 10am–4pm, Sat–Sun noon–4pm.

THE MINNESOTA MUSEUM OF ART, 305 St. Peter St., St. Paul. Tel. 292-4355.

Two historic structures house the Minnesota Museum of Art in St. Paul: the striking 1931 art deco Jemne Building on St. Peter Street at Kellogg Boulevard and, two blocks away, the majestic 1906 Romanesque-style Landmark Center at Fifth and Market streets.

Holdings at the Jemne include works from the ancient as well as the contemporary world. The most recent additions to the museum's collections of American and non-Western art are exhibited at the Jemne, where the building itself is a treasure, with its original terrazzo floors and brass railings.

The museum's temporary exhibition galleries at the Landmark Center include the work of new Midwestern artists as well as major exhibitions. At times, touring exhibitions are on display here too. In the fifth-floor gallery known as "Kidspace," children can enjoy a "hands-on" experience with art.

By the way, there's food for the palate as well as the soul in both buildings. At the Jemne, one of the best Sunday buffets in either town can be found on the fourth-floor Deco Restaurant overlooking the Mississippi River. And at the Landmark, budget-pleasing soup-and-sandwich lunches are a popular weekday feature.

Admission: Free.

Open: Tues–Wed and Fri 10:30am–4:30pm, Thurs 10:30am–7:30pm, Sat–Sun 1–4:30pm.

THE SCIENCE MUSEUM OF MINNESOTA, 30 E. 10th St., St. Paul. Tel. 221-9454.

At the entrance of this immensely popular two-building complex you'll be greeted by Iggy, a 40-foot steel iguana that was sculpted by a 16-year-old St. Paul schoolboy. Boys and girls of all ages have an entertaining and educational time at this massive museum, which offers hands-on exhibits dealing with natural history, science, and technology. Members of an acting troupe turn up here and there to bring to life some of the figures who have played a part in the development of this area.

The East Building holds "Our Minnesota," a permanent exhibit featuring a 12-by-14-foot map of the state that permits visitors to walk or crawl across forests marked in green, croplands marked in gold, mines represented by taconite pellets, and lakes depicted by an expanse of blue plastic. The Hall of Paleontology features the dinosaur lab, in which visitors can watch fossils being cleaned, identified, and assembled. The West Building contains the Hall of Anthropology, the Physics and Technology Gallery, and the Collections Exhibit (miscellaneous artifacts from the collection), as well as a succession of traveling exhibits.

And then there's the Omnitheater, whose screen is a tilted dome, 76 feet in diameter, that puts viewers right into the center of adventures dealing with every time and every place.

Hours for the exhibit halls and the Omnitheater differ according to season; call 221-9454 for information. Call 221-9400 for information about prices for the Omnitheater and for Omnitheater-Museum combination tickets.

   Admission: Exhibit hall $4.50 adults, $3.50 seniors and children under 12.

   Open: Mon–Fri 9:30am–9pm, Sat 9am–9pm, Sun 10am–9pm.

PARKS & GARDENS

More than a million visitors a year make St. Paul's **Como Park** one of the most popular of all Twin Cities attractions. The glorious Como Park Conservatory, site of innumerable weddings and other festive events, is a prime attraction; adjacent to it are two smaller but equally beautiful showplaces: the McKnight Formal Gardens, with their famous Paul Manship sculpture of an Indian boy and his dog, and the Ordway Memorial Japanese Gardens, designed by Masami Matsuda of Nagasaki, St. Paul's Japanese sister city. There is also the popular Como Zoo, not far from a small, privately operated amusement park which has pony rides among its many attractions.

   Golfers will be glad to know about Como Park's elegant new octagonal clubhouse that overlooks one of the city's best 18-hole golf courses. A vast pavilion, restored to its early 20th-century grandeur, is where Twin Citians listen to lakeside concerts. Lake Como provides delightful sunning, and paddleboats are a popular diversion here as well, making their way among the ducks, gulls, and other birds that are at home on the lake.

   If you ever have questions or need help in the park, look for one of the park rangers in their beige-and-brown uniforms; they patrol regularly and are unfailingly courteous and helpful. Como Park is located about 2½ miles north of the juncture of Interstate 94 and Lexington Avenue in St. Paul. See "Sports and Recreation" below for details on park activities, and phone 292-7400 for information on the many beautiful lakes and parks in St. Paul.

SCULPTURE

There are two statues in St. Paul that rank high on any list of sight-seeing attractions. In the St. Paul City Hall/Ramsey County Courthouse, at Fourth and Wabasha avenues, Carl Milles's majestic 36-foot tall onyx figure, *The Indian God of Peace,* stands in regal splendor. This 60-ton statue rotates very, very slowly. It can be seen Tuesday through Friday from 8am to 5pm, Sunday from 1 to 5pm.

   On the slope between the capitol and the cathedral there's an often-overlooked symbolic tribute to a history-making Minnesotan. Charles Lindbergh, who grew up in Little Falls, Minnesota, became in 1927 the first pilot ever to make a nonstop solo flight across the

Atlantic Ocean. Sculptor Paul Granlund has honored him by creating two bronze figures, Lindbergh as a young man and as a small boy.

3. COOL FOR KIDS

The Twin Cities are a mecca for family fun. For those of you with restless youngsters on your hands, this section will head off any threat of boredom.

THE CHILDREN'S MUSEUM, 1217 Bandana Blvd., St. Paul. Tel. 644-3818.

Children get to do all sorts of grown-up things at the Children's Museum, a "hands-on" museum in St. Paul's historic Bandana Square complex. Here, in a two-story reconverted blacksmith's shop, children can control cassette decks and dancing colored lights at a DJ desk. At the telegraph station they can operate Morse code devices that signal simultaneously with a clicker and with blue lights so that deaf children can receive messages of their own. Another top draw is the crane-and-train exhibit, where children can use an electromagnetic crane to pick up and deposit metal discs. At the Now-and-Then fountain, visitors can compare prices in the 1950s with those of the present. At the bank, children can examine foreign and domestic currency on a light table. There are two floors of fun here, and parents seem as intrigued as youngsters are.

Admission: Sept–May $2 weekdays, $3 weekends; June–Aug $3 daily. Free for children one year or younger. Senior citizens $2.

Open: Sun–Tues 10am–6pm, Wed–Sat 10am–8pm. Hours change during summertime; call for specific information. **Closed:** Mon during the school year.

THE CHILDREN'S THEATRE, 2400 3rd Ave. S., Minneapolis. Tel. 874-0400.

Known throughout the world for its imaginative productions for youngsters, the Children's Theatre has portrayed characters from *The Wizard of Oz, Treasure Island, The Jungle Book,* and *500 Hats of Bartholomew Cubbins.* This theater is immense and its sight lines are excellent.

Prices: Tickets $9.75–$21.95 adults, $6.75–$17.45 children under 17 and senior citizens 62 and over.

THE OMNITHEATER, in the Science Museum of Minnesota, 30 E. 10th St., St. Paul. Tel. 221-9400.

The huge curved screen and the world's largest film projector literally propel you out into space, down to the ocean's floor, or to places in between. You can go to the Omnitheater early and wait in line, or phone 221-9456 and pay an extra 50¢ per ticket for advance reservations.

Prices: Tickets $5 adults, $4 senior citizens and children 12 and under.

THE SCIENCE MUSEUM OF MINNESOTA, 30 E. 10th St., St. Paul. Tel. 221-9454.

Children are encouraged to try their hand at everything from grinding grain to operating a computer. Exhibits here cover a wide range of times and places, and one visit may well lead to another.

Admission: $3 adults, $2 children 4–12, children under 4, free. If you attend the Omnitheater on the second floor, your admission to the rest of the Science Museum will be only $1.

Open: Oct–Mar, Tues–Sat 9:30am–9pm, Sun 11am–9pm. Apr–Oct, Mon–Sat 9:30am–9pm, Sun 11am–9pm.

TOWN SQUARE PARK, 445 Minnesota St., St. Paul. Tel. 227-3307.

On the top levels of the Town Square shopping, dining, and office complex is the world's largest indoor park. There's a small playground for children, lots of cozy seating for adults, and a picturesque setting of shrubs, trees, and waterfalls.

THE TWIN CITIES MODEL RAILROAD CLUB, Bandana Sq., 1021 Bandana Blvd. E., St. Paul. Tel. 647-9628.

Here children and their elders have the chance to see a remarkable exhibit in the making. Club members are still assembling historic tracks and artifacts that trace the history of railroading in this area during the past 50 years.

Open: Mon–Fri noon–9pm, Sat 10am–6pm, Sun 1–5pm.

THE COMO PARK ZOO, Midwest Parkway and Kaufman Dr., St. Paul. Tel. 488-5572.

Sparky, the performing seal, is everybody's favorite here, but there are lots of other animals to meet in the Primate and Aquatic buildings and in Wolf Woods. Sparky performs Tuesday through Friday at 11am, 2pm, and 4pm and on weekends at 11am, 2pm, 4pm, and 5pm.

Admission: Free.

Open: Winter daily 10am–6pm, summer daily 10am–6pm.

GIBB'S FARM, 2097 W. Larpenteur Ave., Falcon Heights. Tel. 646-8629.

In this turn-of-the-century farm, children can experience the surroundings of the girls and boys who lived long ago. In addition to the farmhouse, the 7-acre site contains a red barn with old-fashioned tools and another barn with domestic animals.

Admission: $2.50 adults, $2 seniors, $1 children ages 2–18.

Open: May and Sept–Oct, Tues–Fri 10am–4pm, Sun noon–4pm; June–Aug, Tues–Fri 10am–4pm, Sat–Sun noon–4pm.

HISTORIC FORT SNELLING, Hwy. 5 at Hwy. 55, 1 mile east of the Minneapolis–St. Paul airport. Tel. 726-9430.

This restoration of the military post that brought the first settlers to these parts is now one of the most popular of all Twin Cities tourist attractions. Costumed guides encourage visitors to take part in the activities that kept soldiers and their families busy during those early days. Children particularly seem to enjoy the Round Tower, which provided a lookout up and down the Minnesota and Mississippi rivers. The schoolhouse, the blacksmith shop, and the hospital are just some of the fascinating and educational exhibits here.

Admission: $3 adults, $1 senior citizens and children ages 6–15; children under 5, free.

Open: Mon–Sat 10am–5pm, Sun noon–5pm. **Closed:** Nov–Apr.

THE *JONATHON PADDELFORD* STERNWHEELER, Harriet Island, St. Paul. Tel. 227-1100.

Passengers board this authentic 19th-century riverboat on Harriet Island, located on the edge of downtown St. Paul, and sail the Mississippi for a 1½-hour round-trip. A taped narration points out special places, including Fort Snelling, and offers interesting facts. There are three sailings each day from June through August, and one sailing on Saturday, Sunday, and holidays during May and September. Phone for specific details.

Prices: Tickets $8 adults, $5.50 children under 12.

THE LAKE HARRIET TROLLEY, 42nd St. and Queen Ave. S., Minneapolis. Tel. 522-7417.

Many older Twin Citians can remember riding old-fashioned streetcars, but most children have never had the experience—so they have a great time on the mile-long ride between Lake Harriet and Lake Calhoun. Just as in the old days, children buy tokens for the ride and a conductor collects them. This line is manned by volunteers, hence the abbreviated hours.

Fares: 75¢ per person; children 2 and under, free.

Open: Memorial Day to Labor Day Mon–Fri 6:30pm–dusk, Sat 3:30pm–dusk, Sun and holidays 12:30pm–dusk. Labor Day to Oct, weather permitting, Sat 3:30pm–dusk, Sun 12:30pm–dusk. **Closed:** Nov to Memorial Day.

MINNEHAHA FALLS/STATUE OF HIAWATHA AND MINNEHAHA, in Minnehaha Park, near the Mississippi River.

It was reportedly a description of Minnehaha Falls that inspired Henry Wadsworth Longfellow to write his famous poem about Hiawatha and Minnehaha. The two are reunited here in a graceful statue near the falls that bear her name. This whole area is a popular picnicking place for families. It's also the site of many large ethnic picnics, so you may run into costumed Scandinavians of all ages if you get there at the right time.

Directions: From Minneapolis, take Hwy. 55 for about 5 miles; turn left on Minnehaha Parkway and enter the parking lot on the right. From St. Paul, take Hwy. 94 west and get off at the Cretin-Vandalia exit; at the stop sign, turn left and proceed about 3 miles, turning right onto the Ford Parkway, which becomes a bridge that crosses the Mississippi River; one block beyond the Ford Bridge, turn left on 46th Street, proceed one block to Godfrey, turn right on Godfrey, drive about a block, and turn left into the parking lot.

MURPHY'S LANDING, Hwy. 101 near Shakopee. Tel. 445-6900.

Unlike other living-history restorations in the area, Murphy's Landing doesn't confine itself to one point in time. Instead, fifty years of Minnesota Valley history unfolds before visitors as they proceed from the 1840s fur trader's cabin to the 1850 timber farm and ultimately to a village of the 1890s. The costumes of the guides in each of the settings are consistent with the time period they represent. City children in particular enjoy seeing the farm animals roaming through the lanes; they also enjoy watching the churning, spinning, weaving, and other chores being carried on much as they were in the 19th century. Murphy's Landing is located about 11 miles west of the intersection of Interstate 35W and Highway 13, about one mile west of Valleyfair.

Admission: $7 adults, $6 seniors and students 6–18; children under 5, free. Admission includes horse-drawn trolley shuttle and tours of the village.

Open: Tues–Thurs 11am–4pm; Fri–Sun noon–5pm. **Closed:** Nov–Apr.

VALLEYFAIR, Hwy. 101 near Shakopee. Tel. 445-7600.

If you're bringing children to the Twin Cities, you might want to spend a day at Valleyfair, an enormously popular theme park that occupies 60 acres and offers attractions for children and grown-ups alike. This is one of the most popular amusement parks in the entire Midwest. Valleyfair is located about nine miles west of the intersec-

---

IMPRESSIONS

The Falls of Minnehaha
Flash and gleam amoung the oaktrees
Laugh and leap into the valley . . .
From the waterfall he named her
Minnehaha Laughing Water.
—HENRY WADSWORTH LONGFELLOW, *THE SONG OF HIAWATHA*
(1855)

tion of Interstate 35W and Highway 13, about 1 mile from Murphy's Landing.

Admission: $17.50 regular admission, $9.95 children 4 years old to 48 inches tall, $9.95 seniors 62 and older; children under 3, free. Parking $3.50.

Open: May to early Sept daily 10am–8pm; closing time is occasionally later, call for latest hours. **Closed:** Oct to early May; weekdays after first week of Sept.

4. ORGANIZED TOURS

One of the best ways to get your bearings in the Twin Cities is to take a narrated tour. Here are three good options, depending on your preference and pocketbook.

BY BUS

City tours are offered by **Gray Lines,** which in the Twin Cities is run by Medicine Lake Lines. Tours last about four hours and take passengers through both Minneapolis and St. Paul, with time out at Minnehaha Falls and St. Paul Cathedral (if no service is underway). Prices are $15 for adults, $14 for seniors, and $7 for children 7 to 14 (children under seven can ride free as long as they don't take a seat that could go to a fare-paying passenger). Tours run Tuesday through Sunday during June, July, and August. In May and September, tour buses run only on Saturdays and Sundays. Call 591-9099, or ask your concierge or front-desk personnel for further information.

BY MINIVAN

If you prefer seeing the Twin Cities as part of a smaller group in a smaller vehicle, consider **Twin Cities Sightseeing Tours,** operated by Minneapolis and Suburban Airport Limousine Service. This tour lasts 2½ hours, costs $15 for adults, $13 for seniors, and $8 for children under 12 years of age, and will take you to many landmarks in both cities, with a stop en route at Minnehaha Falls. The minivans seat 29 passengers. Individuals can board at a variety of downtown Minneapolis and St. Paul boarding sites; call 827-7777 for specific information. The sights you'll see are pretty well determined in advance, but you'll find that drivers are influenced by their individual preferences. If your interest is primarily historical, literary, or something else, mention that when you call.

BY BOAT

For a change of pace, consider a tape-narrated, round-trip boat trip on an old-fashioned riverboat from Harriet Island in St. Paul to Fort

Snelling. You'll experience a bit of local history as you travel the Mississippi on the *Jonathon Paddelford* or the *Josiah Snelling*, authentic sternwheelers belonging to the Paddelford Packet Boat Company (tel. 227-1100). The company also operates in Minneapolis at the Boom Island landing, where you can board the *Anson Northrop* and the *Betsey Northrop* for a ride downriver past Nicollet Island and through the locks at Upper St. Anthony Falls.

5. SPORTS & RECREATION

SPECTATOR SPORTS

Minneapolis and St. Paul have four professional sports teams: the **Minnesota Vikings** football team, **Minnesota Twins** baseball team, **Minnesota North Stars** hockey team, and the **Minnesota Timberwolves** basketball team. Tickets to Viking games are $25 for any seat, and can be obtained by writing to 500 11th Ave. S., Minneapolis (tel. 333-8828). Twins tickets range in price from $4 to $12; write to 501 Chicago Ave. S., Minneapolis (tel. 375-1366). For ticket information for the Timberwolves, call 989-5151 or write Timberwolves Ticket Office, 500 City Place, 730 Hennepin Ave., Minneapolis.

RECREATION

Minneapolis and St. Paul abound with sports-related activities. For information on recreation in Minneapolis, call 348-2226; for St. Paul, call 292-7400.

CANOEING

If you want to go canoeing, you can literally paddle your way through the neighborhoods of the Twin Cities. Canoeists can start out in Minnetonka, then follow Minnehaha Creek from Gray's Bay through suburban Hopkins, St. Louis Park, and Edina and then go on to a spot not far from the Mississippi River in Minneapolis. **AARCEE Recreational Rental,** 2900 Lyndale Ave. S., Minneapolis (tel. 827-5746), rents 15-foot Coleman canoes for $26 a day, $38 for up to three days, and 17-foot aluminum canoes for $32 a day, $45 for up to three days, including life jackets, paddles, and car-top carriers. Some hardy folks make the round-trip in one outing; others arrange for a car to be waiting for them when they reach the end of the route.

Shorter outings are popular at **Cedar Lake** in Minneapolis, and canoes and rowboats can be rented at **Lake Calhoun** for $4.50 an hour (cash only). A particularly popular course here leads canoeists through the chain of lakes that extends from Lake Calhoun to Lake of the Isles and then to Cedar Lake. In St. Paul, you can canoe or row on **Lake Phalen** for $4.50 per hour with a $25 deposit and photo ID.

FISHING

Want something to show for your day on the water? For fishing, try the lagoon in St. Paul's ever-popular Lake Phalen. You'll pay $5 to rent a fishing boat for the first hour, plus $2.50 for each additional hour (there's a $25 deposit on all boats, and you'll need a photo ID). Call 771-7507 for more information.

GOLF

There are more par-3 courses in the Twin Cities than in any other metropolitan area in the country. If golf is your game, here are a few courses for you to consider.

The **Majestic Oaks Golf Course,** 701 Bunker Lake Blvd., Ham Lake (tel. 755-2142), is privately owned but open to the public; it was rated among the top 50 American public golf courses by *Golf Digest.* There are two courses here. At the Platinum Course you'll pay $18 for 18 holes weekdays, $20 on weekends. The cost of playing the Gold Course, which opened in 1991, is $10 for 9 holes, $16 for 18 holes on weekdays. Carts are available for $10 at the 9-hole course, $20 at the 18-hole courses, and clubs can be rented for $5 (9 holes) or $8 (18 holes).

The **Braemar Golf Course,** 6364 Dewey Hill Rd., Edina (tel. 941-2072), offering an 18-hole regulation course and a 9-hole executive course, has hosted many national tournaments. Rates are $15.50 for 18 holes, $9.25 for 9 holes. There's also a driving range; rates are $4 for a large bucket of balls, $2.75 for a small. Rental carts cost $11 for 9 holes, $19 for 18 holes. Club rental is $5.

The **Francis A. Gross Golf Course,** 2201 St. Anthony Blvd., Minneapolis (tel. 789-2542), charges $10.50 for 9 holes and $14 for 18 holes. Carts are available at $10.50 for 9 holes, $18 for 18 holes, and clubs can be rented at $6 for 9 or 18 holes.

At the **Meadowbrook Golf Course,** 300 Meadowbrook Rd., Hopkins (tel. 929-2077), rates are $10.50 for 9 holes and $14 for 18 holes. Rental carts are available at $10.50 for 9 holes, $18 for 18 holes, and clubs can be rented for $6.

The **Hiawatha Golf Course,** 4553 Longfellow Ave. S., Minneapolis (tel. 724-7715), charges $10.50 for 9 holes and $14 for 18 holes. Carts are rented at $10.50 for 9 holes, $18 for 18 holes, and clubs are available for $6 (18 holes), $3 (9 holes).

In addition, the 18-hole and 9-hole public courses in St. Paul's **Como Park** remain among the best around. Rates are $15 for 18 holes until 4pm; $11.50 from 4 to 6:15pm; $7.50 after 6:15pm. Cost for playing the 9-hole course is $10.50. Call 292-7400 for further information.

At **Edinburgh USA** golf course in Brooklyn Park, 8600 Edinbrook Crossing (tel. 424-7060), green fees are $26 for 18 holes.

A HEALTH CLUB

If you're looking for a health club facility during your stay, consider the **Arena Health Club,** located in downtown Minneapolis at First Avenue North between Sixth and Seventh streets (tel. 673-1200). It offers racquetball, squash, and full-size basketball courts as well as a 75-foot-long swimming pool and a running/walking track. There are three aerobics studios here as well.

SAILING

Colorful sailboats are a familiar part of the summertime scenery in Minneapolis and St. Paul, where the next best thing to sailing is watching the graceful boats gliding through local lakes. Sailboat races are a weekend event each summer at **Lake Nokomis,** at Cedar Avenue and 50th Street in South Minneapolis, but more leisurely boaters are welcome to enjoy the facilities as well. This is one of three Minneapolis lakes designated for sailing; the other two are **Lake Harriet,** at Lake Harriet Parkway and William Berry Road, and **Lake Calhoun,** at 3000 E. Calhoun Parkway, off Lake Street.

If you'd like to try your own hand at sailing, or even wind-surfing, head for **Lake Phalen.** You'll reach the lake from an entrance at Wheelock Parkway and Arcade Street (Highway 61), or Maryland Avenue and Johnson Parkway. Sailboats and wind-surfing boards at the boathouse there rent for $9.50 for the first hour and $6 for every hour thereafter. (A deposit and a photo ID are required for rentals.) Hours are 10am to sundown. Call 771-7507 for more information.

SWIMMING

In St. Paul, **Phalen Park** offers a lovely sandy beach which is adjacent to walking and jogging paths and other park facilities. In Minneapolis, try the beach at **Cedar Lake. Thomas Beach,** at the south end of Lake Calhoun, is a favorite with Twin Cities visitors too. In suburban Eden Prairie, you'll find the popular **Round Lake Park** north of Highway 5 and west of Highway 4. And in northwest Bloomington, you'll enjoy **Bush Lake;** exit onto Bush Lake Road from Interstate 494, proceed south for about 1½ miles, and there you are.

TENNIS

Several local clubs offer guest rates to visitors and offer discounts to those affiliated with the International Racquet Sports Association of America (IRSA).

The tennis club visited by most out-of-towners is likely to be one of the 13 major facilities operated by **Northwest Racquet, Swim, & Health Clubs.** Among the busiest are those at 14600 Burnhaven Rd., Burnsville (tel. 435-7127); 6701 W. 78th St., Bloomington (tel. 835-3113); 1001 W. 98th St., Bloomington (tel. 884-1612); 4001 Lake Breeze Ave. N., Brooklyn Center (tel. 535-3571); and 5525 Cedar Lake Rd., St. Louis Park (tel. 546-6554). The $15 guest fee admission charge for out-of-towners ($10 for those with an IRSA membership card) entitles visitors to full use of the club facilities (including pool, weight equipment, and running track). Hours are 5:15am to midnight, Monday through Friday, 6:45pm to midnight, Saturday and Sunday.

The **Eagan Athletic Club,** 3330 Pilot Knob Rd., Eagan (tel. 454-8790), offers indoor tennis for $10 per hour. Tennis-ball machines are available at $2 per hour. The club is open Monday through Thursday from 6am to 11pm, Friday from 6am to 10pm, and Saturday and Sunday from 7am to 10pm.

The **Nicollet Tennis Center,** 4005 Nicollet Ave., Minneapolis (tel. 825-6844), charges $13 an hour for a court. The center, open daily from 7am to 11pm, is located in Martin Luther King Park. These well-maintained courts are among the most popular in the area.

With more than 100 free public tennis courts located throughout the city of St. Paul, it would be impossible to list them here, but at **Phalen Park** you'll find popular courts at Johnson Parkway and Maryland Avenue, in a particularly attractive location adjacent to Lake Phalen. Tennis is on a first-come, first-served basis. Other beautifully located courts are those in Minneapolis's **Kenwood Park,** at the north end of Lake of the Isles. The most centrally located Minneapolis courts may be the ones in **Loring Park,** at Hennepin Avenue and Harmon Place. On the edge of downtown Minneapolis, these courts have a view of Loring Lake. For information about municipal courts, call the Park Board (tel. 348-2226 for courts in Minneapolis, 292-7400 for courts in St. Paul).

WINTER SPORTS

For serious **skiing,** experienced downhill skiers often head north to **Duluth's Spirit Mountain** during the winter (see Chapter 11), but for cross-country and beginning downhill skiers there's a lot of fun to be had right in town. At **Como Park** in St. Paul there's downhill skiing, with a ski lift and a chalet featuring light food service. In **Wirth Park,** snow machines are ready to help nature along whenever necessary. At **Crosby Farm Park,** with an entrance off Shepherd Road and Mississippi River Boulevard, cross-country skiers can imagine they're off somewhere in the remote wilderness as they traverse the idyllic trails under a canopy of trees.

One of the big surprises of the past couple winters was the popularity of **snowtubing** at Wirth Park, where "Winter at Wirth," a comprehensive program of snow-related activities, has attracted people from throughout the Twin Cities. Adults pay $3 daily, children $1, for an innertube that will whirl round and round while one is sliding down the snowy hill.

You'll see **ice-skating** on virtually all city and suburban lakes; most have warming houses which provide a welcome and considerate touch.

CHAPTER 8

STROLLING AROUND THE TWIN CITIES

1. HISTORIC ST. PAUL
2. HISTORIC MINNEAPOLIS
3. THE NEW MINNEAPOLIS

Since the Twin Cities boast lots of historic buildings and cultural centers, I've provided you with walking tours that highlight their individual and common heritage. I also want you to see the more recent additions to the skyline in downtown Minneapolis.

WALKING TOUR 1 —— Historic St. Paul

Start: Rice Park, 5th Street at Market Street.
Finish: Minnesota History Center.
Time: About 2¾ hours, including brief visits to some of the buildings along the way.

Begin your tour of historic St. Paul at:

1. **Rice Park.** Read the historic marker here explaining how this "urban oasis," which fills a complete city block with its trees, lawns, flowers, and fountain, has served as the site of circuses, celebrations, and concerts for more than 150 years. The park was named for Sen. Henry M. Rice, who came to Fort Snelling from Vermont in 1839, became a fur trader, and later served as an intermediary in treaty negotiations with Sioux and Chippewa tribes.

   On the east side of the park, you'll find the distinguished:
2. **St. Paul Hotel.** Since 1910, this has been one of the finest luxury hotels in the Twin Cities, the destination of choice for businesspersons and tourists. The hotel was extensively renovated in the mid-1980s.

   On the south side of the square you'll find the handsome building that houses two important resources for Twin Citians:
3. **The St. Paul Public Library** and the **James Jerome Hill Reference Library,** both housed in the same structure.

   Continue now to the west side of Rice Park and enter the:
4. **Ordway Music Theatre,** which is well worth a visit whether

or not you're attending a performance here. A beautiful marble staircase will take you to the second floor, where huge windows provide a magnificent view of the city.

On the north side of the park is the:

5. Landmark Center, which looks like a castle but is actually a restored Federal Court Building where you can visit courtrooms in which some of this country's most notorious gangsters came to trial. Despite its upstanding reputation, St. Paul was a refuge in earlier decades for several infamous characters, including John Dillinger and Ma Barker.

Across Washington Street from the Landmark Center you'll see the newly constructed world headquarters of the:

6. St. Paul Companies. A block away you'll find the:

7. World Trade Center, an imposing office complex which opened in the fall of 1987 for the purpose of encouraging and expediting international trade. The adjacent retail area includes a spectacular indoor fountain as well as a diversity of shops and restaurants. The second story Skyway leads to:

8. Town Square, where you'll have a beautiful view of the Minnesota State Capitol, as well as a busy complex of offices and shops.

REFUELING STOP Take the escalator down to the **Food Court** on the lowest level, where you'll find a variety of fast-food stands selling hamburgers, hot dogs, ice cream, yogurt, and ethnic fare. Gather some goodies for a picnic, then take the glass elevator up to:

---

9. Town Square Park, the world's largest indoor park. Here you'll find dining areas nestled in among the trees, bushes, and fountains. If you're so inclined, conclude your stay with a ride on the carousel.

When you're ready to continue your tour, take the escalator or elevator down to the second floor Skyway level and retrace your steps to the World Trade Center; then take the Wabasha Street exit and continue on Wabasha to the:

10. World Theatre. This is where Garrison Keillor, after a hiatus in New York City, has returned to broadcast local performances of his famous radio show. Pass, or enter if time permits, the:

11. Science Museum of Minnesota. Exhibits here range from the anthropological to the technological. Be sure to notice Iggy, the giant steel iguana, who lolls in front of the main entrance serving as a bench for youngsters and their elders. You may want to return at another time to see an exciting and educational film in the circular second story:

12. Omnitheater of the Science Museum of Minnesota. Take the skyway from the Science Museum to the:

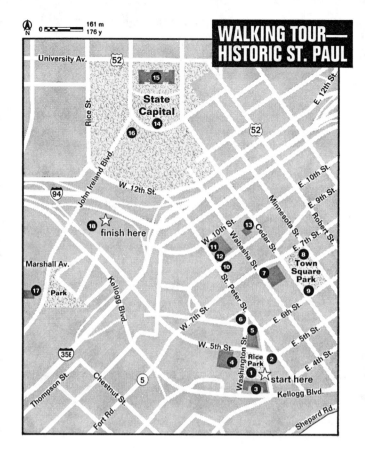

WALKING TOUR—
HISTORIC ST. PAUL

1 Rice Park
2 St. Paul Hotel
3 St. Paul Public Library
4 Ordway Music Theatre
5 Landmark Center
6 St. Paul Companies
7 World Trade Center
8 Town Square
9 Town Square Park
10 World Theater
11 Science Museum of Minnesota
12 Omnitheater
13 Arts and Science Center
14 Capitol Mall
15 Minnesota State Capitol
16 Charles Lindbergh statues
17 Cathedral of St. Paul
18 Minnesota History Center

---

13. Arts and Science Center. As you leave the main entrance, you'll be at 10th and Cedar streets where you'll turn left and then proceed up to the:

14. Capitol Mall, which is bordered by diverse state office buildings, the most prominent of which is the:

15. Minnesota State Capitol, situated on a hill overlooking downtown St. Paul. Flanked by a succession of broad, gray-granite terraces and crowned by the world's largest unsupported marble dome, this magnificent building is the work of Cass Gilbert, who later designed the Woolworth Building in New York City. The interior of the capitol is impressive, with its marble stairways, chambers, and halls, and its classic oil paintings depicting events and persons from Minnesota history.

After leaving the capitol, take John Ireland Boulevard past the lovely:

16. Charles Lindbergh statues. Created by noted Minnesota sculptor Paul Granlund, these two statues depict Lindbergh as a boy and a man. At the far end of John Ireland Boulevard, you'll come to the majestic:

17. Cathedral of St. Paul, which occupies the highest site in the city of St. Paul. Now follow John Ireland Boulevard to the new home of the:

18. Minnesota History Center, where you'll find an astounding assortment of historical documents, artifacts, books, photographs, maps, and manuscripts, as well as a gift shop with a great selection of Minnesota memorabilia at some of the best prices in town.

WALKING TOUR 2 — Historic Minneapolis

Start: Nicollet Mall and Washington Avenue.
Finish: Old Milwaukee Depot.
Time: 2 hours.

Begin your tour of historic Minneapolis at the site of the first bridge ever to span the Mississippi River. The newly constructed:

1. **Hennepin Avenue Suspension Bridge.** The bridge leads to:
2. **Nicollet Island,** where in the mid-19th century sawmills and lumber mills, powered by St. Anthony Falls, established the village of St. Anthony as a prosperous industrial center. Today the northern half of the island is residential, while much of the rest is industrial. Cross the footbridge to:
3. **Main Street,** once literally the main street of Minneapolis. Follow Main Street to East Hennepin Avenue and, after a block, turn right again. There you'll see the:
4. **Our Lady of Lourdes Church,** the oldest continuously used church in Minneapolis. Opened in 1857 by the First Universalist Society, it was bought in 1877 by the French Canadian Catholic

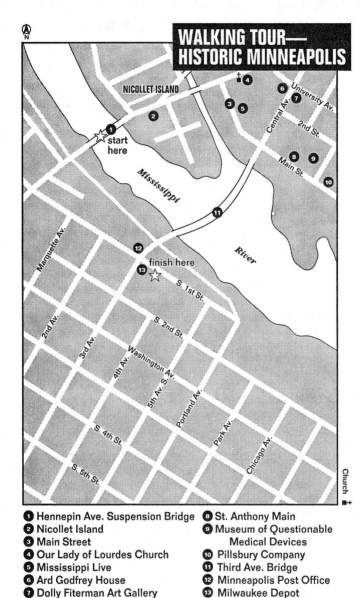

**WALKING TOUR—
HISTORIC MINNEAPOLIS**

NICOLLET ISLAND

Mississippi

River

start
here

finish here

University Av.

Central Av.

2nd St.

Main St.

Marquette Av.

2nd Av.

3rd Av.

4th Av.

5th Av. S.

Washington Av.

Portland Av.

Park Av.

Chicago Av.

S. 1st St.

S. 2nd St.

S. 4th St.

S. 5th St.

Church

❶ Hennepin Ave. Suspension Bridge
❷ Nicollet Island
❸ Main Street
❹ Our Lady of Lourdes Church
❺ Mississippi Live
❻ Ard Godfrey House
❼ Dolly Fiterman Art Gallery
❽ St. Anthony Main
❾ Museum of Questionable
    Medical Devices
❿ Pillsbury Company
⓫ Third Ave. Bridge
⓬ Minneapolis Post Office
⓭ Milwaukee Depot

Community and designated a U.S. Historic Landmark in 1934.
Just across the street at Riverplace there's a huge entertainment
center:
5. Mississippi Live. Located in historic buildings that once
housed late 19th century and early 20th century industries, this
complex houses dining and entertainment facilities.

A short distance east stands tiny Chute Park, which contains the:

6. Ard Godfrey House. Built in 1848, this is the earliest frame house still standing in Minneapolis. Ard Godfrey was a millwright from Maine who came here in 1847 to build a sawmill at St. Anthony Falls.

Across Central Avenue at University Avenue is the:

7. Dolly Fiterman Art Gallery, housed in a historic building which once served as a branch of the Minneapolis Public Library.

Follow University Avenue for one block, then turn to the right and you'll see:

8. St. Anthony Main, another restored industrial complex which was the first retail center in this area and at present is being renovated. Among its most interesting tenants is the:

9. Museum of Questionable Medical Devices, a hands-on exhibit of fraudulent medical instruments, including a phrenology machine which, for $2, will read the bumps on your head and print out more than you want to know about the real you. A block from St. Anthony Main is a portion of the vast milling operation of the:

10. Pillsbury Company, one of the world's largest food manufacturers. From this site you can look across the river at other portions of the Mill District. Among them is the Washburn Crosby Mill, a predecessor of the now world-famous General Mills. (Minneapolis was long known as Mill City, the flour capital of the world.)

Back on Main Street, walk north to your:

REFUELING STOP The **Pracna Historic Dining Saloon** is a popular restaurant and bar where outdoor dining flourishes during the summertime. Menu items include Reuben sandwiches, charbroiled chicken breast, and steak.

After your break continue north. You'll soon reach a circular staircase leading to the:

11. Third Avenue Bridge, which in turn will take you back to downtown Minneapolis. (If you'd rather avoid the stairs, take the Second Street exit from St. Anthony Main's upper level, then turn left to Central Avenue, which leads to the Third Avenue Bridge.) As you cross the bridge, look to the right and get a spectacular view of St. Anthony Falls and the Minneapolis skyline.

After crossing the bridge at the intersection of Third Avenue and First Street, see the:

12. Minneapolis Post Office, a huge sprawling complex that occupies two city blocks, replacing the original Post Office building on the same side of the street two blocks ahead. Across the street is the:

13. **Milwaukee Depot,** now on the National Historic Registry. City officials and developers hope to transform this site into a retail and office complex.

WALKING TOUR 3 — The New Minneapolis

Start: Northwestern National Life Insurance Company.
Finish: The Hubert H. Humphrey Metrodome.
Time: 2 hours.

During the past several decades, the skyline of Minneapolis has changed dramatically as a succession of sleek new buildings replaced their predecessors. One of the most acclaimed newcomers is located at 20 Washington Avenue South:

1. **Northwestern National Life Insurance Company.** This is one of the loveliest and earliest landmarks of the new Minneapolis. Modeled after the Parthenon, this magnificent marble structure with graceful Doric columns was pictured on the cover of *Time.*

   Nearby, at 250 Marquette Avenue, is the:

2. **Federal Reserve Bank Building,** reportedly the first American building designed on the cantilevered suspension system usually reserved for bridges.

   Now walk to 120 Sixth Street South to the:

3. **First Bank Place West,** a gleaming stainless steel building which is connected by skyway to the:

4. **Pillsbury Center** which contains a remarkable eight-story prismatic atrium. At 6th Street and Marquette Avenue, the 57-story:

5. **Norwest Center** lends an elegant tone to downtown Minneapolis. Constructed of a combination of buff-colored stone and white marble, it's considered one of the finest works of architect Cesar Pelli.

   At the center of downtown, you'll find:

6. **City Center,** a 6-acre expanse which occupies the square block between 6th and 7th streets and Nicollet and Hennepin avenues. A newer addition to downtown faces City Center across the Nicollet Mall:

7. **Gavidae Common,** an elegant five-level shopping and entertainment complex anchored by two upscale department stores— Saks Fifth Avenue and Nieman Marcus. The tallest building in

downtown Minneapolis stands across 7th Avenue from Gavidae Common:

8. **Investors Diversified Services Center.** Known locally as the I.D.S. Tower, it is considered one of the finest works of famed architect Philip Johnson. It stands 51 stories high and contains the:

9. **Crystal Court,** which serves as focal point of the city's skyway system.

   On Nicollet Avenue, between 7th and 8th avenues, you'll find:

10. **Dayton's Department Store,** arguably the most popular family business in the Twin Cities. Dayton's is connected by skyway and subway to:

11. **The Conservatory,** a splendid glass-and-marble shopping center containing an upscale collection of shops and boutiques.

   Farther up Nicollet Avenue at 11th Street:

12. **Peavey Plaza** adjoins Orchestra Hall and offers a picturesque outdoor setting for ice skating during the winter and outdoor wining and dining during the festival, Sommerfest. On the way back toward the eastern edge of downtown, you'll pass some particularly handsome and interesting buildings.

   At 222 South 9th Street you'll come upon the:

13. **Piper Jaffray Tower,** a 42-story building that features innumerable panes of aqua-blue glass and provides a particularly dramatic addition to the skyline.

   A few blocks away, at 333 South 7th Street is:

14. **Lincoln Center,** a gray granite building complemented with black, white, and green marble.

   At the corner of 4th Avenue and South 7th Street is the:

15. **Lutheran Brotherhood Building,** a marble and copper-colored glass structure.

   And finally, five blocks away at 900 South 5th Street, there's the:

16. **Hubert H. Humphrey Metrodome,** maybe the most recognizable structure in downtown Minneapolis. Old-time Twin Citians still miss the fun and excitement of outdoor big-league play, but out-of-towners appreciate the certainty that the game they want to attend here won't be rained out.

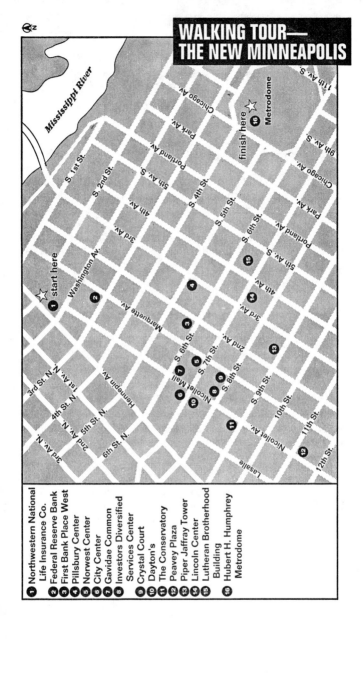

WALKING TOUR—
THE NEW MINNEAPOLIS

Mississippi River

Metrodome

finish here ⑯

start here ①

S. 1st St.
S. 2nd St.
S. 4th St.
S. 5th St.
S. 6th St.
S. 7th St.
S. 8th St.
S. 9th St.
10th St.
11th St.
12th St.

Chicago Av.
Park Av.
Portland Av.
5th Av. S.
4th Av.
3rd Av.
2nd Av. S.
11th Av. S.
9th Av. S.
Chicago Av.
Park Av.
Portland Av.
5th Av. S.
4th Av.
3rd Av.

Washington Av.
Marquette Av.
Hennepin Av.
Nicollet Mall
Nicollet Av.
Lasalle

3rd St. N.
4th St. N.
5th St. N.
6th St. N.
1st Av. N.
2nd Av. N.
3rd Av. N.

① ② ③ ④ ⑤ ⑥ ⑦ ⑧ ⑨ ⑩ ⑪ ⑫ ⑬ ⑭ ⑮ ⑯

① Northwestern National
    Life Insurance Co.
② Federal Reserve Bank
③ First Bank Place West
④ Pillsbury Center
⑤ Norwest Center
⑥ City Center
⑦ Gavidae Common
⑧ Investors Diversified
    Services Center
⑨ Crystal Court
⑩ Dayton's
⑪ The Conservatory
⑫ Peavey Plaza
⑬ Piper Jaffray Tower
⑭ Lincoln Center
⑮ Lutheran Brotherhood
    Building
⑯ Hubert H. Humphrey
    Metrodome

CHAPTER 9

SAVVY SHOPPING

1. THE SHOPPING SCENE

2. SHOPPING A TO Z

In 1956, Southdale, the country's very first fully enclosed, climate-controlled shopping mall, opened its doors in the Twin Cities and changed American life forever. "Going to the mall" has become as American as apple pie, as thousands of communities copied the Twin Cities invention.

Minneapolis and St. Paul have always been a mecca for shoppers. In addition to Southdale and the newly opened Mall of America, there are well over 100 other shopping centers here; while it's impossible to tell you about all of them, what follows will give you an idea of the many and varied shopping experiences awaiting you in the Twin Cities.

1. THE SHOPPING SCENE

HOURS

Shopping hours are generally 10am to 9pm Monday through Friday, 9:30am to 6pm on Saturday, and noon to 5pm on Sunday. During holiday periods, shopping hours are usually extended.

GREAT SHOPPING AREAS

The specialty shopping along **Grand Avenue** in St. Paul has gained enormous popularity during recent years; even if you don't buy anything here, the browsing is bound to be memorable. There are two popular shopping malls on Grand Avenue: Victoria Crossing at 857 Grand Avenue (where you'll find stores like Old Mexico Shop, with lovely imports from across the Rio Grande); and Milton Mall at Milton and Grand. The **Coat of Many Colors,** 1666 Grand Ave. (tel. 690-5255), offers some of the most unusual clothing around.

Downtown St. Paul has its own array of fine shops in two shopping malls which face each other across Cedar Street. At the World Trade Center, with its spectacular indoor fountain, you'll find apparel shops including **J. Riggings** and the **Limited,** while at Town Square, **Peck and Peck, Victoria's Secret,** and **Eddie Bauer,** among others, await you. A few blocks away at Carriage Hill Plaza, you'll find **Sonnie's** and **Frank Murphy,** two fine apparel shops, standing side by side.

In **downtown Minneapolis** three giant department stores dominate Nicollet Mall: **Saks Fifth Avenue, Nieman Marcus,** and **Dayton's.** The Conservatory shopping center is another standout in the Nicollet Mall. Other nearby shops in this area can be found in the City Center (tel. 372-1234) and the IDS Crystal Court (tel. 372-1660).

2. SHOPPING A TO Z

BOOKS

No Twin Cities shopping chapter would be complete without mentioning the abundant bookstores. We have the distinction of being home to the first-ever B. Dalton Bookseller, which opened in suburban Edina back in 1966. There are now nearly two dozen B. Dalton Booksellers in this area. Add to that six Barnes and Noble bookstores, seven Waldenbooks, and a variety of independent and specialty stores and you'll see that people hereabouts do a lot of reading. Here's a partial listing of the bookstores you'll find in the Twin Cities.

THE HUNGRY MIND, 1648 Grand Ave., St. Paul. Tel. 699-0587.

The Hungry Mind boasts an extraordinary selection of books— fiction, biographies, cookbooks, poetry, children's books, and more. The relaxed ambience here is enhanced by easy chairs and couches. Table of Contents, a recently opened café, shares the premises, so there's more than food for thought to be found here. And here's a tip: The store has a 30% off sale every June.

ODEGARD BOOKS, Victoria Crossing, 857 Grand Ave., St. Paul. Tel. 222-2711.

There are actually three separate Odegard bookstores here, one with a general stock, one devoted primarily to books on travel, and one which offers remainder and other deeply discounted books.

ORR BOOKS, 3043 Hennepin Ave., Minneapolis. Tel. 823-2408.

This busy independent store in Minneapolis's uptown area carries fiction, small-press literature; books on psychology, spirituality, Native Americans, and women; and general interest books. The store discounts all new hardcover books and carries paperbacks as well.

RED BALLOON, 891 Grand Ave., St. Paul. Tel. 224-8320.

You'll find all sorts of children's and young adult books at Red Balloon, which claims to have the widest selection of picture books in the Midwest. Besides selling 20,000 titles, the Red Balloon also carries audio- and videotapes, as well as games and toys.

CRAFTS

HEARTLEAF, Diamondhead Mall, 200 W. Burnsville Pkwy., Burnsville. Tel. 890-1233.

There are 19 rooms here in which you'll find a wonderful diversity of items, including the handmade prints, painting, crafts, and pottery. Everything from floral displays to kitchenware, jewelry, Christmas items, toys, and Minnesota souvenirs awaits you here. Certain sections are arranged by the color of the products. Even if you don't buy a thing, you'll have a great time just looking around.

DISCOUNT SHOPPING

BURLINGTON COAT FACTORY, St. Louis Park. Tel. 929-6850.

Burlington has a lot more than coats. You'll find a wide variety of clothing for the whole family here, with periodic arrivals of ultrasuede apparel at very good prices.

LOEHMANN'S, at 98th St. and Normandale Blvd., Bloomington. Tel. 835-2510.

Loehmann's in suburban Bloomington offers discount designer fashions including Donna Karan. Among the items sold here are evening dresses, jackets, blouses, casual clothing, jewelry, purses, and umbrellas.

OPITZ OUTLET, 4320 Excelsior Blvd., St. Louis Park. Tel. 922-9088.

There are some great bargains to be found in this discount store which is only open from Friday through Sunday each week. (When the store is closed, it's being completely restocked.) You'll probably see a newspaper ad for Opitz sometime during your stay, but be aware you may have to read between the lines concerning the week's offerings. For example, if you see the words, "We've got a secret," you can be pretty sure it's Victoria's (meaning the well-known lingerie).

FOOD

BYERLY'S, 3777 Park Center Blvd., St. Louis Park. Tel. 929-2100.

You won't want to leave the Twin Cities without a visit to Byerly's, one of the world's most unusual supermarkets, as well as a self-contained shopping center par excellence. Retailers from throughout the world travel to the Twin Cities regularly to tour this flagship store of Don Byerly's chain. What's all the fuss about? In contrast to the usual supermarket, which carries 15,000 to 18,000 items, Byerly's carries over 25,000. And that includes everything from catsup for 25¢

to mustard for $25 (a French Dijon packaged in a ceramic jar). Besides food, there is a Gift Gallery here selling collectibles at prices ranging from $10 for small hand-carved wooden animals to $75,000 for a gold-plated 6-foot-tall bird cage. Laliques and Hummels are sold here too, as are imported women's accessories by Judith Leiber, whose snakeskin belts go for $50 to $300.

Services as well as goods are available at Byerly's. Particularly popular is the on-site cooking school, with classes in everything from ethnic to microwave to couples' cooking. News of these and other classes are published in the in-house publication, *Byerly's Bag.*

Other nice touches here are the wide carpeted aisles, on-site restaurants, delicatessens, salad bars, and the 24-hour service.

MALLS & SHOPPING CENTERS

THE CONSERVATORY, 808 Nicollet Mall, Minneapolis. Tel. 332-4649.

This remarkable new shopping center opened in downtown Minneapolis in the fall of 1987, and chances are you've never seen anything quite like it. Designed as a "20th-century public square," the block-long Conservatory boasts two dramatic four-story glass atriums, two gracefully winding staircases, an abundance of decorative trees, and a ground-floor dining court.

Connected by skyway and by underground "serpentine" to **Dayton's,** one of the city's premier department stores, the Conservatory offers enticing wares of its own. Among the upscale retailers located here are the fabulous **F.A.O. Schwarz** toy store, a veritable wonderland for children and their elders. Also present are the **Sharper Image,** a shop filled with wondrous electronic gadgetry, and the **Nature Company,** with unique gifts for those you left at home. A local firm that chose to locate at the Conservatory is **Frost and Bud,** a specialty gift shop. What souvenirs you'll discover here! Want to take home a set of bocce balls, a sundial, or a personalized birdhouse? The Conservatory can offer you these—and a whole lot more.

GAVIDAE COMMON, 6th St. on the Mall, Minneapolis. Tel. 372-1222.

Directly across the Nicollet Mall is this elegant downtown shopping complex whose list of tenants reads like a retailing "Who's Who": **Burberry's, Rodier, Laurel, Cactus, Lillie Rubin, Brentano's, Westminster Lace, Eddie Bauer, Ann Klein,** and **Saks Fifth Avenue.** Their presence here indicates a real commitment to the Twin Cities and, in fact, to Minnesota as a whole. In fact, the name "Gaviidae"—Latin for loon—pays tribute to the state bird of Minnesota (a 20-foot wood and metal loon emerging from a pool of water is the focal point for the magnificent five-level atrium here).

CALHOUN SQUARE, at the corner of Hennepin Ave. and Lake St., Minneapolis. Tel. 824-1240.

In the trendy uptown section of Minneapolis (also known as "Yuptown"), you'll find Calhoun Square, a bustling two-story mall offering great shopping, dining, and people-watching. Shops here include Benetton, Bay Street Shoes, Kitchen Window, and Toy Boat.

There are also three galleries featuring works of local artists, and more than 70 other shops and restaurants.

GALLERIA, 69th St. and France Ave., a block south of Southdale, Edina. Tel. 925-4321.

A fashionable upscale center with 60 shops and restaurants, the Galleria has a picturesque setting, with lush greenery, soft lighting, and cobblestone walkways. You'll find stores specializing in handbags, books, swimwear, furs, cookware, dolls, gourmet foods, pottery, and a great deal more. When Galleria advertises a sale, run do not walk. At other times, be advised that prices—and quality—tend to be high.

RIDGEDALE, on I-394 (Wayzata Blvd.), 1 mile east of I-494, Minnetonka. Tel. 541-4864.

Ridgedale first opened in August 1974 with two anchor department stores, **Dayton's** and **Donaldson's.** Five months later **J. C. Penney** and **Sears** moved in as well. A graceful fountain stands among palm trees in the skylit center court. Four sections extend in a pinwheel pattern that contains more than 130 specialty shops representing national and local retailers. A sidewalk café is one of the 11 restaurants and snack bars here. Unlike many other suburban malls, Ridgedale contains a **Woolworth's** variety store.

SOUTHDALE, 66th St. and France Ave., Edina. Tel. 925-7885.

There were lots of unanswered questions when Southdale opened its doors for the first time. Would there really be enough business in the quiet community of Edina to support two of the area's largest department stores, as well as 64 specialty shops, under one roof? Well, today more than 30 years after that grand opening, **Dayton's** and **Carson Pirie Scott** face each other across Southdale's busy courtyard, while a third department store, **J. C. Penney,** has been doing a brisk business as well. And nearly 200 specialty shops thrive elsewhere in the mall.

A splendid new four-story Dayton's opened right next door to the original store in 1990. The greatly enlarged new space made a variety of welcome innovations possible, including a full-service **Estee Lauder Spa,** complimentary coat checking, and a drive-through parcel-pick-up area accommodating six cars at one time. Serving as a backdrop to the dramatic display of top-quality merchandise throughout the elegant Southdale Dayton's are striking works of art, including three lovely murals.

Southdale is south of crosstown Highway 62, n
494, and between Interstate 35W and Highway 10
the three big-name department stores, Southdale
known shops like **Peck and Peck, Eddie Baue.,**
Gantos, and **Florsheim.** But what may interest you more a..
dozens of specialty shops with less-familiar names that feature fine
apparel, jewelry, toys, mementos, and more. You'll also find a
self-service post office here, along with a Northwest Airlines ticket
office and two 1-hour photo-processing shops.

THE MALL OF AMERICA, 60 East Broadway, Blooming-
ton. Tel. 851-3500.

Opened in 1992, The Mall of America (or "Megamall," as it's
known locally) is the largest and most diversified complex of its kind
in the country. In addition to providing four major stores—**Macy's,**
Bloomingdale's, Nordstrom's, and **Sears**—Mall of America
also houses some 400 specialty shops and a variety of off-price
retailers, including **Filene's, Marshall's,** and **Linen 'n Things.**
There are also unique kinds of stores that you're unlikely to have
encountered before. Consider, for instance, **Oshman's Super-**
Sports USA, with areas that give customers the opportunity to try
out the items they're considering: On-site here is a basketball court, a
tennis court with automatic ball machine, an archery range, a boxing
ring, and a computerized video golf course!

The Mall of America prides itself on being customer-friendly,
with its four family rooms, each equipped with TV, microwaves, and
other comfort features. Ample vertical transportation is provided by
44 escalators and 17 elevators. Electric golf carts provide transportation for those who'd prefer to ride than walk.

Also on site is Camp Snoopy, the world's largest enclosed
amusement park, along with a 14-theater movie complex, a variety of
restaurants and nightclubs, and a two-level golf course. Suffice it to
say, this remarkable complex is being watched nationally and even
internationally as an indication of things to come.

CHAPTER 10

TWIN CITIES NIGHTS

The Twin Cities offers a diverse selection of evening entertainment, but you'll be amazed by the prevalence of high-quality theater awaiting you here. Over the course of a month you can attend dozens of productions in the metropolitan area. The standards are high, but the cost of tickets remains surprisingly low here in the birthplace of American regional theater.

Other performing arts flourish in the Twin Cities as well: Music, dance, and art exhibits attract large and loyal audiences. And with two world-class music halls and two famous art museums, the facilities in Minneapolis and St. Paul complement rather than compete with each other.

You'll find upcoming events listed every Friday in the daily newspapers, *St. Paul Pioneer Press* and *Star Tribune*. There are, in addition, a number of widely available weekly and monthly local periodicals, some of them free, that provide useful information on current activities and performances.

1. THE PERFORMING ARTS

PERFORMING ARTS COMPANIES

OPERA & CLASSICAL MUSIC

THE MINNESOTA ORCHESTRA, Orchestra Hall, 1111 Nicollet Mall, Minneapolis. Tel. 371-5656.

The Minnesota Orchestra was born in 1903, the eighth major orchestra to be established in the United States. In 1923 it was heard on crystal radio sets; one year later it became the second major American orchestra to make recordings of its performances. Under the leadership of Eugene Ormandy from 1931 to 1936, the orchestra gained international recognition through its recordings and its concerts abroad.

Dmitri Mitropoulos served as conductor from 1937 to 1949,

THE MAJOR CONCERT & PERFORMANCE HALLS

Guthrie Theater, 725 Vineland Place, Minneapolis. Tel. 377-2224.

Northrop Auditorium, 84 Church St. S.E., University of Minnesota. Tel. 624-2345.

Orchestra Hall, 1111 Nicollet Mall, Minneapolis. Tel. 371-5656.

Ordway Music Theatre, 345 Washington St., St. Paul. Tel. 224-4222.

University of Minnesota Theatre, Rarig Center, University of Minnesota West Bank Campus. Tel. 625-4001.

---

during which time the orchestra made a 34,000-mile tour of the Middle East sponsored by the State Department.

During the 19-year tenure of Stanislaw Skrowaczewski, the Minnesota Orchestra increased in size to 95 musicians and took up residence in its new home at Orchestra Hall. The Minnesota Orchestra also performs at St. Paul's Ordway Music Theatre (tel. 224-4222), and makes guest appearances throughout the nation and the world. Since September 1986 the orchestra has been led by the distinguished conductor Edo de Waart.

Prices: Tickets $10–$32.

ST. PAUL CHAMBER ORCHESTRA, 75 W. 5th St., St. Paul. Tel. 291-1144.

The St. Paul Chamber Orchestra, the nation's only full-time professional chamber orchestra, may be performing at the Ordway Music Theatre while you're here, or you may find them in one of the shopping centers, churches, or school auditoriums that used to welcome them during their homeless years when they were identified as "Music on the Move." The group originated in 1959 when a group of St. Paulites decided to find a conductor to head a group of freelance professional musicians who performed educational programs. They eventually established a 10-concert season, went on tour, and gained enough backing to incorporate under the name St. Paul Chamber Orchestra.

By the late seventies the group had undertaken a number of important tours—to 140 American cities and to Western and Eastern Europe and the Soviet Union. During this time they also gained a reputation for regularly combining classical works and world premiers on the same program.

From 1980 to 1987, under the leadership of Pinchas Zukerman, the chamber orchestra hosted such music greats as Isaac Stern and

Misha Dichter. Under Zukerman's leadership the local season expanded to 80 concerts and the St. Paul Chamber Orchestra gained fame as one of the country's best musical groups, with frequent guest appearances at Carnegie Hall, Avery Fisher Hall, and the Kennedy Center.

The orchestra now performs 150 concerts during a 40-week season that extends from September to June. In addition to performing at the Ordway, they take their music to seven metropolitan locations throughout the Twin Cities.

Prices: Tickets $9–$31.50.

THE SCHUBERT CLUB, 301 Landmark Center, St. Paul. Tel. 292-3267.

Vladimir Horowitz, Isaac Stern, Robert Casadesus, and Beverly Sills are among the renowned artists who've been brought to St. Paul several times by the Schubert Club, founded in 1882 and now one of the oldest musical organizations in the United States. If you're a music lover, you might want to inquire about whether one of the 50 or so recitals they offer each year will be at the Ordway Music Theatre during your stay.

In addition to bringing celebrated artists from throughout the world to perform in the Twin Cities, the Schubert Club regularly commissions work from selected composers. One of these works, "From the Diary of Virginia Woolf" by Dominick Argento, won the Pulitzer Prize in music in 1975. This work was sung by Dame Janet Baker both here in St. Paul and at Carnegie Hall in New York City.

Among the club's other projects has been the establishment and maintenance of a musical museum containing over 75 keyboard instruments dating back to the mid-16th century.

Prices: Tickets $14–$25.

DANCE COMPANIES

No cities except New York and Washington, D.C., offer a more active professional dance scene than the one you'll find in Minneapolis and St. Paul. Whatever the season, there's likely to be at least one major performance during your stay. Calendars of local and touring dance programs are published weekly in local newspapers and magazines, and the **Minnesota Dance Alliance** (tel. 340-1900) will provide specific information about current and upcoming presentations.

You'll find the price of tickets to dance performances is remarkably low in the Twin Cities. Prices for touring dance productions range from $8 to $23; for local companies, $5 to $15.

The **O'Shaughnessey Dance Series**, a 6-week program offered during the spring of each year, is the only one of its kind in the country. Committed to spotlighting local professional dance companies, it undertakes a major selection process, then presents its annual series in the beautiful 1,800-seat O'Shaughnessey Auditorium, 2004

Randolph Ave., St. Paul (tel. 690-6700), on the campus of the College of St. Catherine. Among the local troupes that have appeared in the O'Shaughnessey series have been the dynamic **Zorongo Flamenco Dance Theatre,** one of only five professional Spanish Gypsy dance troupes in the country.

Summerdance, a 2-week series sponsored by the Minnesota Dance Alliance in June, also showcases the work of selected local companies and choreographers. In 1987 this festival took place in the intimate McKnight Playhouse at the Ordway Music Theatre (see above). The Minneapolis Children's Theatre (see below) and the Hennepin Center for the Arts, 528 Hennepin Ave. (tel. 332-4478), also play host to these programs from time to time.

ETHNIC DANCE THEATRE, 1940 Hennepin Ave., Minneapolis. Tel. 872-0024.

Ethnic Dance Theatre has made an international name for itself. Comprised of nearly 50 dancers and musicians, this company travels to distant destinations at home and abroad, learning traditional dances and then using these as the basis for original choreography. A recent premiere piece was researched in the Soviet republic of Tadzhikistan and concerns the legendary Tamara Khanum, the first Muslim dancer in the Soviet Union to risk execution by casting aside her veil while performing in public.

Prices: Tickets $12–$15.

BALLET OF THE DOLLS, 400 3rd Ave. N., Minneapolis. Tel. 332-2792.

Ballet of the Dolls is a company of professional dancers whose work is primarily a combination of ballet and jazz dance. This inventive troupe evolved from a succession of late-evening spontaneous performances directed by Myron Johnson, who also directs frequently at the Minneapolis Children's Theatre.

Prices: Tickets Thurs and Sun $10, Fri and Sat $12.50.

THEATER COMPANIES

Although Twin Cities theater didn't gain international prominence until the establishment in 1964 of the Tyrone Guthrie Theater, first-rate productions had been attracting theatergoers for a long time before that. The Old Log, one of the country's oldest stock companies, began staging professional productions in 1941. Theater in the Round, one of the country's longest-lived community theaters, staged its first performance in 1952. The Brave New Workshop, the country's oldest satirical revue, was founded in 1958, five years before Chicago's Second City company.

What's best about today's Twin Cities theater is that it's a year-round activity for audiences of widely different tastes. There's mainstream theater and avant-garde theater, dinner theater and coffeehouse theater, theater in the park and theater in the round, children's theater, historical theater, showboat theater, and a lot more.

In the Twin Cities theater is not primarily a business but an art; it's supported in large part by contributions from individuals and corporations. Ticket prices are relatively low in Minneapolis and St. Paul; a good seat will seldom cost more than $15 to $20, and student, senior citizen, and standby rates are lower still. Also, transportation poses few problems here: even outlying theaters are easy to reach by highway and freeway, and parking is either free or inexpensive.

What follows is a listing of some of the theatrical companies that await you in Minneapolis and St. Paul.

BRAVE NEW WORKSHOP, 2605 Hennepin Ave., Minneapolis. Tel. 332-6620.

For nearly 30 years, Dudley Riggs's Brave New Workshop has been fulfilling its self-proclaimed role as loyal opposition to all parties. It is by now the oldest satirical company in the United States. Company members write their own material, and after each evening's series of sketches the company does improvisations based on audience suggestions. Past productions, which have toured in New York, Boston, Miami, and San Francisco, include *I'm OK, You're a Jerk; National Velveeta,* or *What a Friend We Have in Cheeses;* and *The Vice Man Cometh.* Performances are at 8pm Tuesday through Thursday, at 8 and 10:30pm on Friday and Saturday.

Prices: Tickets $12–$15.

CHILDREN'S THEATRE, 2400 3rd Ave. S., Minneapolis. Tel. 874-0400.

In the large and lovely building that houses the Minneapolis Institute of Art, the 746-seat Children's Theatre presents productions geared for kids of all ages. Based primarily on tales familiar to children and teenagers, the plays are lavishly produced and skillfully acted by a company of child and adult players.

Authors are often invited to participate in the staging of their plays at Children's Theatre; the late Dr. Seuss (Theodore Geiss) worked with the company on its production of *The 500 Hats of Bartholomew Cubbins* and Astrid Lindgren gave advice on the play based on her book *Pippi Longstocking.*

Prices: Tickets $12–$23.50 adults, $9.50–$19.00 full-time college students, children, and senior citizens.

CRICKET THEATRE, 9 W. 14th St., Minneapolis. Tel. 871-2244.

Founded in 1968, the Cricket Theatre mostly presents contemporary plays by living playwrights, some of whom have already made a name for themselves, some whose reputations are emerging. Modern classics presented here include *Streamers, Fool for Love,* and *Who's Afraid of Virginia Woolf?*

In 1987 the Cricket made two important changes: it moved to a new home in a beautifully renovated old theater on the southern edge of downtown Minneapolis and it decided to include one guest production by a foreign theater company each season.

Performances are at 7:30pm Thursday, 8pm Friday and Saturday, 5 and 8:30pm Sunday.

Prices: Thurs and Sun evenings and Sat matinees $14.75; Fri–Sat evenings $16.75.

FRANK THEATRE, no address at press time. Tel. 377-0501.

Founded in 1989 by two determined women, director Wendy Knox and actor Bernadette Sullivan, the Frank Theatre is in search of a permanent home. The company stages interesting and provocative productions including *Sincerity Forever* by Mac Wellman, *Miriam's Flowers* and *Lucy Loves Me* by Migdalia Cruz, and a satiric Afrocentric production of *Medea*.

GREAT AMERICAN THEATER, in Weyerhauser Auditorium at St. Paul's Landmark Center, 75 W. 5th St. Tel. 292-4323.

The Great American Theater commissions, produces, and tours plays that dramatize the history, folklore, and social issues of this region.

Prices: Tickets Thurs and Sun, $12; Fri and Sat, $14.

GUTHRIE THEATER, 725 Vineland Place, Minneapolis. Tel. 377-2224.

Whatever your taste in theater entertainment, you'll surely want to include a Guthrie performance in your Twin Cities agenda. In 1964 the Tyrone Guthrie Theater gained worldwide fame as the home of a new classical repertory company, selected by the distinguished director for whom it was named. Lately there has been a succession of record-breaking presentations, among them the 1992 production of a cycle of Greek tragedies by Euripides, Aeschylus, and Sophocles.

There are several reasons to arrive early for a Guthrie performance: you'll want to see one of the country's largest public sculpture gardens just across the street and to explore the theater itself. Before you enter the auditorium, you'll be surrounded by a tempting array of dining, drinking, and shopping choices. The Guthrie shares an entry lobby with the adjacent Walker Art Center and is just steps away from the Walker's extensive, and often expensive, selection of gifts and souvenirs. The Guthrie's own smaller gift shop carries a variety of theater-related items.

Performances begin at 7:30pm Tuesday through Thursday, 8pm Friday and Saturday, and 7pm on Sunday (the theater is closed on Monday). Matinees are usually presented at 1pm on Wednesday and Saturday with an occasional matinee on Sunday, but call to confirm specific days and times.

Prices: Tickets $6–$38.

HEART OF THE BEAST PUPPET AND MASK THEATRE,
1500 E. Lake St., Minneapolis. Tel. 721-2535.

The success of the Heart of the Beast Puppet and Mask Theatre is a perfect example of one good turn begetting another. Established in 1973 with the stated purpose of serving a racially mixed community in one of the oldest business areas in the Twin Cities, this company of artists performed at outdoor sites and in rented theater spaces for nearly 15 years before being asked by the community to move into a former x-rated movie house. Now, with a 300-seat playhouse to call their own, Heart of the Beast Puppet and Mask Theatre has increased its audience more than 700% with family-oriented shows like *La Befana,* based on an Italian folk story, and *Invisible Child,* inspired by a traditional Swedish tale. Among its adult productions is *The Reapers Tale,* which provides a history of Columbus's arrival in the New World from the Native Americans' point of view. The company also produces an annual festival on the first Sunday of each May (participants numbered about 21,000 in 1990).

Prices: Tickets $9 adults, $5 children aged 3–12, free for children under 3. Those willing to usher are admitted free.

ILLUSION THEATRE, 528 Hennepin Ave., Minneapolis.
Tel. 339-4944.

Headquartered at the Hennepin Center for the Arts, this eight-member company has pioneered a new form of theater: in 1977 the group became the first in the country to use drama as a means of preventing sexual abuse and interpersonal violence. *Touch,* an original play for children, has been performed throughout the country in schools and churches. So have two other works, *No Easy Answers,* written for adolescents, and *For Adults Only,* designed for grown-up audiences. Most recently, three new plays have been added to the repertoire: *Family,* dealing with relationships among family members, as well as *Amazing Grace* and *The Alphabet of Aids,* both of which deal with HIV/AIDS.

In addition to the touring productions of these plays, the theater performs in the Twin Cities from February to July. All performances are at 8pm, except on Sunday when they begin at 7pm.

Prices: Tickets $10 Thurs and Sun, $15 Fri and Sat.

LAKESHORE PLAYERS, 4280 Stewart Ave., White Bear
Lake. Tel. 429-5674.

Lakeshore Players, one of the oldest community theaters in the area, has provided musical comedies and other family entertainment to suburbanites and city folk alike for nearly 40 years. Recent hits include *Dames at Sea* and *The Foreigner.* Six productions are staged here each year.

Prices: Tickets $6–$8, with discounts for children and seniors.

MIXED BLOOD THEATER, 1501 S. 4th St., Minneapolis.
Tel. 338-6131.

This professional theater was founded in 1976 to produce works with an ethnically diverse cast. Mixed Blood has by now received numerous local awards for productions like *The Boys Next Door, A My Name Is Alice,* and *For Colored Girls Who Have Considered Suicide When a Rainbow Is Enuf.* Founder Jack Reuler has also received national awards for his theater's commitment to hiring minority actors.

Mixed Blood productions are presented in a 100-year-old firehouse with a large, flexible space and various settings. Show time is 8pm on Thursday, Friday, and Sunday; on Saturday there are two performances at 7 and 9:30pm.

Prices: Tickets $10 Thurs and Sun, $12.50 Fri, $15 Sat.

OLD LOG THEATER, 5175 Meadville St., Excelsior. Tel. 474-5951.

This popular playhouse on the shores of Lake Minnetonka is a family affair where Don Stolz has been staging Equity productions since 1941. In fact, the Old Log is the Twin Cities' oldest theater company. The small original theater, now used as a scenery shop, was replaced in 1960 by the present Old Log, which is closer to the water's edge and, with 655 seats, one of the largest theaters in the Twin Cities area.

Comedies are the specialty of this house, and eldest son Tom Stolz has developed through the years into an adept comic actor, notable for his droll deadpan delivery in productions as diverse as *Brighton Beach Memoirs* and *Bedfull of Foreigners.* Other family members make their own contributions behind the scenes and at the front of the house.

From time to time more serious work has been presented at the Old Log, including admirable productions of *Look Homeward, Angel* and *84 Charing Cross.* If you're in the Twin Cities during the Easter season, you might want to phone the theater for word on Tom Stolz's annual tour-de-force performance in *The Gospel According to Saint Mark.*

Shows are at 8:30pm Wednesday through Saturday and at 7:30pm on Sunday.

Prices: $14 Sat, $12.50 all other performances.

PARK SQUARE THEATRE, Minnesota Museum of Art, St. Peter St. at Kellogg Blvd., St. Paul. Tel. 291-7005.

The Park Square Theatre offers two distinctly different seasons, the main Classic Season and the summertime Festival Season, when new American plays are staged, usually in conjunction with their authors.

PENUMBRA THEATRE, 270 N. Kent St., St. Paul. Tel. 224-4601.

At the Penumbra Theatre you'll find Minnesota's only black professional theater company. Penumbra has another claim to fame as well; at this writing, it's the only Twin Cities professional troupe to have staged the plays of August Wilson. Their production of the renowned St. Paul playwright's *Fences,* starring Penumbra founder Lou Bellamy, won high praise in 1990. (Wilson's *Fences* is the only play in American theatrical history to have won the Pulitzer Prize, the Tony Award, the New York Theater Critics Award, the Outer Critics Circle Award, and the American Theater Critics Association Award.) Call for information about current productions—you won't be disappointed.

Prices: Tickets $12.50 Wed, Thurs, Fri, Sun; $14.50 Sat.

PLYMOUTH PLAYHOUSE, the Kelly Inn, 2705 Annapolis Lane, Plymouth. Tel. 553-1600 or 989-5151.

At this intimate theatre you'll have an evening of first-rate entertainment if past history is any guide. Previous hits here have included long runs of *Nunsense, Pump Boys and Dinettes,* and, since November 1992, *Ain't Misbehavin',* the Tony Award–winning musical about Fats Waller. Productions at the Plymouth Playhouse are presented by Troupe America, a nationally known entertainment company which was founded in the Twin Cities by producer/director Curt Wollan, whose touring productions have entertained audiences coast to coast.

RED EYE COLLABORATION, 126 N. Washington Ave., Minneapolis. Tel. 870-0309.

The only resident experimental theater company in the Twin Cities, Red Eye Collaboration performs in a 70-seat studio theater in the downtown Minneapolis Warehouse District. You'll know you've found the theater when you see a warehouse with a large neon sign featuring a blue fish. Four mixed-media productions are staged each year by the Red Eye Collaboration, along with one work-in-progress series. All performances are at 8pm.

Prices: Tickets Thurs, $8 or $14 for two; $10 Fri; $12.50 Sun.

THÉÂTRE DE LA JEUNE LUNE, 105 1st St. N. Minneapolis. Tel. 333-6200.

This company began in 1978 when a fledgling international theater group was founded by four students, two Twin Citians and two Parisians, who met while studying at the École Jacques-Lecoq in Paris. Productions by this constantly interesting group tend to be highly physical and visually exciting, reflecting elements of clowning, farce, mime, and vaudeville. Recent hits include the wild comedy *Yang Zen Froggs in Moon over a Hong Kong Sweatshop* and a production of *Romeo and Juliet* in which the title characters were portrayed as middle aged.

Prices: Tickets $8–$17.

THEATER IN THE ROUND, 245 Cedar Ave., Minneapolis. Tel. 333-3010.

Since 1952 talented Twin Citians have participated in the productions of Theater in the Round, or TRP as it's known locally. More than half a million theatergoers have attended this community theater housed in a one-story brick building in the west-bank theater district. Some of the Twin Cities' top directors have worked here with aspiring actors and technicians who have gone on to professional careers in theater, TV, and film.

Play selection here is eclectic: The biggest hits to date have been *Equus, Of Thee I Sing, The Mousetrap, Mrs. Warren's Profession,* and *Cyrano de Bergerac.* Plays by aspiring authors are produced as well. Performances are held at 8pm Friday and Saturday and at 7pm on Sunday.

Prices: Tickets $9.50.

UNIVERSITY OF MINNESOTA THEATRE DEPARTMENT, Rarig Center at the University of Minnesota West Bank Campus. Tel. 625-4001.

The University of Minnesota Theatre Department's four separate stages at the handsome Rarig Center theater complex consistently present a wide variety of enjoyable entertainment. You'll also enjoy the perennially popular productions aboard the university's Centennial Showboat, where audiences are welcomed aboard for summertime productions of 19th-century melodramas.

Prices: Tickets at Rarig Center $9; summertime Showboat $10 Tues–Sat, $8 Sun.

MAJOR CONCERT HALLS & ALL-PURPOSE AUDITORIUMS

NORTHROP AUDITORIUM, on University of Minnesota's main campus at 84 Church St. S.E., Minneapolis. Tel. 624-2345.

Since 1929 the 4,800-seat Northrop Auditorium has hosted performances by acclaimed touring companies such as the American Ballet Theatre, the Joffrey Ballet, the National Ballet of China, and the Sakailuku, a brilliant Paris-based Japanese company. International stars, including the late Margot Fonteyn, Mikhail Baryshnikov, and Twyla Tharp, have performed here too. Touring Broadway shows make stops here as well from time to time.

Prices: Ticket prices vary. Call 624-2345 for information.

ORCHESTRA HALL, 1111 Nicollet Mall, Minneapolis. Tel. 371-5656.

As its name implies, Orchestra Hall was built as a home for the internationally acclaimed Minnesota Orchestra. Since it opened in 1974, this 2,300-seat hall has offered diverse programs featuring a range of famous artists, from Isaac Stern and Itzhak Perlman to Andy Williams and the late Pearl Bailey.

Since 1980 the annual Viennese Sommerfest featuring guest conductors has drawn very large audiences to Orchestra Hall for programs including everything from light classics to orchestral masterworks.

Prices: Tickets $15–$32.

ORDWAY MUSIC THEATRE, 345 Washington St., St. Paul. Tel. 224-4222.

After St. Paul's only major downtown performing arts building was closed in 1980 because of structural deterioration, the family of Lucius Ordway offered to donate $10 million toward a new music hall if public and private interests in the Twin Cities would match that commitment and that contribution.

Since its triumphant opening on January 1, 1985, the Ordway Music Theatre has been praised not only for the programs it presents, but for the beauty it imparts to the historic Rice Park area of St. Paul. The Ordway's design combines the new and the old, with its glass walls set into a facade of brick and copper and its state-of-the-art acoustics. Doormen await theatergoers at the entrance to the handsome lobby; a magnificent spiral stairway leads to the Grand Foyer and upper Promenade, both of which offer spectacular views of the city. The spacious lobby provides upholstered couches and window-wall mahogany benches just right for conversation, refreshments, and people-watching.

The 1,800-seat Main Hall and the 315-seat McKnight Theatre have hosted distinguished musicians from the Twin Cities as well as famous acts like Leontyne Price, Mel Tormé, and the Ballet Folklórico Nacional de Mexico.

A series of touring Broadway shows appears at the Ordway each year. Past productions have included *Les Miserables, West Side Story,* and *The Heidi Chronicles.*

Prices: Ticket prices vary according to event. Students can get discounts prior to some performances; call for more information.

2. THE CLUB & MUSIC SCENE

COMEDY CLUBS

Twin Cities comedy clubs have become something of a one-man show thanks to Scott Hanson, a local impresario and comic whose own credits include local performances at the Guthrie Theater and at Riverfest. On the national scene, he's opened for Jay Leno, Roseanne Barr, and Rodney Dangerfield.

More recently, though, Hanson has developed a series of comedy "galleries" in Minneapolis at St. Anthony Main, 219 SE Main St. You'll find three rooms here: **Scott Hanson's Comedy Gallery,**

Wild Bill's Comedy Safari, and the **Padded Ce**
is $7 to each, Sunday through Thursday; $10 on Frida
The phone number for all three spots is 331-JOKE.

ROCK

FIRST AVENUE CLUB, 701 1st Ave. N., Minneapolis. Tel. 338-8388.

A cavernous former bus depot serves as the site of one of Minneapolis's largest, busiest, and most famous nightspots. The 1,200-seat First Avenue Club is familiar to moviegoers around the world as the setting for Prince's movie *Purple Rain.*

There's recorded music for dancing four times each week at First Avenue, where hi-tech sounds and lights provide a noisy and exciting atmosphere. Live acts are presented here too, in styles ranging from country to pop to jazz.

Admission: Prices vary on concert nights. Tickets Thurs–Sat $1 8–9pm, $3 9–10pm, $5 10pm to closing; Sun $5; Tues two-for-one night, call for details.

GLAM SLAM, 110 N. 5th St., Minneapolis. Tel. 338-3383.

Since its September 1990 opening, Glam Slam has been the only Twin Cities nightclub offering in-person performances by Prince and other celebrated Paisley Park recording artists. And, thanks to another exclusive Glam Slam agreement, this is the only place you'll hear unreleased material produced at Paisley Park, Prince's widely admired state-of-the-art recording complex.

The second-floor private area at Glam Slam is reserved for members only, but don't fret. There's plenty to enjoy on the main floor of this 20,000-square-foot nightclub, where nationally known artists perform rock, country, hip-hop, and jazz. Located in Minneapolis's Warehouse District, Glam Slam, which is open five nights a week, Tuesday through Saturday, boasts the area's most advanced sight, sound, and lights.

Admission: Ticket prices vary; call for specific information.

7TH STREET ENTRY, 701 1st Ave. N., Minneapolis. Tel. 338-8388.

While some promising unknowns play First Avenue from time to time, the usual launching pad for new talent is the adjoining 7th Street Entry, which is open daily and features at least three live bands each night. Formerly a storage area, this room has become the club in which publicists try to book their young clients, hoping to catch the eye of scouts who've made this a regular stop in their search for new talent.

You'll find drinks of all kinds here, and the small kitchen serves nachos and pizza. Phone 332-1775 for daily recorded information about performances. If you'd rather speak to a real person, call the number listed above Monday through Friday from noon to 5pm.

Admission: Prices vary; call for specific information.

JAZZ

If you want specific information about the jazz entertainment being offered during your stay in the Twin Cities, call **Jazzline** (tel. 633-0329), a service of the Twin Cities Jazz Society. They provide a lengthy rundown on the artists appearing throughout the Twin Cities at clubs, bars, restaurants, hotels, parks, plazas, and even on local radio. During the summer months, much of the jazz hereabouts is performed outdoors.

DAKOTA BAR AND GRILL, at Bandana Sq., 1021 E. Bandana Blvd., St. Paul. Tel. 642-1442.

The Dakota Bar and Grill, which offers live jazz seven nights a week, has developed into one of the top jazz venues in America, featuring artists like Harry Connick, Jr., Wynton Marsalis, Max Roach, Betty Carter, and Carmen McCrae. The Twin Cities' finest local jazz musicians appear here regularly as well.

See Chapter 6 for a description of the fine restaurant here.

Admission: Prices vary; call for specific information.

MIXED BAG

FINE LINE MUSIC CAFÉ, 318 1st Ave. N., Minneapolis. Tel. 338-8100.

Unlike thematic nightclubs that limit themselves to one musical niche or another—jazz, rock and roll, or blues, for example—this is a "showcase room," which according to owner Joel Conner means the Fine Line is free to put any kind of music onstage, so long as it's of a high quality.

Groups performing here have included Bonedaddies, a Cajun group from New Orleans; Zvuki Mu, rock-and-rollers from the Soviet Union; and bellAmitri, a group from Scotland.

Situated in the Warehouse District of downtown Minneapolis, the Fine Line somehow manages an aura of intimacy while accommodating some 460 patrons at small tables on two levels.

The eclectic dinner menu, with prices ranging from $6 to $14, includes a lot of fish, pasta, and chicken, as well as a wide variety of appetizers and drinks.

It's a good idea to call before coming to see whether the fare being offered will suit your taste. And keep this place in mind for its Sunday brunch, a long-standing tradition. Evening hours at the Fine Line are Monday through Friday 5pm until 1am and Saturday and Sunday 6pm until 1am.

Admission: $6.95–$14.95 plus an additional cover charge that varies according to the artist. Call for specific information.

NEW RIVERSIDE CAFÉ, 329 Cedar Ave. S., Minneapolis. Tel. 333-4814.

At the New Riverside Café you'll hear a variety of music by Twin Cities bands and vocalists. In this 20-year-old collective, where the owners also serve as managers and maintenance staff, the often first-rate musicians are paid by tips from patrons and a meal from the café. You'll find the work of local artists mounted on the wall here as well. "The Riv" is a vegetarian, alcohol-free restaurant with a reputation for tasty food in a wholesome environment. Check it out. Music entertainment begins at 7:30pm Tuesday through Thursday and at 9pm Friday and Saturday and lasts until 11pm on weekdays, until midnight on Saturday.

Admission: Free.

O'GARA'S BAR AND GRILL, 164 N. Snelling, St. Paul. Tel. 644-3333.

At O'Gara's you'll find a complex that's far outgrown the pub founded in March 1941 by James Freeman O'Gara of County Sligo. The pub originally served food and liquor to locals who manufactured World War II munitions. Nowadays you can enjoy music in O'Gara's piano bar and listen to a variety of bands in the Garage on Friday and Saturday from 7:30pm to 1am. Food and drink are served in the expanded dining and drinking areas. Students, professors, and white-collar types mix affably with the blue-collar regulars.

Admission: Prices vary; call for specific information.

DANCE CLUBS/DISCOS

CATTLE COMPANY, 4470 W. 78th St. Circle. Tel. 835-1225.

On the strip in Bloomington, this nightspot has D-jays on hand seven nights a week from 8pm to 1am (Sunday until midnight). A wide mix of dance music, from the fifties and sixties to the current Top 40, is featured here.

Admission: $3 cover on Sunday only.

3. THE BAR SCENE

CHAMPPS SPORTS BAR AND GOURMET HAMBURGER GRILL, 2431 W. 7th St., at Sibley Plaza in St. Paul. Tel. 698-5050.

People of all ages, sizes, backgrounds, and temperaments mix merrily here amid large TV screens showing, of course, sports events. When visiting the Twin Cities, sports celebrities from out of town head for Champps, and local sports figures congregate here as well. The atmosphere is jovial, and food and drink prices are moderate.

Known as "one of the top six sports bars in the nation," Champps is always busy.

There are five other Champps Sports Bars in the Twin Cities in Richfield at 66th and Lyndale Ave. S. (tel. 861-3333); in Minnetonka at 1641 Plymouth Rd., (tel. 546-3333); in New Brighton at 2397 Palmer Dr. (tel. 639-0339); in Maplewood at 1734 Adolphus St. (tel. 487-5050); and in Burnsville at 1200 W. County Rd. 42 (tel. 898-5050).

FITZGERALD'S, in St. Paul's Galtier Plaza, Sibley St. between 5th and 6th Aves. Tel. 297-6787.

At Fitzgerald's you'll find a lounge, a bar, and a restaurant with an open contemporary air; huge windows offer a lovely view of Mears Park below. Featured here is a wide variety of scotches and cognacs, after-dinner cordials, and premium imported and domestic wines. Fitzgerald's is popular at lunchtime with local businesspeople. Dinner is served starting at 5pm seven days a week.

Fitzgerald's comes to life late at night, when it's frequented by out-of-towners staying at nearby hotels with skyway access. This is also a popular place for after-theater audiences. The bar is open from 11am to 1am Monday through Saturday and from 11am to midnight on Sunday. There's live jazz entertainment on Friday and Saturday nights from 8:30pm to 12:30am, with a $1 cover charge.

J. COUSINEAU'S, 15 Main St. S.E., Minneapolis. Tel. 623-3632.

On the ground floor of Riverplace, the trendy shopping and entertainment complex on the shores of the Mississippi River, you'll find this popular pub with a large outdoor patio. It's famous for its enormous half-yard and full-yard ale glasses, reproductions of the glasses used in England during the 17th and 18th centuries. After quaffing your selection, feel free to purchase the 1-foot glass at $29.95, half-yard glass at $35.75, or the full-yard glass at $59.95. (Less hearty or less thirsty souls can imbibe from smaller vessels.)

SWEENEY'S SALOON, 96 N. Dale St., St. Paul. Tel. 221-9157.

At Sweeney's Saloon you'll find a boisterous place with a large selection of beers, to say nothing of daily food specials that really are special. Thirteen tap beers, including a few brewed in New Ulm, Minnesota, are also available. The saloon is open Monday through Friday from 11am to 1am and Saturday and Sunday from 9am to 1am.

CHAPTER 11

EASY EXCURSIONS FROM THE TWIN CITIES

By now you know that the Twin Cities could easily keep you occupied throughout your entire stay. If time permits, though, you might want to see for yourself some of the places that lure local folks out of town for weekend excursions. Stillwater is a popular destination with pleasant shops and restaurants. Rochester, home of the famous Mayo Clinic, is close enough for a 90-minute drive, a bit of sight-seeing, and a return on the same day. For the river town rambles, though, or a visit to Duluth, you'll probably want to set aside at least one night, maybe more. In any case, these excursions will give you an idea of the diversity to be found in marvelous Minnesota.

1. STILLWATER

This is where it all began. It was on August 28, 1848, that 61 delegates gathered in Stillwater to draft a petition asking Congress and President James K. Polk for the "organization of the Territory of Minnesota." The following year, under the sponsorship of Sen. Stephen A. Douglas, the bill was passed, and the rest, as they say, is history.

Nestled in the picturesque St. Croix River Valley, Stillwater today is readily reached by boat or car, and during the summer pleasure craft from throughout Minnesota and nearby Wisconsin occupy the docks that are located a block or two from the city's main street.

Once you get to town, your first stop should be the **Stillwater Chamber of Commerce,** 423 S. Main St. (tel. 612/439-7700).

You'll find maps here, along with brochures about minitours, lodgings, antiques, and other information of interest.

WHAT TO SEE & DO

As you approach Stillwater on Highway 36, you'll pass one of the area's most popular destinations. Turn left on Manning Avenue North (Highway 15) and you'll find **Aamodt's Apple Farm,** 6428 Manning Ave. N. (tel. 439-3127), a 180-acre orchard with its own processing plant, gift shops, bakery, and lunchroom. A large carving of Johnny Appleseed stands in the renovated 1800s barn, where visitors munch contentedly on apple goodies—apple-cheese soup, apple salad, and most popular of all, giant apple-oatmeal cookies. And of course they're washing it all down with tasty apple cider. At this writing, Aamodt's is open from August to March, with cross-country skiing available through 30 kilometers of groomed, tracked trails. (Call from the Twin Cities to check on the hours.) If you're lucky enough to be here in spring, enjoy the visual and aromatic pleasure of apple-blossom time at Aamodt's.

There's a diversity of outdoor fun to be found at such Stillwater picnic sites as **Pioneer Park,** on a bluff at Second Street overlooking the scenic St. Croix River, and **Lowell Park,** two blocks east of Main Street, which borders downtown from north to south. In the large amphitheater at Pioneer Park, musical events are held all summer, and during the town's annual spectacular, **Lumberjack Days,** local talent shows are presented along with a variety of lumber-related activities, including log-rolling, tree-climbing, and cross-chop-sawing demonstrations by professional lumberjacks. Call the Chamber of Commerce (tel. 612/439-7700) for the particular July weekend on which it will be held during your stay. On Sunday the festivities end with a grand parade that features marching and musical groups from all over the state.

On July 19, 1987, the **Minnesota Zephyr** made its inaugural run from the old depot at 601 N. Main St. and promptly became one of Stillwater's most popular dining and sight-seeing attractions. Passengers board these meticulously restored 1949 dining cars for a trip that carries them through some of the most beautiful landscape in Minnesota. You'll pass the meandering St. Croix River on one side and picturesque limestone river bluffs on the other, then make your way through forests where maple, ash, oak, walnut, white birch, and other state trees abound. The entire journey proceeds at about 5 miles per hour and takes about 3¼ hours; a delightful four-course dinner is included. The cost of this visit to the past is $49.50 per guest, with one glass of wine included in the price of the meal; cocktails and gratuity are not included. On Thursdays through Saturdays, you'll board at 6:30pm, depart at 7pm, and return at 10:15pm. On Sundays, you'll board at 11:30am, depart at noon, and return at 3:15pm. For reservations and further information, call 430-3000, a local phone call from Minneapolis and St. Paul.

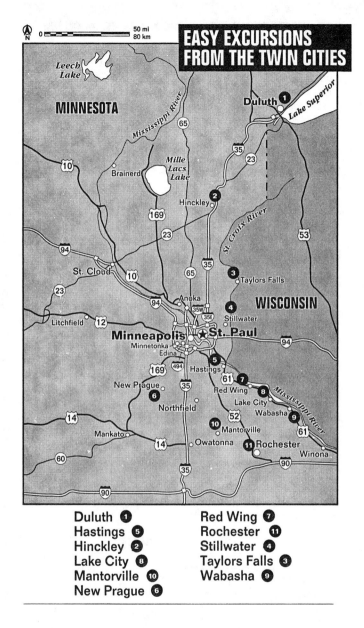

EASY EXCURSIONS FROM THE TWIN CITIES

0 ⎯⎯⎯ 50 mi
        80 km

Leech Lake

MINNESOTA

Mississippi River

Duluth **1** · Lake Superior

35

23

Mille Lacs Lake

Brainerd

Hinckley **2**

St. Croix River

53

St. Cloud

Taylors Falls **3**

WISCONSIN

94

Anoka

35W

35E

Stillwater **4**

Litchfield 12

Minneapolis ★ **St. Paul**

Minnetonka
Edina

94

169 494 Hastings

New Prague 61 **7**

6 Red Wing **8** Mississippi River

Northfield Lake City

Wabasha **9**

14

52

Mankato 61

14 **10** Mantorville

Owatonna **11** Rochester

60

Winona

35 90

90

Duluth **1**	Red Wing **7**
Hastings **5**	Rochester **11**
Hinckley **2**	Stillwater **4**
Lake City **8**	Taylors Falls **3**
Mantorville **10**	Wabasha **9**
New Prague **6**	

Shopping is especially enjoyable in Stillwater because so many of the stores are located in historic structures. On Main Street you'll find a group of fine specialty shops in a complex called the **Grand Garage and Gallery,** 324 S. Main St. At the **Brick Alley Mall,** 423 S. Main St., two 19th-century structures separated by an old alley have been connected by an enclosed walkway. Elsewhere in town,

River Town Galleries, 236 S. Main St. (tel. 439-9393), attracts art collectors from throughout the Midwest, while sweater and outerwear collectors have a fine time in another restored building where the **Winona Knitting Mills Factory Outlet,** 215 S. Main St. (tel. 430-1711), offers a wide selection of apparel at prices about 30% to 50% lower than in department and specialty shops.

WHERE TO STAY

LOWELL INN, 102 N. 2nd St., Stillwater, MN 55082. Tel. 612/439-1100. 21 rms. TV TEL

$ Rates: Fri–Sat $209–$279 per person including meals; Sun–Thurs $99–$169. MC, V.

A beautiful three-story structure with large white columns, arched windows, and a comfortably furnished veranda, this inn first opened in 1930. Sumptuously furnished with a mixture of French provincial and Victorian reproductions and antiques, the romantic rooms are much in demand by couples who find this the perfect place for an anniversary celebration. In fact the demand is so great that you might have trouble getting a room here, so do call ahead for reservations. Rates depend on the room's size, location, and accoutrements. Four of the rooms have Jacuzzis (presumably these don't date back to the 18th century); one room has its own adjoining living room, and one boasts a shower-in-the-round, with fixtures imported from Italy.

AFTON HOUSE, 3291 S. St. Croix Trail, Afton, MN 55001. Tel. 612/436-8883. Fax 612/435-6859. 15 rms. TV TEL

$ Rates (including continental breakfast): $60 basic room; $120–$135 room with river view and Jacuzzi. AE, DISC, MC, V.

Just minutes away from Stillwater, about 15 miles south on Highway 95, you'll find the delightful Afton House. On the banks of the St. Croix River, the inn's guest rooms have been furnished individually with antiques that include trundle beds, clipper chairs, and English armoires. Four of the rooms have small private balconies, with a larger one available to all guests.

WHERE TO DINE

FREIGHT HOUSE RESTAURANT, 435 S. Water St. Tel. 439-5718.

Cuisine: AMERICAN. **Reservations:** Not accepted.

$ Prices: Lunch $4.95–$10.95; dinner $6.95–$12.95. AE, CB, DC, DISC, MC, V.

Open: Nov–Feb Mon–Thurs 11am–10pm, Fri–Sat 11am–11pm, Sun 9:30am–10pm.

A block off Main Street, this restaurant overlooks the St. Croix River. The building it's housed in is listed on the National Register of Historic Places and was once occupied by an old railroad company. The large picture windows here provide diners with a panoramic view of the river. Prices are moderate, with a lunch of a salad, sandwich, or hamburger going for about $6. Barbecued ribs at $13 remain a longtime favorite for dinner.

VITTORIO'S, 402 S. Main St. Tel. 439-3588.

Cuisine: ITALIAN. **Reservations:** Recommended for dinner.
$ Prices: Lunch $5.50–$8.75; dinner $11.75–$17.75. AE, MC, V.
Open: Lunch Mon–Sun 11am–3pm; dinner Sun–Thurs 3–11pm, Fri–Sat 3pm–midnight.

Vittorio's features tasty northern Italian food in a large restaurant with four dining rooms and a lounge where a 19th-century brewery once stood. Popular dinner entrées, served here with antipasto salad and garlic toast, include ravioli carne (meat-filled pasta prepared with the house red sauce) and pollo alla cacciatora (chicken sautéed in wine and served with a portion of baked cannelloni rossi).

BRINE'S OLD FASHIONED MEATS, 219 S. Main St. Tel. 439-7556.

Cuisine: AMERICAN.
$ Prices: Sandwiches $2.95–$3.95; all-you-can-eat rib dinner $8.95. MC, V.
Open: Sun–Thurs 8am–9pm, Fri–Sat 8am–10pm.

A general store back in the 1860s, Brine's Old Fashioned Meats offers first-floor grocery shopping with informal dining on the second floor. Old-World delicatessen items, along with hamburgers and milk shakes, are the specialties of the house. The all-you-can-eat rib dinner starts at 5pm.

LOWELL INN, 102 N. 2nd St. Tel. 439-1100.

Cuisine: AMERICAN. **Reservations:** Recommended.
$ Prices: Lunch $10.95–$19.95, dinner $19.95–$32.95. MC, V.
Open: Lunch noon–2pm; dinner in Matterhorn room Fri–Sat seatings at 6pm and 9:30pm; Sun–Thurs 6–8:30pm; other rooms Sun–Sat 6–8:30pm.

The Lowell Inn attracts diners from throughout the state. You can dine in one of three rooms: The elegant George Washington Room with its sheffield silver, dresden china, and antique sideboards; the Matterhorn Room, notable for its acid-etched stained-glass windows and authentic Swiss carvings; and the Garden Room, which contains an indoor trout pool. The Matterhorn Room features a beef-and-shrimp fondue dinner with a European wine-tasting for $92 per couple; the George Washington Room and the Garden Room have the same varied American menu. Lunch and dinner hours vary from room to room, so phone ahead for specifics.

AFTON HOUSE, 3291 S. St. Croix Trail, Afton. Tel. 436-8883.

Cuisine: AMERICAN. **Reservations:** Recommended.
$ Prices: Lunch $3.95–$6.95; dinner $11.95–$21.95; Sun brunch

$10.95, holiday brunch $12.95; Sun cruise brunch, $21. AE, DISC, MC, V.

Open: Lunch Mon–Sat 11:30am–2:30pm; dinner Mon–Thurs 5:30–9pm, Fri–Sat 5–10pm, Sun 4:30–9pm; Sun brunch 10am–2pm.

Just minutes away from downtown Stillwater, the Afton House is accessible by road and by river. Close enough to the Twin Cities to make it a special dinner destination, this beautiful inn, now on the National Register of Historic Places, caters to a wide variety of patrons throughout the year. Skiers from nearby Afton Alps make this a mandatory stop during the winter months. And during the summer boaters tie up at the on-site dock.

In the elegant Wheel Room, dinner favorites include steak Diane garnished with fresh vegetables and poached salmon served with champagne sauce. The Catfish Salon features a variety of burgers, sandwiches, and soup selections. The Sunday cruise brunch includes a 2-hour cruise.

2. TAYLORS FALLS

For a view of the St. Croix River Valley, follow Highway 95 from Stillwater. Drive past lush farmlands, magnificent bluffs, and dramatic waterways until you reach Taylors Falls, nestled on the northern end of 900-acre Interstate Park, which extends from one side of the St. Croix to the other and includes within its scope the towns of St. Croix Falls, Wisconsin, and Taylors Falls, Minnesota. (This was the first interstate park ever established in the United States.)

WHAT TO SEE & DO

Taylors Falls is famous for its **hiking, camping, boating,** and **swimming,** as well as its good **fishing,** with plenty of catfish, smallmouth bass, northerns, and walleyes to be caught here. But this area's greatest claim to fame derives from **potholes** and **log jams.** You can see for yourself an enormous pothole more than 60 feet deep that was created out of volcanic rock during the meltdown of ancient glaciers. No remnants of the Taylors Falls logjam remain, but the legend endures: In 1886 when lack of rain prevented logging companies from floating their wood downriver, huge piles of logs accumulated on the riverbanks. When heavy rains did begin, there was a mad dash to get the wood on its way. Since the St. Croix River narrows and bends just below Taylors Falls, a logjam developed that eventually reached a height of 30 feet and a length of more than 2 miles. Another tie with the past is Taylors Falls' famous **historic residential area** where 19th-century homes and churches have been carefully preserved.

WHERE TO STAY

TAYLORS FALLS JAIL, 102 Government Rd., Taylors Falls, MN 55084. Tel. 612/465-3112. 3 rms.

$ Rates: Jail $100 with continental breakfast, second night $70; Cave $110 with continental breakfast, second night $80. No credit cards.

Taylors Falls Jail, now a unique two-story guest house, started life as the lockup for unruly locals. It still has bars on its windows, but in recent years it's welcomed some very estimable citizens indeed. The jail's outside appearance was restored after consultation with the Historic Preservation Office of the Minnesota Historical Society. Its interior has been turned into a comfortably furnished living room, well-equipped modern kitchen and bathroom, and a cozy loft bedroom. At certain times of year you'll need a reservation to spend the night in jail. In all three accommodations provisions are left for you in the refrigerator so that you can do your own cooking at your convenience. There are also accommodations available in the neighboring Schottmuller Building, an old saloon now known as the Cave, and on the third floor of the jail building.

SPRINGS INN, one block west of the junction of Hwys. 8 and 95, Taylors Falls. Mailing address: P.O. Box 11, Taylors Falls, MN 55084. Tel. 612/465-6565, toll free 800/851-4243. 27 rms. TV TEL

$ Rates: Sun–Thurs double $40.40, Fri–Sat double $45.80. AE, DISC, MC, V.

The pleasant, economical, and centrally located Springs Inn features a popular hot tub and Jacuzzi, housed in an adjoining geodesic dome. The three-story wood-frame inn offers rooms with one or two double beds. Free coffee is available in the lobby.

3. NEW PRAGUE

Whether you're getting away for a day or a weekend or longer, you'll do well to consider nearby New Prague, located just 35 miles southwest of the Twin Cities.

WHAT TO SEE & DO

A visit to **Sponsel's Minnesota Harvest Apple Orchard** (tel. 612/492-2785) in nearby Jordan is a good bet. There's a wonderful array of fruit to be picked from the tree or from the bin. Minnesota Harvest's hours vary according to the season: In July, August, September, and October, hours are 9am to 7pm Monday through Thursday and 9am to 8pm Friday, Saturday, and Sunday; in November and December hours are 9am to 6pm daily; January and February hours are 9am to 5pm Friday, Saturday, and Sunday only. There's also an assortment of other attractions, including an animal farm, hiking trails, and, from time to time, helicopter rides.

WHERE TO STAY

SCHUMACHER'S NEW PRAGUE HOTEL, 212 W. Main St. Tel. 445-7285. 11 rms. TEL
$ Rates: Fri–Sat $130–$150 double, Sun–Thurs $104–$120 double. AE, DISC, MC, V.

This remarkable hotel has been featured in such national magazines as *Gourmet, Good Housekeeping,* and *Better Homes and Gardens.* It was designed by famed architect Cass Gilbert, whose other work includes the U.S. Supreme Court Building in Washington, D.C., and the Woolworth Building in New York City.

Each of the guest rooms has been named for a month of the year and decorated in a manner consistent with that month and its season. TV's are available upon request. Czech glasswork and Bavarian folk art enhance the accommodations, along with antique wall sconces and chandeliers. Nearby attractions include golf, tennis, cross-country skiing, biking, canoeing, and, of course, shopping.

A favorite getaway for Minnesotans with an event to celebrate, New Prague is also famous for its cuisine. Innkeeper and head chef John Schumacher and his wife Kathleen offer a wide variety of authentic Bavarian dishes, featuring everything from paprikash and Wiener Schnitzel, to the house specialty, Czechoslovakian roast duck. Kathleen, a registered dietitian, has added a "healthy heart" section to the menu, including dishes which are at once delicious and low in fat and cholesterol. Everything here is prepared to order from scratch, so special dietary requirements pose no problem. Lunchtime entrées are served with a choice of accompaniments which include dumplings, homemade sauerkraut, German potato salad, and the vegetable of the day. Dinner is served with hot or cold soup, German salad plate, choice of two Bavarian side dishes, and homemade kolache and rye roll. Reservations are required at this popular restaurant.

4. ROCHESTER

Rochester, Minnesota, about 80 miles south of the Twin Cities, may be the most cosmopolitan community of its size in the entire country. That's because nearly a quarter of a million visitors from throughout the world arrive here each year to visit the famous Mayo Clinic.

The pleasant drive to Rochester from the Twin Cities takes you along Highway 52 through some of the state's loveliest rolling countryside and luxuriant farmland. If you'd prefer to leave the driving to **Greyhound** (tel. 612/371-3311), the fare each way from the Twin Cities for the 2-hour trip is about $10. **Northwest Airlines** (tel. 612/726-1234) has a 30-minute flight from the Twin Cities to Rochester, with prices ranging from $52 to $135 each way.

WHAT TO SEE & DO

With a staff of more than 800 physicians, surgeons, and medical scientists, in addition to 1,500 medical trainees and more than 5,000 paramedical personnel, the **Mayo Clinic,** 200 1st St. S.W. (tel. 507/284-2511), is the largest and probably the most prestigious group medical practice in the world. It also maintains the largest graduate school of medicine in the world, with an international student body that adds further to the cosmopolitan atmosphere in Rochester.

How did so famous a medical complex happen to develop in a small Midwestern city? The story began back in 1883, when a devastating tornado struck this obscure farming community, leaving 26 people dead and the entire northern part of the town demolished.

Dr. William Worral Mayo was a local English-born physician who had practiced in Rochester for 20 years, after first coming here as an examining surgeon for the Union Army Enrollment Board. After the tornado struck, he worked with other Rochester doctors and with the nuns from the Convent of St. Francis to treat the injured, but their efforts were severely hampered by the lack of adequate medical facilities.

Shortly after the disaster, the mother superior at the convent suggested to Dr. Mayo that he head the medical staff of a hospital which the sisters were planning to build and maintain. At first reluctant, Dr. Mayo agreed, although he knew that hospitals then were frightening to the public, who viewed them as places where people went to die. When St. Mary's Hospital was opened in 1889, other local doctors refused to associate with it, leaving Dr. Mayo and his two physician sons, Will and Charlie, to serve as the entire medical staff.

Both Will and Charlie had been trained in the antiseptic methods introduced by Joseph Lister, and both began to practice the relatively new field of surgery as staff members of St. Mary's Hospital. Word soon got around that patients suffering from chronic ailments like ulcers, appendicitis, and gallstones were being made well again, quickly and permanently, by these young physicians.

Even as patients in Minnesota helped spread the word about Drs. Will and Charlie Mayo, physicians from around the country and even from Europe began coming to Rochester to see for themselves the kind of work that the young Mayos had described at medical meetings and written about in medical journals.

By the mid-1890s their growing practice made it necessary for the Mayos to enlarge their medical staff, and by 1914 they opened a building they called the Mayo Clinic. The group medical practice they established was unique in that it encouraged a sharing of knowledge among a group of medical specialists for the purpose of promoting more comprehensive care for patients. That remains the practice and the purpose of the Mayo Clinic to this day. Free tours of the impressive clinic facilities are available from 10am to 2pm Monday through Friday.

The **Mayo Medical Museum,** open free to the public, offers a variety of films and videotapes as well as exhibits that enable visitors to examine the human body and its functions, to learn about some of the illnesses and injuries that pose a threat around the world, and to become acquainted with some of the methods by which the medical profession deals with these problems. Hours are Monday through Friday from 9am to 9pm, Saturday 9am to 5pm, and Sunday from 1 to 5pm.

Perhaps the most beloved local attraction in downtown Rochester is the **Rochester Carillon,** in the tower of the Plummer Building. This set of 56 stationary bells of various sizes, sounded with levers pressed by a carillonneur's fist, was bought by Dr. Will Mayo during a trip to Europe in the 1920s. With a range of 4½ octaves, it's the most complete carillon in North America. Concerts are offered at 7pm on Monday and at noon on Wednesday and Friday. Additional recitals are held on holidays and for special events.

Mayowood, the splendid home of two generations of the Mayo family, was built in 1911 by Dr. Charles H. Mayo. He and his wife, Edith, brought up four daughters and two sons in this large, gracious home. Later, Dr. Charles (Chuck) W. Mayo, his wife, Alice, and their four sons and two daughters resided here. Perched on 3,000 acres overlooking the Zumbro River Valley, Mayowood has welcomed such famous figures as Helen Keller, Franklin D. Roosevelt, and Adlai Stevenson. Over 38 rooms are furnished in American, English, French, Spanish, and Italian antiques. The only way to get to Mayowood is via an Olmstead County Historical Society shuttle bus; phone 282-9447 for information concerning tours.

Another popular home tour is offered at the **Plummer House,** 1091 Plummer Lane (tel. 281-6182), once the residence of Dr. Henry Plummer. Dr. Plummer joined the Mayo Clinic staff in 1901, and he is credited with having devised the pneumatic tube and the clinic's remarkable communication and recordkeeping systems. When he and his family moved into this Tudor-style mansion in 1924, they were the first in the area to make use of natural gas and the first to have burglar alarms. It's still notable for its exquisite rose garden and for its 11 acres of parkland, open to the public throughout the year from sunrise to sunset. House tours are available June through August on Wednesday from 1 to 7pm. The cost is $1.50 per adult and $1 per child or student; children under 5 are admitted without charge.

Perhaps the unlikeliest of all clinic-related attractions in Rochester are the hordes of giant **Canada geese** that winter here each year.

They were first attracted by a small flock of geese donated by a grateful patient in 1947 and released in Silver Lake Park, at North Broadway and 13th Street. The following year, Rochester's new power plant began using Silver Lake for cooling water, with the result that the lake remained free of ice throughout the winter. The Canada geese stayed on that winter—and have ever since. Now numbering in the tens of thousands, these amiable birds are welcomed in Rochester by people of all ages, who bring them bread crumbs, popcorn, and other goodies. Silver Lake Park has more than geese to offer, though. Paddleboats and canoes can be rented during the warmer months, and picnicking is popular then too.

Other outdoor activities can be enjoyed on the city's six 18-hole golf courses and 30 outdoor tennis courts. There's a popular 9-mile nature trail here as well. For sports information, phone 289-7414.

Cultural attractions in Rochester include the fine **Rochester Art Center,** 320 E. Center St. (tel. 282-8629), open Tuesday through Saturday from 10am to 5pm, and the highly regarded **Rochester Symphony Orchestra,** 109 City Hall, 200 1st Ave. S.W. (tel. 285-8976).

WHERE TO STAY

KAHLER HOTEL, 20 2nd Ave. S.W., Rochester, MN 55902. Tel. 507/282-2581, or toll free 800/533-1655. Fax 507/285-2775. 720 rms and suites. MINIBAR.

$ Rates: $54–$125 double. AE, DISC, MC, V.

Some of the most famous people in the world have stayed at Rochester's Kahler Hotel. Elegant enough for the most festive of getaways, this hotel serves primarily as a comfortable home away from home for those who have come to Rochester to visit the Mayo Clinic.

Accommodations are comfortable and cheery, nearby medical facilities notwithstanding. Along with fine restaurants (see "Where to Dine," below) and shops, the Kahler offers a domed recreation center with swimming pool, sauna, and whirlpool.

The Mayo Clinic and the Kahler Hotel are very careful to protect the privacy of the hotel's visitors, but word does get around town when celebrities like Lady Bird Johnson, Bill Cosby, or Jim Nabors check in.

CLINIC VIEW INN, 9 3rd Ave. N.W., Rochester, MN 55901. Tel. 507/289-8646. Fax 507/282-4478. 142 rms.

$ Rates: $59.95 single, $69 double; $79.95 suite for one, $84.95 suite for two. AE, DISC, MC, V.

Another property with connections to the Mayo Clinic is the more modest Clinic View Inn. It offers a swimming pool, whirlpool, sauna, and restaurant and the choice of standard rooms or more luxurious suites, all at remarkably low cost.

WHERE TO DINE

ELIZABETHAN ROOM, at the Kahler Hotel, 20 2nd Ave., S.W. Tel. 282-2581.

Cuisine: AMERICAN. **Reservations:** Recommended.

$ Prices: Lunch $8.50–$11; dinner $15–$22.

Open: Lunch Mon–Fri 11:30am–2pm; dinner Mon–Fri 5:30–9pm, Sat 6–10pm; Sun brunch 10am–2:30pm. AE, DISC, MC, V.

You won't find a more elegant setting for a memorable dinner than the famous Elizabethan Room. The coats-of-arms on dark paneled walls, the stained-glass panels, the red velvet, and large, double-tiered wrought-iron chandeliers give a majestic ambience to this handsome room. A romantic air is provided by the Elizabethan Strings, strolling violinists who make a lovely musical contribution to your dining pleasure. The irresistible blend of impeccable service and fine fare—for example, breast of chicken or rack of lamb for two—make for a terrific evening out.

The adjoining Lord Essex Room is a perfect complement to the Elizabethan Room. Similar in decor but smaller in size, this room provides a delightfully intimate setting. Primarily a cocktail lounge, the Lord Essex becomes a small dining room during the Elizabethan Room's elaborate Sunday brunch. Overflow brunchers are directed to the Lord Essex Room, a very pleasant alternative indeed!

If you're interested in another cocktail lounge, try the Kahler's Penthouse, a delightful retreat where you can sink into overstuffed chairs amid towering plants and enjoy a commanding view of the city. And there's a third bar down on street level, the Greenhouse, with a terrarium, an aquarium, an oversize TV screen, and 2,000 hanging plants, all of them for sale.

MICHAEL'S, 15 S. Broadway. Tel. 941-9828.

Cuisine: AMERICAN. **Reservations:** Recommended.

$ Prices: Lunch $5.95–$7.95; early dinner (3:30–5pm) $7.95–9.95, late dinner (5–10pm) $11.95–$14.95.

Open: Lunch Mon–Sat 11am–3pm; dinner Mon–Thurs and Sun 3–9pm, Sat 3–10pm.

No Rochester dining spot is better known than Michael's, a family restaurant started in 1951. Now six times larger than it was then, Michael's somehow manages to retain an air of intimacy and cordiality. But there's a cosmopolitan touch here as well. Although the decor in most of the rooms will remind you of an old English country home, one area, the Harkala Room, is decidedly Greek, as is the Pappas family that owns and runs Michael's. A section of the menu includes Greek dishes, but primarily this is an American steak-and-seafood spot. The food will please you, and so will the tab.

WONG'S CAFÉ, 4 Third St. S.W. Tel. 507/282-7545.

Cuisine: CHINESE/AMERICAN. **Reservations:** Recommended for parties of 5 or more.

$ Prices: $5–$9.95.

Open: Mon–Sat 11am–9:30pm, Sun 11am–9pm.

Another well-known family restaurant in these parts is Wong's Café. Now being run by second-generation owners, brothers Michael and Dennis Wong and their cousin Steve Wong, this restaurant was opened in 1952 by Ben and Mae Wong and Neil and Poya Wong. It was in 1982 that the second generation took over and two years later moved the restaurant into a remodeled 100-year-old bank building. (Just 50 feet from where the original restaurant stood, the "new" Wong's Café increased its seating capacity from 150 to 240.) Although American dishes occupy a prominent place on the menu seven days a week, Wong's is probably best known for its Chinese cuisine, particularly for such dishes as the ever-popular moo goo gai pan (sweet and sour chicken with pork-fried rice). Children have their own menu here on place mats that feature games and puzzles.

5. MANTORVILLE

About 65 miles south of the Twin Cities and 20 minutes west of Rochester, you'll find the historic town of Mantorville, whose entire 12-block downtown area is listed on the National Register of Historic Places. Limestone quarries were this town's claim to fame during the 19th century, and a great many important buildings throughout the country are constructed of "Mantorville stone," among them St. Mary's Hospital in Rochester. The Dodge County Courthouse, Minnesota's oldest operating courthouse, is also made of local limestone.

WHAT TO SEE & DO

Among the historically significant buildings to be visited here are a 19th-century one-room **schoolhouse,** a recently restored **log house** (one of the earliest buildings in town), and the **Grand Old Mansion,** 501 Clay St., Mantorville (507/635-3231), an imposing Victorian building that serves today as a bed-and-breakfast remarkable not only for its fine cuisine but for its original woodwork, its hand-carved staircase, and the many antiques with which it's been furnished by owner/hostess Irene Selker. Rates range from $30 for a double-bed room with shared bath to $53 per couple for accommodations in a remodeled schoolhouse. (There's an $8 charge for each additional person.)

WHERE TO DINE

HUBBELL HOUSE, Hwy. 57, Mantorville. Tel. 507/635-2331.

Cuisine: AMERICAN. **Reservations:** Recommended.
$ Prices: Lunch $5.95–$7.95; dinner $9.95–$29.95. AE, DC, DISC, MC, V.
Open: Tues–Sat 11:15am–2pm and 5–10pm, Sun 11:30am–9:30pm.

Perhaps the most frequently visited old building in Mantorville is the Hubbell House, an old country inn established in 1854 and today one of the state's most famous restaurants. Its guests have included Sen. Horace Greeley, best remembered for his advice "Go west, young man. Go west . . ." Alexander Ramsey, Minnesota's first U.S. senator, dined here as well. So, more recently, did a variety of other luminaries, including circus impresario John Ringling North, Gen. Dwight D. Eisenhower, and baseball great Mickey Mantle. Facsimiles of their signatures and those of more than a dozen other famous guests decorate the place mats that have become popular as souvenirs.

Many Twin Citians regularly drive down for dinner at Hubbell House, where the elegant decor in no way detracts from the casual, comfortable atmosphere. The chateaubriand served here is justly famous. It's also reasonably priced, and comes with appetizer or soup, salad, vegetable, and potato. Jumbo shrimp slowly broiled and served over pasta and walleye pike amandine are other dinner specialties. Luncheons represent a particularly attractive buy, with entrées like stuffed pork chops or pasta seafood salad served with potato, vegetable or salad, and beverage.

6. RIVER TOWNS

Follow the Mississippi south from the Twin Cities and you'll find a succession of quaint river towns that retain much of the architecture and atmosphere of bygone days.

Combine the historical interest of this area with the natural beauty of the surrounding Hiawatha Valley, add the unique attractions each community has to offer, and you'll see why Hastings, Red Wing, Lake City, and Wabasha are popular Twin Cities getaways for a day, an evening, a weekend, or longer.

HASTINGS

Just 25 miles from the Twin Cities, Hastings was one of the earliest river towns in Minnesota. A trading post was established here as early as 1833, and the town was incorporated in 1857. Three rivers—the Mississippi, the St. Croix, and the Vermillion—made Hastings readily accessible to other markets, and the spectacular Vermillion waterfalls provided power for the mills that made this one of the great wheat centers of the Northwest.

WHAT TO SEE & DO

Today, there are 61 buildings in Hastings that have been listed on the National Register of Historic Places. The newest of these is a contemporary work by Frank Lloyd Wright, who in 1957–59 built the dramatic **Fasbender Medical Clinic** at the southeast corner of Highway 55 and Pine Street. Situated on land that blends into an adjacent park, the clinic, which is largely submerged in the ground, is readily identified by its folded roof.

As part of the National Trust program known as "Main Street," all of downtown Hastings has been designated a historic district. See the helpful **Hastings Chamber of Commerce,** at 220 Sibley St. (tel. 612/437-6775), for a handy guide to your own walking tour of these fascinating buildings, foremost among them the **Le Duc-Simmons Mansion,** 1629 Vermillion St. (Highway 61). This imposing limestone structure, with its pointed arched windows, high tower, and intricate scrollwork, dates back to 1856.

The **Alexis Bailly Vineyard,** 18200 Kirby Ave. (tel. 437-1413), was founded in 1973 and has since won more than a dozen awards from Wineries Unlimited, an international competition involving wineries all over the United States and Canada. From June through October the winery is open to the public from noon to 5pm Friday through Sunday. And in fact individuals and small groups are welcome to walk through the vineyards and to sample and purchase wines anytime during working hours. By the way, it was the original Alexis Bailly who selected the site for the trading post that would one day develop into the town of Hastings.

The **Carpenter St. Croix Valley Nature Center,** 12805 St. Croix Trail (tel. 437-4359), conducts a number of programs, including the rehabilitation of raptors (birds of prey such as bald eagles and hawks), the banding of birds, and the maintenance of orchards. It also organizes maple syruping in the spring, organic gardening in the summer, and animal tracking in the winter. The center is open to the public on the first and third Sunday of the month.

WHERE TO STAY

THORWOOD BED AND BREAKFAST, 649 W. 3rd St., Hastings, MN 55033. Tel. 612/437-3297. 8 rms (all with bath).
$ Rates (including full breakfast and evening snack): $75–$225 for two persons.

Thorwood is a reconverted 1880 mansion that's been turned into a delightful accommodation by Pam and Dick Thorsen. There are eight rooms here, some with fireplaces, some with whirlpools, and each with its own distinctive decor. Breakfast, brought to your door in an oversize basket, includes oven omelets, warm pastries, sausages, muffins, coffee or tea, and juice. Reservations are recommended.

A new B&B, also owned by the Thorsens, is **Rosewood,** 620

Ramsey St., Hastings, MN 55033 (tel. 612/437-3297). There are seven rooms in this lovely home; the prices are the same as those for Thorwood.

WHERE TO DINE

MISSISSIPPI BELLE, 101 E. 2nd St. Tel. 437-5694.

Cuisine: AMERICAN. **Reservations:** Recommended.

$ Prices: Lunch $3.50–$6.50; dinner $7.95–$16.95. AE, DC, DISC, V.

Open: Tues–Sat 11am–1:30pm and 5–9pm, Sun 11am–6pm.

Perhaps the best-known restaurant in Hastings is the Mississippi Belle, a replica of the side-wheel packet steamers that traveled the Mississippi during the golden era of riverboats, from 1855 to 1875. A perennially popular dinner entrée here is baked seafood au gratin, which combines shrimp, scallops, crabmeat, and lobster in a sherry sauce. A smaller version is available at lunchtime as well. Oven-fried chicken, broiled center-cut pork chops, and Port of Hastings steak (a boneless New York cut) are among the items that have made Mississippi Belle a drawing card. The pies here are legendary, with lemon angel, sour-cream raisin, and southern pecan among the delicious offerings.

RED WING

As you continue your river town ramble southward from the Twin Cities, you'll find Red Wing, a town whose beginnings date back to 1680, when Father Hennepin came upon an Indian village here. The town was later named in honor of the area's Sioux Indian chiefs, whose emblem was a swan's wing that had been dyed red. In 1837 white settlers came to Red Wing, and by the 1870s it had become a primary wheat market.

As railroads assumed a greater role in the transportation of products, Red Wing's importance as a shipping center began to diminish, even as the town's manufacture of two products, pottery and shoes, began to draw widespread attention.

WHAT TO SEE & DO

The Minnesota Stoneware Company, which began production in the late 1800s and eventually became known as Red Wing Pottery, made use of local raw materials and soon established a national reputation. In 1967, after nearly a century of operation, the company closed its plant as the result of a prolonged and bitter labor dispute. But the historic factory and salesroom have been turned into a major tourist attraction. At **Red Wing Pottery Sales,** 1995 W. Main St. (tel. 338-3562), you'll be able to find some remaining pieces of the original Red Wing pottery, along with collectibles from around the world. You can also browse among a variety of country items, and in the candy section you'll find such old-fashioned sweets as homemade fudge.

Winona Mills, 1902 W. Main St. (tel. 338-5738), one of a statewide network of factory outlet stores, offers a wide assortment of high-quality, reasonably priced apparel, all of it made in the United States, with one notable exception—the genuine Icelandic sweaters, which sell for much lower prices here than elsewhere.

And then there's **Loons and Ladyslippers,** 1890 W. Main St. (tel. 388-9418), a delightful shop where you'll find a miscellany of gifts, crafts, and collectibles, all of them related in some way to Minnesota, whose official bird is the loon and whose official flower is the lady slipper.

At nearby **Pottery Place,** you'll find a two-level mall containing factory outlets, specialty shops, and restaurants.

WHERE TO STAY

ST. JAMES HOTEL, 406 Main St., Red Wing, MN 55066.
Tel. 612/388-2846. Fax 612/388-5226. 41 rms. TV TEL
$ Rates: $70–$135 double. AE, DISC, DC, MC, V.

After making a national name for itself as the manufacturer of fine leather products, the Red Wing Shoe Company took a step in an entirely different direction in 1977, when it bought the 100-year-old St. James Hotel. The subsequent restoration was meticulous and skillful.

The 60 original guest rooms were reduced to 41 in order to accommodate private modern baths and facilities. Each room is individually decorated with period wallpaper, period pieces, and coordinated handmade down quilts. In a discreet bow to modernity, handcrafted Victorian wardrobes open to reveal television sets. Delightful examples of Victorian workmanship have been displayed throughout the corridors.

A popular gathering place at the St. James Hotel is **Jimmy's Pub,** which offers not only a fine fifth-story view of the city, but a warm, friendly ambience enhanced by antique stained-glass panels, old English hunting scenes in antique frames over the oak bar, and upholstered armchairs facing the massive fireplace. Jimmy's Pub should really be called Jimmy's Bar—no food is served in this otherwise hospitable room. But you can get a bite at breakfast or lunchtime at the delightful **Veranda Coffee Shop,** with its lovely view of the Mississippi. You have your choice here of a table in the cheery informal dining room or on the adjoining enclosed porch.

WHERE TO DINE

PORT OF RED WING, in the St. James Hotel, 406 Main St.
Tel. 388-2846.

Cuisine: AMERICAN. **Reservations:** Recommended.
$ Prices: Lunch $5–$8; dinner $15–$20.
Open: Lunch Mon–Sat 11am–2pm; dinner daily 5–9:30pm. AE,
DC, DISC, MC, V.

Only an hour from the Twin Cities, this restaurant is close enough for
a lunch or dinner date. Port of Red Wing, the St. James's major
restaurant, retains its original limestone walls and a variety of period
antiques, which have been put to ingenious use. The original
safe-deposit vault, for example, serves now as a fine wine cellar. Port
of Red Wing offers a traditional American menu, with specials every
evening.

LAKE CITY

Picturesque bluffs overlook Highway 61 as you approach Lake City,
situated on Lake Pepin, the widest expanse on the Mississippi River.
Lake City takes pride in the fact that the sport of waterskiing was
invented here back in 1922, when 18-year-old Ralph Samuelson
steamed and then bent into shape two pine boards. His theory was
that if people could ski on snow, they could also ski on water, and the
corroboration of that theory put Lake City on the map and enabled
millions of men, women, and children throughout the world to ski, if
not walk, on water.

WHAT TO SEE & DO

This small city features a variety of activities that center on its major
claim to fame, the largest marina on the Mississippi River. Following
a recent expansion, 625 sailboats can now be docked here, while a
90-foot breakwater makes **fishing** possible from three 60-foot
platforms. Northerns, walleyes, crappies, and bass are among the
varieties most often caught in these waters. But fish are not the only
wildlife that draws tourists to Lake City. There are also the majestic
bald eagles that have made their home in the bluffs overlooking
Highway 61, south of Lake City at Read's Landing. These imposing
birds can be seen from time to time swooping down onto the open
water for food, and as the season progresses they do their ice fishing
on the shoreline before it too freezes over.

WABASHA

You'll be visiting the oldest city in Minnesota when you arrive in
Wabasha. Named for Indian Chief Wapashaw, a peacemaker during
the Sioux Indian uprising of 1862, Wabasha was by the 1880s a center
of lumbering, milling, and boat building. Many of the buildings of
that period, constructed of local materials, still stand today. In fact,
Wabasha's entire downtown business district has been placed on the
National Register of Historic Places.

There are two marinas here, offering 400 open slips and 200

closed slips, and the city dock provides launching to the public as well. Many sailors take advantage of the shuttle service provided at the docks by the Anderson House, the state's oldest operating hotel.

WHERE TO STAY

ANDERSON HOUSE, 333 N. Main St., Wabasha, MN 55981. Tel. 612/565-4524. Fax 612/565-4003. 27 rms (15 with bath).

$ Rates: $35–$54 double with shared bath, $55–$85 double with bath, $95–$105 suite. MC, V.

Run by the members of the same family since it first opened in 1896, the Anderson House has received national TV, magazine, and newspaper coverage as the Minnesota hotel that gives new meaning to the term "cathouse." Here guests can reserve a complimentary overnight cat when they register for a room; a feline, its food, and even a litter box will be delivered to their door that evening. Daytime visits can also be arranged—usually at nap time for children or their elders.

There are other homey touches at the Anderson House as well. Home-baked cookies are available in a large jar on the front desk 24 hours a day. Heated bricks are provided for those who opt for that sort of bed warmer. Guests with the sniffles can have a mustard plaster delivered to their door. And those who remember to leave their shoes outside the door at night will find them there brightly shined the next morning.

Besides its meticulous services, the Anderson House is also famous for its home cooking. Grandma Ida Hoffman Anderson brought her Pennsylvania Dutch recipes from Lancaster, Pennsylvania, at the turn of the century, and the family has been using them ever since. Today Ida's granddaughter Jeanne Hall and great grandson John share the operation of the Anderson House. They've also shared authorship of a number of cookbooks for those who want to try their hand at this kind of fare.

The cinnamon and praline breakfast rolls at the Anderson House are massive, and so is the selection of home-baked breads and rolls that waitresses bring to your table at dinnertime. Entrées include Dutch oven steak, Pennsylvania Dutch beef rolls, and batter-fried cod, as well as such standbys as roast turkey and dressing, baked ham, and barbecued ribs. And then there's the Friday-night seafood buffet, an all-you-can-eat selection of seafood gumbo, shrimp, deep-fried pike, crab sections, oven-baked cod and white fish, along with potato and vegetable and, of course, the bread tray, all for $6.95. Lunches here, served from 11am to 3pm, range from $5.50 to $8. Dinners, served from 5 to 8:30pm, range from $10.95 to $15.95. Never mind that the river recreation is top notch in Wabasha. The Anderson House itself is reason enough to visit this historic river town.

7. DULUTH

About halfway between the Twin Cities and the Canadian border is Duluth, the third largest city in Minneapolis, but second to none in its importance as an international inland port. Ships from all over the world arrive and depart each day from April to December, imparting a truly cosmopolitan air to this northern Minnesota city.

Like Minneapolis and St. Paul, Duluth is linked to a "twin"—in this case one that resides in a different state. Superior, Wisconsin, and Duluth, Minnesota, have always shared a natural harbor on Lake Superior, the huge inland sea that Henry Wadsworth Longfellow immortalized in 1855 as the birthplace of Hiawatha: "By the shores of Gitche Gumee, By the shining big-sea water. . . ."

Like any siblings, these cities have disagreed at times, most memorably perhaps one April weekend in 1871, after Duluth had decided to do something about the 6½-mile sandbar, Minnesota Point, around which its fishing ships had to travel before reaching open water. The city of Superior enjoyed a natural advantage because Wisconsin Point, less than 3 miles long, gave its boats readier access to the lake.

On this April day in 1871, Duluth officials authorized the digging of an artificial channel through Minnesota Point. A steam shovel had already started work when Superior officials contacted Washington, D.C., with a request that the excavation be halted. Word reached Duluth on a Friday afternoon that an army engineer was on his way with an injunction to halt the excavation. By the time he actually arrived early on Monday, the entire town had bent to the task, working ceaselessly throughout the weekend and finishing the entryway in time for a little tugboat, *Fero,* to toot its way through while Duluthians cheered.

In 1873 the federal government assumed control of the canal and the harbor, and ten years later named it the Duluth-Superior Harbor. Today an aerial lift bridge oversees the nearly 40 million tons of domestic and international cargo that passes through each year.

These international ships carry grain to Europe and beyond, while ore boats take on taconite for shipment to cities in the American East. And of course the presence here of ships from all over the world has become a prime tourist attraction for the city of Duluth.

WHAT TO SEE & DO

One of the "musts" in any visit to Duluth is a drive along **Skyline Parkway,** a 26-mile strip of city that hugs the crest of a hillside at the western end of town. Day or night, winter or summer, this is a beautiful drive, looking out on Lake Superior, St. Louis Bay, and many residential areas. Part of the route goes through another sight-seeing attraction, **Hawks Ridge Nature Reserve,** a place where bird-watchers gather each fall to watch the migratory flights of hawks and eagles.

At the other end of town, **Spirit Mountain** (tel. toll free 800/247-0146) has been bringing ever-increasing numbers of skiers to Duluth during the past decade to enjoy such innovations as the 444 Express, a chair lift that raises four skiers in a bubble-domed quad to a height of 4,000 feet in just four minutes. The first of its kind in Minnesota, the 444 Express is one of only three or four similar lifts in the entire country. Work is constantly under way not only on lengthening and improving existing runs, but also on developing programs for individual skiers and families. One of the most notable events at Spirit Mountain takes place each New Year's Eve when instructors and members of the ski patrol lead a torchlight parade down the slopes before fireworks erupt into the cold, clear winter sky.

One of the long-range development plans here is to extend runs as far as the **Lake Superior Zoological Garden,** at Seventh Avenue West and Grand Avenue (Highway 23) (tel. 624-1502), which boasts more than 500 animals from around the world, including a variety of "night animals" that recently took up residence in their own newly constructed nocturnal building. Another popular spot here is the **Children's Zoo Contact Building,** where children, under staff supervision, are invited to touch and pet a variety of animals. Admission to the zoo from April 15 to October 15 is $1.50 for adults, 75¢ for children 6 to 12. Zoo hours during this period are 9am to 6pm seven days a week. There's no entrance fee during the rest of the year, when the zoo is open from 9am to 4pm. Closed Thanksgiving, Christmas, and New Year's Day.

Another favorite sight-seeing attraction, for children and grown-ups alike, is the **Depot,** 506 W. Michigan St. (tel. 727-8025). An interesting series of exhibits and museums leads visitors through two centuries of local history, with an early stop at the Immigrants' Waiting Room. Elsewhere along the way, children enjoy the two-story walk-through Habitat Tree, and visitors of all ages admire the wonderful mid-19th-century collection of Ojibwa Indian portraits by Eastman Johnson. Elsewhere at the Depot you'll find a fascinating assortment of antique trains, dolls, and furnishings. Open daily from 10am to 5pm during the summer months. During the winter, the hours are Monday through Saturday from 10am to 5pm and on Sunday from 1 to 5pm.

And then there's **Glensheen,** a most popular attraction during the past several years, but maybe for the wrong reason. This magnificent mansion, at 3300 London Rd. (Highway 61 North), was donated by the wealthy Congdon family to the University of Minnesota at Duluth and stands in the lakeside neighborhood where logging and mining barons built lavish homes nearly a century ago. The much-publicized murder in this mansion of a member of the Congdon family and the subsequent trial and acquittal of an adopted daughter may have something to do with the renewed interest in the property, but tourists should know in advance that the Junior League docents who lead the tours avoid any reference whatever to the crime—so don't visit Glensheen on that account. If, on the other hand, you'd like to see for yourself a dazzling array of exquisite architecture, interior design, art, and horticulture, you'll find your visit to this 39-room Jacobean manor house one of the highlights of your visit to Duluth. Call 724-8863 for recorded information regarding hours, tours, and admission charges, or 724-8864 for reservations and additional information.

For information about other attractions, call or write the **Duluth Convention and Visitors Bureau Information Center,** Fifth Avenue West and the Waterfront, Duluth, MN 55802 (tel. 218/722-6024, or toll free 800/862-1172 in Minnesota).

WHERE TO STAY

Theoretically, you could make a 1-day excursion from Minneapolis to Duluth, but since the drive takes about three hours each way, I strongly suggest that you plan to spend the night. There's a lot to see and do in this lovely city.

THE MANSION, 3600 London Rd., Duluth, MN 55804. Tel. 218/724-0739. 10 rms.

$ Rates (including country breakfast): $85–$105 double. MC, V.
Just two doors away from Glensheen, the Mansion was from 1928 to 1932 the 10-bedroom home of another member of the Congdon family, Marjorie Congdon Dudley, and her husband, Harry C. Dudley. Accommodations here are named for the color of the rooms and the view they command.

A hearty country breakfast, served in the formal dining room, is included in the rates. So is access to the oak-paneled library, the pine-paneled living room, and the sun porch and dining room. As of this writing the Mansion is open to overnight guests only from Memorial Day to October 15 and most winter weekends, with certain other periods available by special arrangement. For the doctor's family that runs it, this beautiful and gracious home has become a labor of love, and you'll find all kinds of delightful reasons to come back again.

FITGER'S INN, 600 E. Superior St., Duluth, MN 55802. Tel. 218/722-8826, or toll free 800/726-2982. Fax 218/727-8871. 48 rms and suites. TV TEL

$ Rates: Peak season $84.95–$104.95 double; off season $69.95–$89.95 double. AE, CB, DC, DISC, MC, V.
Another notable place to stay is Fitger's Inn. Listed on the National Register of Historic Places, this restored 19th-century structure offers individually styled rooms, some of them with a view of Lake Superior

and some with original stone walls from the days when the building served as a famous Duluth brewery.

EDGEWATER INN WEST, 2211 London Rd., Duluth, MN 55804. Tel. 218/728-5141. Fax 218/728-3727. 280 rms. A/C

$ Rates (including continental breakfast): Lake-view double $84, street-side double $77, new lakeside wing double $99. AE, MC, V.

Less expensive but very comfortable accommodations are available at the Edgewater Inn, with another location, the Edgewater East, at 2330 London Rd., Duluth, MN 55804 (tel. 218/728-3601). Rates include breakfast delivered to your door. The more expensive rooms, not surprisingly, are those that look out on Lake Superior. Edgewater East, the original lakeside complex, faces Edgewater West, located on the other side of busy London Road. A new lakeside building also has rooms.

WHERE TO DINE

GRANDMA'S SALOON AND DELI, 522 Lake Ave. S. Tel. 218/727-4192.
Cuisine: ITALIAN/AMERICAN.
$ Prices: $5.95–$14.95. AE, DISC, MC, V.
Open: Winter daily 11:30am–10pm; summer daily 11am–11pm.

Grandma's is something of an institution throughout the state, not so much because of its food, which is very good, or its decor, which is very imaginative, but because of its marathon, which is very famous and getting more so year after year. In 1977 Grandma's agreed to sponsor a North Shore run that attracted about 150 participants. One decade later the same route from Two Harbours to Duluth attracted 8,000-plus runners. By now there's a prerace $5 all-you-can-eat spaghetti fest to fortify the runners with carbohydrates and $50,000 worth of prize money awaiting the winners. Please note that Grandma's Marathon, which attracts runners from throughout the country, is the only race on record that ends at a bar. Tents, bands, and vendors with balloons, T-shirts, and other memorabilia are also on hand for the occasion.

Oh yes, the food and decor. You'll find absolutely everything hanging on the wall or from the ceiling at Grandma's. That means antique neon signs, stained-glass windows, brass beds and cribs, and even a stuffed black bear (the one, supposedly, that ran into the Hotel Duluth some years ago and thereby achieved immortality). The food is Italian-American—equal proportions of each, actually—and all of it well prepared and reasonable in cost.

PICKWICK, 508 E. Superior St. Tel. 218/727-8901.
Cuisine: AMERICAN. **Reservations:** Recommended.

$ Prices: Lunch $2–$7.50, dinner $8–$30. AE, MC, V.
   Open: Mon–Sat 11am–11pm.

The family-owned Pickwick has been serving fine food at reasonable prices since 1914. The decor here is 19th-century German, the cuisine is primarily American, and the beer is imported from a number of European countries.

   The service will make you think of an earlier, more gracious time; so will the across-the-board senior citizens' 10% discount, which may account for the somewhat advanced average age here. Or the explanation may be that older folks know value when they run into it and return because of it. At any rate, the Pickwick is a beautiful, unique, and very popular Duluth tradition.

THE CHINESE LANTERN, 402 W. 1st St. Tel. 722-7486.
   Cuisine: CHINESE.
$ Prices: $8–$12. AE, DISC, MC, V.
   Open: Mon–Thurs 11am–11pm, Fri 11am–12:30am, Sat noon–12:30am, Sun noon–10pm.

The Chinese Lantern was the first Cantonese restaurant in Duluth when it opened in 1965. By now, as photos on the walls attest, diners have included Bob Hope, Loretta Lynn, Pearl Bailey, Barry Manilow, and Tom Jones. The only restaurant north of Minneapolis to be listed in *Who's Who of American Restaurants*, the Chinese Lantern is owned by Wing Y. Huie, whose family fled China in the mid-1930s. His father, Joe Huie, ran a famous 24-hour Duluth café for many years; he claimed that it was open all day and all night because he'd lost the key. He questioned Wing's decision to offer Chinese cuisine to a primarily blue-collar clientele, but lived long enough to admit with enormous pride that his son's judgment in that regard was better than his own. After dinner, climb the stairs to the second-story Brass Phoenix Night Club, another gamble that paid off handsomely for the enterprising Wing Huie.

8. HINCKLEY

Hinckley, Minnesota, is the site of the distinguished **Hinckley Fire Museum** that memorializes the famous 1894 Hinckley fire storm, second only to the Great Chicago Fire in terms of total destructiveness. Located in a train depot that's listed on the National Register of Historic Places, this museum allows visitors to examine the turn-of-the-century waiting rooms (one for women and one for men), the beanery and freight room, and the depot agent's five-room apartment, furnished with late Victorian antiques. A large diorama shows the town of Hinckley and local landmarks, including the river, where logs were floated to the local lumber mill, and the gravel pit, where many Hinckley residents sought and found safety as the fire storm swept through the town. A slide show, presented hourly, tells more about Hinckley before, during, and after the fire. Admission to the museum is $2 for adults, $1.50 for senior citizens 62 and older and for children 13 to 18. Children 6 through 12 pay 50¢, and those 5 and under accompanied by an adult are admitted free.

But this community may be even better known for another claim to fame. For the past several decades the word "Hinckley" has meant just one thing to thousands of travelers—finger-lickin' caramel and cinnamon rolls, specialties of **Tobie's Eat Shop & Bus Stop,** situated since 1947 on Interstate 35 halfway between the Twin Cities and Duluth. Tobie's has been for travelers the traditional place to fill up cars and people. The establishment has gone far beyond its humble origins: The bakery now employs 17 full-time bakers. A handsome restaurant, bar, and lounge have been added to an enlarged coffee shop. And there's a 29-unit motel with sauna and hot tub, not to mention a shopping center complete with women's wear, sporting goods, country gifts, and a year-round Christmas store. Call 612/384-7600 for information on prices and events at any of Tobie's facilities and attractions.

9. SPAS

The brief spa getaway is a concept that's caught on with increasing numbers of Twin Citians. Whether you're taking time out from a business trip, a long vacation, or just the everyday stay-at-home routine, you might want to consider one or more of the following facilities. They differ in location and amenities, but not in their primary purpose—to offer the kind of relaxing or invigorating activity that induces a healthful sense of well being and rejuvenation.

THE MARSH

The Marsh, 15000 Minnetonka Blvd., Minnetonka, MN 55345 (tel. 612/935-2202), a self-described "center for balance and fitness," offers state-of-the-art equipment and a whole lot more. The rustic three-story building, set on the edge of a picturesque area of untouched suburban wetland, offers a wide variety of facilities and programs. The circuit training/Nautilus room is equipped with a Versa-climber, a Concept II rowing ergometer, and a "Heart Mate," whose computerized display not only monitors the heart rate as you bicycle, but tells how many calories are being burned per hour and per session. (This supersophisticated machine also has a built-in TV

and an AM/FM radio that will exercise your mind—to a degree—
while you're exercising the rest of you.)

The Marsh also offers two fully equipped exercise studios,
outfitted with spring-cushioned wood floors to absorb the shock of
aerobic workouts. At 30 feet by 60 feet, this is the largest spring-
cushioned floor in the Midwest. As directed and inspired by Ruth
Stricker, the Marsh is also interested in your mental, spiritual, and
emotional fitness. Classes, seminars, and lectures by nationally
known fitness experts help in this regard. And there is a small dining
room serving three healthful meals a day. Membership is open to
those 16 and older.

For guests who can only spend a limited number of hours here,
there's a variety of facials, massages, and body wraps, in addition to
cosmetic make-overs and other health and beauty services. Prices
vary according to method and time. A 1-hour session of Swedish and
Esalen massage is $40 for nonmembers, while there's a $45 charge for
nonmembers for Shiatsu, neuromuscular, and sports massage and a
$40 charge for nonmembers who'd like a half-hour of acupuncture.
Call 935-2202 for more specific information about services and
prices.

Inquire about full-day, 2-day, and 3-day Marsh "minivacations" at
prices ranging from $150 to $375 for nonmembers. (Although an
expansion is being planned that will include overnight accommodations for the Marsh, it's not yet available. Personnel here will make
reduced-rate reservations for you, at your expense, in the nearby
Minnetonka Marriot Hotel. Phone the Marsh for more specific
information.)

BIRDWING

You'll find a very different kind of spa-getaway at Birdwing Spa,
Route 2, Box 104, Litchfield, MN 55355 (tel. 612/693-6064).
Opened in spring 1986, this beautiful getaway has lured guests from
the Twin Cities (about a 70-mile drive) and from more far-flung places
as well. In fact, guests have come from 37 states and four foreign
countries to visit this luxurious retreat situated on 300 acres of woods
and prairie. Names of the groomed trails impart information about
the kinds of wildlife you'll encounter here: "Swan's Flight," "Hawk's
Prairie," "Pelican Loop," and "Woodduck Cove." Summertime
guests enjoy hiking these trails when they're not canoeing, biking, or
doing aqua aerobics in the small outdoor swimming pool. During
winter at this picturesque property, exercise takes the form of
walking, snowshoeing, and cross-country skiing. Wintertime aerobic
workouts, though, are held indoors.

But don't get the idea that exercise is all there is at Birdwing Spa.
Would you rather have breakfast in bed than in the dining room? No
problem. Would you like to skip some of the fitness session? That's
for you to decide. What you won't want to skip, though, are the

"beauty services" which are included, one per day, in the price of your stay. If you come for a week (at a cost of $1095 per person double occupancy, $1195 single), you'll receive three massages, a European facial, a manicure, a pedicure, and a beauty make-over. The weekend package ($315 per person double, $385 single) includes a full body massage, a facial, and two tanning sessions. Additional services can be secured on an individual basis, of course, at rates ranging from $5 for a tanning session to $60 for an "ultimate" 2-hour massage as well as a body wrap and other services.

Meals here are worth writing home about, with gourmet items that somehow make 1100 to 1300 calories a day seem sufficient. The small shop that's open briefly during your stay sells a cookbook with which you'll be able to reproduce at home the delicacies you enjoyed here. It makes an appropriate and practical souvenir. The attention really is personalized here, so call to see what Birdwing can offer you.

ESTEE LAUDER SPA

When the Estee Lauder Spa (tel. 612/924-6638) opened at Dayton's Department Store at the Southdale Center in Edina at 66th Street and France Avenue South, it became only the ninth such full-service spa in the entire country. It also became a place where Twin Cities women, men, and teenagers can find "an island of tranquillity" right in the heart of one of the busiest centers in the Twin Cities. The services here—everything from facials to body massage to manicures—have proved popular with a diverse clientele. For example, the spa features a specially tailored "Lauder Men's Facial Treatment" designed to clean, energize, and maintain a healthy skin. (Cost: $55 for one treatment, $275 for a series of six.) Then there's the "Teenage Problem Skin Facial Treatment, to regularize oil and eliminate break outs." (Cost: $25 for one treatment, $125 for six.)

But the majority of clients at this Southdale spa are women, and for them there's a wide variety of services, available individually or as part of a package. Facials come in many forms and at many costs, from the $55 "Skin Perfecting or Thorough Cleansing" treatments to the $80 "Four-phased Detoxifying Facial." Body massage, maybe the most popular treatment of all, ranges from the "Re-Vitalizing" ½ hour back massage at $35 to the "Tension Relieving Body Massage" at $55.

Hand and foot treatments include manicures, individual nail wraps, foot massage, toenail shaping and polishing.

Since the name Estee Lauder means makeup to millions of women, there are, of course, makeup applications and makeup lessons available, with the cost of each service applicable toward the price of any Estee Lauder product.

One last point of pride here is that this is the first full-service Estee Lauder spa in the country to offer three features: a shower, dry brushing for hands and feet, and seaweed body wraps. Sooner or later these will probably be available in Estee Lauder spas elsewhere, but they originated here at Southdale.

AVEDA SPA OSCEOLA

And finally you'll want to know about Aveda Spa Osceola, a holistic retreat located at 1015 Cascade St., Osceola, Wisconsin (tel. 715/294-4465). Set on the banks of the St. Croix River about 50 miles from downtown Minneapolis or St. Paul, this beautiful European-style spa complex stands amid 80 acres of unspoiled land in an area long noted for the purity of its air and its natural medicinal waters.

Aveda Spa Osceola, which opened in August 1990, was founded by Austrian-born Horst Rechelbacher, who made his name in the sixties as one of the top hairdressers in the world. (His distinctions include the coveted Intercoiffure Chevalier Award.)

In the late sixties, after opening the first of his six current Horst-and-Friends salons and establishing the Horst Education Center, from which salons throughout the country now recruit stylists, Rechelbacher turned to the intensive study of medicinal herbs, plants, and flowers. During this time he traveled to the Himalayas, which he still visits annually, to study with experts in aromatology. By 1978 he'd founded the Aveda Corporation, which uses the science of flower and plant essences in natural products for the hair, skin, body, and environment. Aveda products are now marketed internationally, and they are, of course, used exclusively on these premises. Given Rechelbacher's philosophy concerning beauty products, it won't surprise you to learn that the meals here are strictly organic; all foods are grown on-site. The menu changes every day.

Full-day and overnight packages are particularly popular here with guests who drive in from the Twin Cities or those who fly into the Twin Cities and are then provided shuttle service from Minneapolis/St. Paul International Airport at a charge of $50 each way.

The 1-day package for women and men includes a choice of full body massage or face and body treatment, natural essence scalp treatment, haircut and style, and a choice of a flower essence whirlpool session with body wrap or a body polishing treatment. In addition women receive a makeup lesson, while men are provided a skin-care consultation. The total cost, which includes an organic gourmet lunch, is $175.

The overnight package includes all the above plus a night's lodging in one of the truly beautiful guest rooms, gourmet dinner on arrival, breakfast and lunch the following day, one session of professional instruction in stretching and stress-relieving exercise, and use of the spa steam room. Fitness and weight-training equipment are available and so is unlimited outdoor activity and exploration. Mountain bikes, tennis courts, and wintertime snowshoeing and cross-country skiing are available. Prices are $265, single occupancy,

$230 per person double occupancy. Aveda Spa Osceola is open year-round. Handicapped accommodations are available. Some rooms have shared baths. For further information and for reservations, call 715/294-4465.

NEARBY PLACES TO STAY OR DINE

If you'd like to spend another night or two in Osceola, you'll enjoy the **St. Croix River Inn Bed-and-Breakfast,** 305 River St., Osceola, Wisconsin 54020 (tel. 715/294-4248). Rates for a room are $100 to $200 on Friday and Saturday, and $85 to $150 from Sunday to Thursday. The business person's special costs $58 for a midweek room with breakfast. Situated high on a bluff overlooking the picturesque St. Croix River, this meticulously restored 80-year-old limestone house provides a few amenities that the original structure lacked. Each of the seven rooms has, in addition to its Victorian decor, a private bath with Jacuzzi. To enhance the atmosphere, you'll also find a stereo cassette player and tapes in your room. (If the cookies at the front desk didn't make you feel at home, the soft fluffy robe hanging in your room's armoire surely will.) A full breakfast will be brought to your door in the morning, so be sure to indicate when you register whether you prefer coffee or tea.

For lunch or dinner, try the **Royal Christie's Restaurant,** (tel. 612/433-5141) at 2232 100th Ave. in Dresser, Wisconsin. This lovely rustic room has fieldstone walls, a huge fireplace, a fine view of the slopes and, during much of the winter season, a great view of skiers as well. You'll enjoy fine fare here at very reasonable prices. Appetizers range from $1.75 to $4 and dinner main courses from $5.95 to $22.95. The Friday night fish fry with salad bar is one of the area's best buys at $6.50 and the same can be said for the Sunday buffet, noon to 8pm at the low cost of $7.50.

INDEX

GENERAL INFORMATION

SIGHTS & ATTRACTIONS

OUTSIDE THE TWIN CITIES

ACCOMMODATIONS

KEY TO ABBREVIATIONS: *B* = Budget; *E* = Expensive; *M* = Moderate; * = Author's favorite; *$* = Super-value choice

RESTAURANTS

MINNEAPOLIS AND ENVIRONS

KEY TO ABBREVIATIONS: *B* = Budget; *E* = Expensive; *M* = Moderate; * = Author's favorite; *$* = Super-value choice.

ST. PAUL AND ENVIRONS

OUTSIDE THE TWIN CITIES

FROMMER GUIDES

	Retail Price	Code		Retail Price	Code
Alaska 1990–91	$14.95	C001	Jamaica/Barbados 1993–94	$15.00	C105
Arizona 1993–94	$18.00	C101	Japan 1992–93	$19.00	C020
Australia 1992–93	$18.00	C002	Morocco 1992–93	$18.00	C021
Austria/Hungary 1991–92	$14.95	C003	Nepal 1992–93	$18.00	C038
Belgium/Holland/ Luxembourg 1993–94	$18.00	C106	New England 1992	$17.00	C023
Bermuda/Bahamas 1992–93	$17.00	C005	New Mexico 1991–92	$13.95	C024
Brazil 1991–92	$14.95	C006	New York State 1992–93	$19.00	C025
California 1992	$18.00	C007	Northwest 1991–92	$16.95	C026
Canada 1992–93	$18.00	C009	Portugal 1992–93	$16.00	C027
Caribbean 1993	$18.00	C102	Puerto Rico 1993–94	$15.00	C103
The Carolinas/Georgia 1992–93	$17.00	C034	Puerto Vallarta/ Manzanillo/Guadalajara 1992–93	$14.00	C028
Colorado 1993–94	$16.00	C100	Scandinavia 1991–92	$18.95	C029
Cruises 1993–94	$19.00	C107	Scotland 1992–93	$16.00	C040
DE/MD/PA & NJ Shore 1992–93	$19.00	C012	Skiing Europe 1989–90	$14.95	C030
Egypt 1990–91	$14.95	C013	South Pacific 1992–93	$20.00	C031
England 1993	$18.00	C109	Switzerland/Liechtenstein 1992–93	$19.00	C032
Florida 1993	$18.00	C104	Thailand 1992–93	$20.00	C033
France 1992–93	$20.00	C017	USA 1991–92	$16.95	C035
Germany 1993	$19.00	C108	Virgin Islands 1992–93	$13.00	C036
Italy 1992	$19.00	C019	Virginia 1992–93	$14.00	C037
			Yucatán 1992–93	$18.00	C110

FROMMER $-A-DAY GUIDES

	Retail Price	Code		Retail Price	Code
Australia on $45 a Day 1993–94	$18.00	D102	Israel on $45 a Day 1993–94	$18.00	D101
Costa Rica/Guatemala/ Belize on $35 a Day 1991–92	$15.95	D004	Mexico on $50 a Day 1993	$19.00	D105
Eastern Europe on $25 a Day 1991–92	$16.95	D005	New York on $70 a Day 1992–93	$16.00	D016
England on $60 a Day 1993	$18.00	D107	New Zealand on $45 a Day 1993–94	$18.00	D103
Europe on $45 a Day 1993	$19.00	D106	Scotland/Wales on $50 a Day 1992–93	$18.00	D019
Greece on $45 a Day 1993–94	$19.00	D100	South America on $40 a Day 1991–92	$15.95	D020
Hawaii on $75 a Day 1993	$19.00	D104	Spain on $50 a Day 1991–92	$15.95	D021
India on $40 a Day 1992–93	$20.00	D010	Turkey on $40 a Day 1992	$22.00	D023
Ireland on $40 a Day 1992–93	$17.00	D011	Washington, D.C. on $40 a Day 1992	$17.00	D024

FROMMER CITY $-A-DAY GUIDES

	Retail Price	Code		Retail Price	Code
Berlin on $40 a Day 1992–93	$12.00	D002	Madrid on $50 a Day 1992–93	$13.00	D014
Copenhagen on $50 a Day 1992–93	$12.00	D003	Paris on $45 a Day 1992–93	$12.00	D018
London on $45 a Day 1992–93	$12.00	D013	Stockholm on $50 a Day 1992–93	$13.00	D022

FROMMER TOURING GUIDES

Amsterdam	$10.95	T001	New York	$10.95	T008
Australia	$10.95	T002	Paris	$ 8.95	T009
Barcelona	$14.00	T015	Rome	$10.95	T010
Brazil	$10.95	T003	Scotland	$ 9.95	T011
Egypt	$ 8.95	T004	Sicily	$14.95	T017
Florence	$ 8.95	T005	Thailand	$12.95	T012
Hong Kong/Singapore/ Macau	$10.95	T006	Tokyo	$15.00	T016
Kenya	$13.95	T018	Turkey	$10.95	T013
London	$12.95	T007	Venice	$ 8.95	T014

FROMMER'S FAMILY GUIDES

California with Kids	$16.95	F001	San Francisco with Kids	$17.00	F004
Los Angeles with Kids	$17.00	F002	Washington, D.C. with Kids	$17.00	F005
New York City with Kids	$18.00	F003			

FROMMER CITY GUIDES

Amsterdam/Holland 1991–92	$ 8.95	S001	Miami 1991–92	$ 8.95	S021
Athens 1991–92	$ 8.95	S002	Minneapolis/St. Paul 1991–92	$ 8.95	S022
Atlanta 1991–92	$ 8.95	S003	Montréal/Québec City 1991–92	$ 8.95	S023
Atlantic City/Cape May 1991–92	$ 8.95	S004	New Orleans 1993–94	$13.00	S103
Bangkok 1992–93	$13.00	S005	New York 1992	$12.00	S025
Barcelona/Majorca/ Minorca/Ibiza 1992	$12.00	S006	Orlando 1993	$13.00	S101
Belgium 1989–90	$ 5.95	S007	Paris 1993–94	$13.00	S109
Berlin 1991–92	$10.00	S008	Philadelphia 1991–92	$ 8.95	S028
Boston 1991–92	$ 8.95	S009	Rio 1991–92	$ 8.95	S029
Cancún/Cozumel/Yucatán 1991–92	$ 8.95	S010	Rome 1991–92	$ 8.95	S030
Chicago 1991–92	$ 9.95	S011	Salt Lake City 1991–92	$ 8.95	S031
Denver/Boulder/Colorado Springs 1990–91	$ 7.95	S012	San Diego 1993–94	$13.00	S107
Dublin/Ireland 1991–92	$ 8.95	S013	San Francisco 1993	$13.00	S104
Hawaii 1992	$12.00	S014	Santa Fe/Taos/ Albuquerque 1993–94	$13.00	S108
Hong Kong 1992–93	$12.00	S015	Seattle/Portland 1992–93	$12.00	S035
Honolulu/Oahu 1993	$13.00	S106	St. Louis/Kansas City 1991–92	$ 9.95	S036
Las Vegas 1991–92	$ 8.95	S016	Sydney 1991–92	$ 8.95	S037
Lisbon/Madrid/Costa del Sol 1991–92	$ 8.95	S017	Tampa/St. Petersburg 1993–94	$13.00	S105
London 1993	$13.00	S100	Tokyo 1992–93	$13.00	S039
Los Angeles 1991–92	$ 8.95	S019	Toronto 1991–92	$ 8.95	S040
Mexico City/Acapulco 1991–92	$ 8.95	S020	Vancouver/Victoria 1990–91	$ 7.95	S041
			Washington, D.C. 1993	$13.00	S102

Other Titles Available at Membership Prices—
SPECIAL EDITIONS

	Retail Price	Code		Retail Price	Code
Bed & Breakfast North America	$14.95	P002	Marilyn Wood's Wonderful Weekends (within 250-mile radius of New York City)	$11.95	P017
Caribbean Hideaways	$16.00	P005			
Honeymoon Destinations	$14.95	P006			
			New World of Travel 1991 by Arthur Frommer	$16.95	P018
			Where to Stay USA	$13.95	P015

GAULT MILLAU'S "BEST OF" GUIDES

Chicago	$15.95	G002	New England	$15.95	G010
Florida	$17.00	G003	New Orleans	$16.95	G011
France	$16.95	G004	New York	$16.95	G012
Germany	$18.00	G018	Paris	$16.95	G013
Hawaii	$16.95	G006	San Francisco	$16.95	G014
Hong Kong	$16.95	G007	Thailand	$17.95	G019
London	$16.95	G009	Toronto	$17.00	G020
Los Angeles	$16.95	G005	Washington, D.C.	$16.95	G017

THE REAL GUIDES

Amsterdam	$13.00	R100	Morocco	$14.00	R111
Barcelona	$13.00	R101	Nepal	$14.00	R018
Berlin	$11.95	R002	New York	$13.00	R019
Brazil	$13.95	R003	Able to Travel (avail April '93)	$20.00	R112
California & the West Coast	$17.00	R102	Paris	$13.00	R020
Canada	$15.00	R103	Peru	$12.95	R021
Czechoslovakia	$14.00	R104	Poland	$13.95	R022
Egypt	$19.00	R105	Portugal	$15.00	R023
Florida	$14.00	R006	Prague	$15.00	R113
France	$18.00	R106	San Francisco & the Bay Area	$11.95	R024
Germany	$18.00	R107	Scandinavia	$14.95	R025
Greece	$18.00	R108	Spain	$16.00	R026
Guatemala/Belize	$14.00	R109	Thailand	$17.00	R114
Holland/Belgium/Luxembourg	$16.00	R031	Tunisia	$17.00	R115
Hong Kong/Macau	$11.95	R011	Turkey	$13.95	R116
Hungary	$12.95	R012	U.S.A.	$18.00	R117
Ireland	$17.00	R110	Venice	$11.95	R028
Italy	$13.95	R014	Women Travel	$12.95	R029
Kenya	$12.95	R015	Yugoslavia	$12.95	R030
Mexico	$11.95	R016			